Autonomous

VALA AFSHAR | HENRY KING

Autonomous

WHY THE FITTEST BUSINESSES EMBRACE AI-FIRST STRATEGIES AND DIGITAL LABOR

WILEY

Copyright © 2026 by John Wiley & Sons, Inc. All rights reserved, including rights for text and data mining and training of artificial intelligence technologies or similar technologies.

Published by John Wiley & Sons, Inc., Hoboken, New Jersey.
Published simultaneously in Canada.

No part of this publication may be reproduced, stored in a retrieval system, or transmitted in any form or by any means, electronic, mechanical, photocopying, recording, scanning, or otherwise, except as permitted under Section 107 or 108 of the 1976 United States Copyright Act, without either the prior written permission of the Publisher, or authorization through payment of the appropriate per-copy fee to the Copyright Clearance Center, Inc., 222 Rosewood Drive, Danvers, MA 01923, (978) 750-8400, fax (978) 750-4470, or on the web at www.copyright.com. Requests to the Publisher for permission should be addressed to the Permissions Department, John Wiley & Sons, Inc., 111 River Street, Hoboken, NJ 07030, (201) 748-6011, fax (201) 748-6008, or online at http://www.wiley.com/go/permission.

The manufacturer's authorized representative according to the EU General Product Safety Regulation is Wiley-VCH GmbH, Boschstr. 12, 69469 Weinheim, Germany, e-mail: Product_Safety@wiley.com.

Trademarks: Wiley and the Wiley logo are trademarks or registered trademarks of John Wiley & Sons, Inc. and/or its affiliates in the United States and other countries and may not be used without written permission. All other trademarks are the property of their respective owners. John Wiley & Sons, Inc. is not associated with any product or vendor mentioned in this book.

Limit of Liability/Disclaimer of Warranty: While the publisher and the authors have used their best efforts in preparing this work, including a review of the content of the work, neither the publisher nor the authors make any representations or warranties with respect to the accuracy or completeness of the contents of this work and specifically disclaim all warranties, including without limitation any implied warranties of merchantability or fitness for a particular purpose. No warranty may be created or extended by sales representatives, written sales materials or promotional statements for this work. The fact that an organization, website, or product is referred to in this work as a citation and/or potential source of further information does not mean that the publisher and authors endorse the information or services the organization, website, or product may provide or recommendations it may make. This work is sold with the understanding that the publisher is not engaged in rendering professional services. The advice and strategies contained herein may not be suitable for your situation. You should consult with a specialist where appropriate. Further, readers should be aware that websites listed in this work may have changed or disappeared between when this work was written and when it is read. Neither the publisher nor authors shall be liable for any loss of profit or any other commercial damages, including but not limited to special, incidental, consequential, or other damages.

For general information on our other products and services or for technical support, please contact our Customer Care Department within the United States at (800) 762-2974, outside the United States at (317) 572-3993 or fax (317) 572-4002.

Wiley also publishes its books in a variety of electronic formats. Some content that appears in print may not be available in electronic formats. For more information about Wiley products, visit our web site at www.wiley.com.

Library of Congress Cataloging-in-Publication Data is Available:

ISBN: 9781394357925 (Cloth)
ISBN: 9781394357932 (ePub)
ISBN: 9781394357949 (ePDF)

Cover Design and Image: © Wiley
Author Images: Courtesy of the Authors

SKY10124600_082125

This book is dedicated to our families.

Contents

Introduction   ix

Chapter 1   What Is a Fit Company?   1
In an <u>AI-powered</u> economy, the companies that are the <u>fittest</u> (best positioned to win) are <u>Autonomous</u> using <u>digital labor</u>.

Chapter 2   Blockages Kill Companies   19
<u>Blockages</u> are the number one cause of <u>death</u> in living organisms and businesses alike. <u>Autonomous</u> companies are <u>living organisms</u> that are <u>immune</u> to blockages.

Chapter 3   A New Autonomous Operating Model   43
Autonomous companies have <u>operating models</u> for <u>decision dominance</u> and action at <u>machine speed and scale</u> (mSUDA).

Chapter 4   Relational Intelligence for Digital Labor   73
Autonomous companies are <u>hyper-talented</u>, integrating <u>human and digital resources</u> and building deep <u>relational intelligence</u>.

Chapter 5   AI-First Design and Nonlinearity   103
Adopting an <u>AI-first</u> strategy is the <u>only</u> path from assistive to <u>Autonomous</u> capabilities, producing <u>nonlinear</u>, exponential outcomes.

Chapter 6	Autonomy and Boundless Principles	127
	Becoming an <u>Autonomous business</u> requires the seven <u>Boundless principles</u> shaping the <u>mindset</u> and business <u>operating model</u>.	
Chapter 7	AI Is the New UI	141
	<u>Taking our hands off the steering wheel</u>: the road to Autonomous maturity for AI, the company, and its humans requires bold leadership and a new playbook.	
Chapter 8	Summary of Key Insights	175
	This is what defines the world's most successful companies: Autonomy.	
Chapter 9	Ten Tenets of Autonomous Businesses	185
	These are the 10 key takeaways from this book.	

Notes	*187*
Glossary of AI Terms	*191*
Acknowledgments	*197*
About the Authors	*199*
Index	*201*

Introduction

The fittest companies in the world are Autonomous companies. With management committed to future-proofing their organizations, they are building a digital labor force powered by Agentic artificial intelligence (Agentic AI) to nonlinearly scale the health, conditioning, and talent of their teams, business, and ecosystem. They are enabling 24 × 7 × 365 continuity and responsiveness, removing blockages and waste that trap or reduce value creation and positioning themselves for Boundless business success in an AI-first economy. They are machine-led and human-assisted, no longer vice versa. This is what it means for a business to be Autonomous. This is what it takes to be the fittest.

Our goal in writing this book is to persuade business leaders, strategists, and designers that this evolution of AI's role from digital tool to digital labor, and humans' role from operational control to mission control, is real and urgent. We aim to lay out the implications of this evolution and help them transform their companies from being human-first to becoming AI-first. We have developed seven key insights for this transformation, and our book is focused on explaining and exploring each one to prepare leaders for the journey to Autonomy.

The Seven Key Insights

Let's discuss the insights.

> **Insight 1: In an <u>AI-powered</u> economy, the companies that are the <u>fittest</u> (best positioned to win) are <u>Autonomous</u> using <u>digital labor</u>.**

What does it mean for companies to be fit in the AI economy? We believe that the answer is that they need to be fit in the sense of being adaptable to the ever-changing needs of the customer, the market, and the economy as a whole, and in the more usual sense nowadays of being in top physical shape. This means being healthy, conditioned, and talented. The fittest companies are healthy without blockages or waste slowing them down and destroying value; they are conditioned to perform at a high level, at speed that is routine, not a matter of heroics. They are talented, employing a digital workforce alongside their human one to create a new, hybrid resource pool that takes what's best from both types of intelligence. And they prioritize AI-first strategies and designs to generate nonlinear or exponential outcomes. The fittest companies have leaders that are committed to the future and are willing and able to let go of the steering wheel to enable those nonlinear outcomes to happen. We have a word for the fittest companies in the age of AI: Autonomous.

> **Insight 2: <u>Blockages</u> are the number one cause of <u>death</u> in living organisms and businesses alike. <u>Autonomous</u> companies are <u>living organisms</u> that are <u>immune</u> to blockages.**

A healthy living organism, from complex ones like humans to the individual cells that we're composed of, is one that optimizes flow. Optimal flows of matter, energy, and information between the organism and its environment, and flows within the organism itself, keep us all alive and healthy.

Optimal flow is also essential to the health or optimal functioning of a whole variety of machines and systems. From the flow of electricity that animates nearly all systems nowadays, to hydraulic flows, data flows, fuel flows, airflow, and so on, our constructed and built world relies on uninterrupted flow to work properly.

This same principle of optimal flow also applies to business. Healthy companies have optimal flows of money, raw materials, electricity, expertise, data, and other resources coming in and flows of value to the customer coming out (product, service, information, and so on), as well as flows of money back out to providers, investors, and so on. When these flows are obstructed, business suffers in all sorts of ways. Blockages cause the deterioration and even death of companies of all shapes and sizes.

Insight 3: Autonomous companies have <u>operating models</u> for <u>decision dominance</u> and action at <u>machine speed and scale</u> (mSUDA).

Overall health is a prerequisite for fitness but conditioning is what sets Autonomous companies apart and enables them to perform at the highest level. They are able to act at speed routinely because they are built on mSUDA (machine-scale Sense, Understand, Decide, Act). mSUDA is the operating model for decision dominance and competitive advantage in the AI age, tuned to minimize the gap between sensing any event, like a customer query or competitor pricing change or supplier inventory shortage for instance, and acting on it. Adopting mSUDA requires predictive, Generative, Agentic, and physical AI-powered solutions, driving the evolution of enterprise applications from systems of records to systems of engagement and from there to systems of action and impact.

Insight 4: Autonomous companies are <u>hyper-talented</u>, integrating <u>human and digital resources</u> and building deep <u>relational intelligence</u>.

At the core of all successful businesses are successful relationships: relationships built on trust and commitment, providing moments of delight, delivering mutual and sustained value. The advent of AI as digital labor, as an integrated part of the workforce, will bring its own relationship opportunities and challenges. Relational intelligence (RI) is the ability to design, cultivate, nurture, and enhance successful relationships in the age of AI and smart machines. RI integrates human individuality, creativity, and empathy with the efficiencies, contextual awareness, and data-driven insights of AI agents at machine scale and speed to deepen the connections that matter most, with customers, employees, and with other valued stakeholders.

AI brings a new talent pool to the company, enabling new levels of performance at speed and scale previously unimagined. These resources need to be integrated and harnessed thoughtfully, not randomly assigned to stand-alone pain points, to increase the effectiveness and performance of the whole.

> **Insight 5: Adopting an <u>AI-first</u> strategy is the <u>only</u> path from assistive to <u>Autonomous</u> capabilities, producing <u>nonlinear</u>, exponential outcomes.**

Conventionally, airplanes were designed with an inherent compromise between stability and performance. Human pilots, even the most skilled and experienced, have a limit to the degree of instability they can handle in their aircraft. But the aircraft have a limit in their performance when their stability is maximized. In other words, human limitations put constraints on the kind of airplanes and their performance that could be built. Fly-by-wire systems removed or at least significantly reduced that compromise, leading to extraordinary developments in speed, stealth, maneuverability, recoverability, and more, and future AI enhancements to those systems, known as intelligent flight control systems, promise to extend the possibilities of aircraft still further.

When we look at business through this lens, we realize that there are other human qualities that we have always considered neutral or actually beneficial that might now be regarded as limitations in the age of AI. Experience may not be so relevant when AI systems can learn complex tasks quickly and improve their performance continuously. Effort may not be so relevant when AI can work $24 \times 7 \times 365$ without reward. Corporate hierarchies and management practices might not be so relevant when AI can choreograph, orchestrate, and mentor without higher salary, better perks, or a larger office. Many of the ways in which we do business are now up for grabs. An Autonomous company is designed for AI and machine strategies first, and in the future will likely be designed by them, too.

> **Insight 6: Becoming an <u>Autonomous business</u> requires the seven <u>Boundless principles</u> shaping the <u>mindset</u> and business <u>operating model</u>.**

Autonomous companies will rest on the principles of connection, integration, distribution, Autonomy (naturally enough), mobility, continuity, and shared success. Agentic AI means new and more connections. Data is the lifeblood of AI success and integration is key to data access. Distribution becomes automated and scaled. Mobility and continuity accelerate Autonomy, and shared success now applies to human and digital labor alike, enabling a shift in focus from economies of scale to ecosystems of success.

Introduction xiii

We introduced these principles in our previous book *Boundless* to describe a business mindset that is the opposite of conventionally siloed organizations. We've since realized that these very principles are the perfect frame on which to build the AI-first company.

> **Insight 7: Taking our hands off the steering wheel**: the road to Autonomous maturity for AI, the company, and its humans requires bold leadership and a new playbook.

Companies will not transform from human-led to AI-led Autonomous companies overnight. We have created a seven-level maturity model to help companies anticipate and plan and track their expansion of digital labor and progress toward Autonomy, with two main phases and inflection points at which the impact of AI becomes nonlinear. A car's autonomous capabilities provide only incremental, linear value to the human driver while they are in the driver's seat with their hands on the steering wheel but have exponentially greater potential as soon as those conditions are removed. In the same way, the impact of AI on an organization will only be incremental until a level of Autonomous maturity is achieved at which point we can only begin to imagine what might be possible if we cede operational control to our new digital colleagues and collaborators and mentors and orchestrators.

What's in This Book?

This book explains the journey ahead and helps business leaders, strategists, and designers take it for themselves and their organizations, and ultimately reach autonomy for their companies, their technologies, and themselves. We have organized the book according to each of our seven key insights.

> **Chapter 1: What Is a Fit Company?** In an **AI-powered** economy, the companies that are the **fittest** (best positioned to win) are **Autonomous** using **digital labor.**

In our first chapter we introduce the animating insight for the entire book. We had asked ourselves what kind of a company will not only survive in an AI economy but also win in it, meaning not just its ability to compete successfully but also its ability to collaborate successfully. What kind of company would, in other words, be among the fittest? We believe that the answer is the Autonomous business, one that is healthy without blockages or waste slowing it down and destroying value, one that is conditioned to perform at a high level, at speed that is routine, not a matter of heroics.

> **Chapter 2: Blockages Kill Companies. <u>Blockages</u> are the number one cause of <u>death</u> in living organisms and businesses alike. <u>Autonomous</u> companies are <u>living organisms</u> that are <u>immune</u> to blockages.**

In this chapter we focus on health as a prerequisite for fitness. We note that all living organisms are dependent on the flow of resources, energy, and matter for their health and continued life. Blockages cause them to deteriorate and fail. The average company is full of blockages that prevent optimal performance but AI may help predict, detect, and prevent them in a variety of ways.

Speed is one of the currencies of the information—and now AI—age, and companies that can process all the signals coming in from the market, make decisions, and take action at speed will outperform those that can't and render them irrelevant. Some companies achieve speed in the short term by piling pressure on their employees and, where necessary, bypassing standard processes and controls.

But speed cannot be sustained by a dependence on heroics and shortcuts. For this, a company needs instead to focus on creating flow—of information, expertise, finance, and other resources—across the entire organization to ensure that the right resources get to the parts that need them most. And the first step to creating flow is to get rid of anything that prevents flow. In a word, blockages.

We have already written an entire book about one type of blockage, namely organizational silos. Silos are not easy to get rid of, largely because—as we argue—they work, at least for those who manage them. Not only that, they are also our default way to manage our resources, our choice without even realizing that we're making a choice. In order to get rid of silos, therefore, companies need to embrace a new mindset, one that we call Boundless.

But the process of removing other blockages can be started without needing a new mindset. All that is required is a sense of urgency, coming from the realization that blockages in the human body cause up to 50% of all deaths and that all death is ultimately determined by the cessation of flows, the flow of breath and the flow of blood. While companies are not the same as bodies in the literal sense, they are nevertheless alive and they are just as dependent on flows to stay healthy.

Blockages—of information, money, expertise, decision-making, human resources, and so on—cause them to slow down and become less effective. Ultimately, we believe that blockages have a similar impact on company success as they do on individual human health and life (although to our knowledge no one has ever done a deep dive to measure their impact). In *Autonomous*, we will identify dozens of business blockages that are hard to detect, harder to root cause, and nearly impossible to immediately resolve without the adoption of AI, specifically predictive, Generative, and Agentic AI.

AI today can identify blockages in the coronary arteries based on angiogram images with 90% accuracy, based on research that shows this innovation could significantly reduce the need for pressure wire testing, saving health care providers time and reducing patients' discomfort. More research on AI's ability to identify people at risk of a heart attack in the next 10 years has been hailed as "game changing" by scientists. The AI model detects inflammation in the heart that does not show up on CT scans. Early detection of blockages in humans is hard, and in business, it is incredibly difficult.

To start removing blockages, first you will need to know where to look, and then create a list of high-potential blockages, that is, those that lead to the greatest delays in getting things done *and* that can be removed or redesigned with the least effort. To help you in your search, in this chapter we discuss the most common blockage types and their typical impact.

Fortunately, AI is not only the change catalyst for removing blockages but it can also be a powerful change agent, a valuable tool for identifying and removing various types of blockages across different aspects of business operations.

All waste is costly but not all costs are wasteful. Removing waste from all aspects of a company's operations focuses the organization on creating value both for the customer and itself—as well as for other stakeholders. The key message of our book *Boundless* was this: silos kill. And business leaders must adopt a Boundless mindset in order to deliberately remove silos. But our support comes with a word of warning: when you smash your silos but don't have an alternative way to manage your resources, you risk creating a spill instead of a flow. A spill is a waste of resources that can even become a pollutant or a hazard. A Boundless organization, by contrast, creates and then directs flows of resources to wherever it most needs them. Our message, therefore, is that Boundless can, and should, become the alternative for any organization looking for continued success in this increasingly turbulent world.

This focus on waste is an important point worth reemphasizing—especially in light of the more demanding market conditions that have visited us over the last few years. Shared success among key stakeholders is both the goal and the outcome of a Boundless mindset. But that does not make it a free-for-all. The risk is that the term *Boundless* may be misunderstood to stand for unfettered growth, signifying a lack of discipline and insensitivity to issues like cost and productivity demands.

But nothing could be further from the truth! The real question is, How are these issues handled in the Boundless model compared to the silo model?

The most common business response to softening demand and/or deteriorating market conditions is to focus on cost cutting. This seems to be true, more or less, regardless of industry and company status. In other words, big or small, incumbent or new entrant, mature or fast growth, traditional or cutting edge, when things are not going as well as they were and pressure to respond is being felt at the executive level, cost cutting is the go-to strategy.

The problem with this—at least from a Boundless perspective—is that cost cutting is a silo-based strategy. In other words, cost cutting is focused on resource management rather than on value creation. Even in market conditions or business cycles that favor margin growth over revenue or customer growth, we believe that a focus on reducing waste is a better strategy than cutting costs. There are four main reasons why:

- First, all waste is costly but not all costs are wasteful. Cost cutting, especially when it is carried out "across the board" to appear impartial or fair (also known as "peanut buttering"), risks harming value, quality, effectiveness, employee satisfaction, customer experience, and reputation. But all efforts to reduce or even eliminate waste will cut the right kinds of costs, costs that generate no value. At a minimum, this means that they will not cut into the "muscle" of the organization and make it less fit. More likely they will improve its fitness and

responsiveness. In other words, waste reduction is a path to becoming Boundless, one we would recommend in any cycle, and is thus more disciplined and more constructive than pure cost cutting.
- Second, and of particular interest to us from a Boundless perspective, cost cutting by itself does nothing to improve the flow of data, decision-making, and action taking across the organization, and may make it worse. As we argue in the book, silos can literally kill. All forms of silos, blockages, friction, bottlenecks, and roadblocks slow or stop people, projects, and processes in their tracks and threaten responsiveness and resilience.
- Third, waste has a negative impact on value to the customer, quality, and/or sustainability. Reducing waste therefore has a positive impact on value, quality, and/or sustainability. This means that reducing waste is always a good strategy regardless of business or market cycle.
- Fourth, some waste bears a cost not just for the company but also the world beyond it. This type of waste is known in economics as an externality, a by-product that is borne unwittingly by a third party. Reducing or eliminating externalities has particular relevance in terms of sustainability and helps achieve shared success.

Identifying wasteful processes in business is not an easy task. It's standard accounting practice to identify, measure, and report on an organization's costs. However, not all forms of waste are so easily identifiable or measurable. In particular, outside of the manufacturing industry, which focuses deeply on waste, as typified by the Toyota Production System's "muda" principle, business processes rarely get scrutinized in any formal way for waste.

Also, business complexity has grown to the point where it can be difficult to trace activities back to customer or stakeholder value. To compound matters further, people naturally favor their own ways of completing tasks and solving problems, even when those ways may be objectively more complicated and more time-consuming than consistent, standardized, or shared approaches. So waste can be difficult to pinpoint and even more difficult to eliminate.

Despite these challenges, removing waste from all aspects of a company's operations focuses the organization on creating value both for the customer and for itself—as well as for other stakeholders. Removing waste prioritizes the flow of resources including data and decisions, and increases responsiveness to new challenges and opportunities. A key tool in sustainability and profitability, continuous waste elimination is always a good practice and goal regardless of the economic cycle. And, perhaps surprisingly, it is always Boundless.

> **Chapter 3: A New Autonomous Operating Model. Autonomous companies have <u>operating models</u> for <u>decision dominance</u> and action at <u>machine speed and scale</u> (mSUDA).**

In this chapter we focus on conditioning. Conditioning is the second of three components of fitness and goes beyond basic health to set up a company for competition and customer satisfaction. The SUDA operating model (Sense, Understand, Decide, Act), especially one powered by AI, provides that conditioning, minimizing the delay between detecting any event that requires the company to act and taking the appropriate action.

Machine power multipliers applied to each stage of the SUDA operating model will create abilities beyond human capabilities. AI will not merely progress to being more productive compared to individual human full-time equivalents or being measured in workforce units. AI will come to be measured in machine power—not simply in terms of GPUs/CPUs or transactions per second but probably as some function of complexity, accuracy, and speed.

AI is advancing so rapidly that we are creating a new digital workforce to do our jobs for us. AI-powered capabilities are growing in orders of magnitude annually. By leveraging AI's predictive and analytical capabilities, companies make informed decisions that benefit their bottom line, society, and the environment.

As Agentic AI adoption increases in business, and actions can be taken 24/7 on behalf of human workers, we will see the emergence of a new measure of productivity: "machine power" or something similar. This measure will be needed to represent how machines will no longer just do "human" jobs faster, more accurately, and cheaply. They'll also be doing jobs that we can't do, jobs far more complex, with more inputs to handle, more moving parts to orchestrate, and less time to solve.

Managing robo-taxi fleets, the latest innovation in the centuries-old ride-for-hire service that no longer employs human drivers or horse "engines," will be an early example of this new machine power. Managing fully autonomous companies will be another.

What does Agentic AI and mSUDA business operating models mean for the future of work?

Decision dominance, achieved through mSUDA operating models and powered by Agentic AI capabilities, will enable businesses to massively shrink the time between sensing, understanding, deciding, and acting to nearly zero. To stay relevant in an AI-powered economy, the currencies that matter most are speed, scale, intelligence, personalization, and—most importantly—trust.

Businesses must plan and design for instability. AI will play a crucial role in assisting leaders and their teams in making strategic—as well as immediate—data-driven decisions and taking effective action.

> **Chapter 4: Relational Intelligence for Digital Labor. Autonomous companies are <u>hyper-talented</u>, integrating <u>human and digital resources</u> and building deep <u>relational intelligence</u>.**

The third component of fitness is talent, and in this chapter we discuss what talent means when it includes digital as well as human talent. At the heart of all successful companies are successful relationships. The advent of AI as digital labor supporting customers, partners, and human colleagues. At least in principle AI will help companies serve their customers better and support their business ecosystem more effectively. But they will also change company dynamics. When AI is taking over more and more of the operations, what's left are the relationships, those between humans and humans, humans and AI (including robots), AI and AI.

Companies will need to become more intentional about designing all their relationships, internally and externally. We call this *relational intelligence (RI)*, the ability to design, cultivate, nurture, and enhance successful relationships in the age of AI and smart machines. RI integrates human individuality, creativity, and empathy with the efficiencies, contextual awareness, and data-driven insights of AI agents at machine scale and speed to deepen the connections that matter most, with customers, employees, and other valued stakeholders.

In this chapter we discuss the characteristics of successful business relationships, including also the human qualities of curiosity (who, why, what, when, where?) and imagination (If this is now possible, what else is? What's next, what if?), which seem to be perfectly matched with AI's capabilities to answer, predict, and model and test.

Finally we will examine the role of human resources (HR), its opportunity and challenges, when humans aren't the only resources.

> **Chapter 5: AI-First Design for Nonlinearity. Adopting an <u>AI-first</u> strategy is the <u>only</u> path from assistive to <u>Autonomous</u> capabilities, producing <u>nonlinear</u>, exponential outcomes.**

For as many centuries as we have been conducting business, despite the many differences in culture and language, region, technological progress, and so on, all of our organizations have been designed by humans for humans. And more recently, over the last couple of decades or so, being "human-centered" has become a mantra for good product, experience, and service design. But now, in this chapter, we argue that the only path to future business Fitness and nonlinear outcomes is through AI-first strategy and design. If you don't take your hands off the steering wheel you won't allow the car to become autonomous and unlock its future potential.

In this chapter we identify a few of the many ways in which companies are designed for human capabilities and characteristics and show how those may no longer be relevant in the age of AI, how far from being strengths they may be constraints.

Again we review other systems and situations into which automation and AI have been introduced and the surprises and learning that came with them. We discuss the design of airplanes for stability, a performance characteristic that is highly desirable and even necessary when humans are piloting the plane but that might be a limitation and compromise when AI takes over.

One of the things we're hearing a lot recently from leaders and independent contributors alike is that they're "waiting for the dust to settle" before they make their next move or their next major decision. This is understandable given the tumultuous and unpredictable nature of the last few years, from COVID-19 to business restructurings to banking collapses to the rise of Generative and Agentic AI, and everything in between.

But here's a newsflash for all of us: it's never going to happen. The dust is not going to settle. So let's stop waiting and wasting time. We need to become more sensitive to the changes all around us and more responsive to them, not more passive or more resistant. If we want to build high-performance organizations of the future, Boundless organizations, we need to throw our ideas about stability out the window. We need to organize and plan and design our businesses to be inherently unstable themselves.

But what would it mean to be inherently unstable?

Most airplanes are built to be stable, meaning that after a disturbance they will return to aeronautical equilibrium with minimum pilot effort. In everyday circumstances, this is a highly desirable characteristic. It makes the plane comparatively easy for a human to fly, even one with limited expertise, and consequently makes flight accessible to more people. So this is all good. But it comes at a cost. The more stable the aircraft, the less maneuverable it is. In everyday situations, this is hardly a problem. But in challenging situations, when environmental or competitive forces are at play and responsiveness is in high demand, this trade-off starts to become one.

In the case of fighter aircraft, for example, lack of maneuverability would be a real problem during combat. So fighter jets are designed for the exact opposite set of characteristics. They are built for the greatest possible maneuverability, and as a result, they are inherently unstable (also known by the friendlier-sounding term *relaxed stability*).

The problem is that inherently unstable aircraft are nearly impossible for humans—even highly trained pilots—to control by themselves. So pilots rely on computerized fly-by-wire flight control systems that sense flight conditions, take thousands of measurements per second, and continuously manipulate the plane's control surfaces. This combination of designed instability and computerized control systems using real-time feedback loops gives the human pilot the best of both worlds: maneuverability and stability.

In short, fighter pilots need help simply to keep their planes in the air. The planes are so optimized for maneuverability that without assistance from onboard computers, they would be unflyable by any human, however expert. But with that help, pilots can maximize the maneuverability of the plane to accomplish their objectives while giving the task of keeping the plane aloft to the AI system.

What does this have to do with leadership and dust settling? Quite a lot as it happens. Today's businesses, like most airplanes, are built for stability. They withstand change rather than respond to it. What they are not built for is maneuverability. Waiting for the dust to settle means battening down the hatches and hunkering down until normality returns, not being active in the prevailing conditions.

But making decisions and taking action, being maneuverable or responsive, is precisely what the company of the present and future is going to need. The conditions of business are going to continue to be turbulent. There will be more and more information flowing in from customers, partners, competitors, and the market in general, and it's going to be out of the realm of human leadership to process it in real time. There will simply be too many inputs, too many decisions to be made, and too many actions to be taken for humans to do it all on their own.

We believe that leaders need to act against their natural reactions. They need to stop thinking that they have to be in control of everything and everyone to be "good" managers and executives. In fact, they have to go in the opposite direction and demand so much data to be generated from every part of their operations that no one could possibly handle it or make sense of it without help. In the words of Ming Zeng, the chair of Alibaba's Academic Council, they need to "datafy" everything. And then they need to set AI on it.

Generative, Agentic, and physical AI will revolutionize the way we work. AI is the electricity of the 21st century. Ignore it and your business will be left in the dark. Accenture notes that 97% of global executives agree AI foundation models will enable connections across data types, revolutionizing where and how AI is used. Generative AI integrated with the right customer processes will improve the customer experience.

AI can play a crucial role in assisting leaders and their teams in making strategic, as well as immediate, data-driven decisions and taking effective action. AI empowers organizations to deliver powerful customer experiences by driving efficiency through automation and building trust by securing customer data.

It's important to note that while AI can provide valuable support in decision-making, human expertise and judgment are still crucial for considering ethical, legal, and contextual factors in business decision-making processes. Today's businesses and their leaders are facing unprecedented complexity and turbulence. But there are no signs that it's going to get any easier or smoother any time soon. And so the time is ripe for a fundamental rethink, a new mindset that abandons hope of stability and that embraces the exact opposite. It is a mindset that intentionally pushes the organization out of equilibrium, out of the hope of human control, and that learns to apply computerized systems using data, AI, and real-time feedback loops to enhance humans' power of strategic decision-making.

We ask what it means for human qualities and virtues like experience and effort when they're up against AI that can go from novice to master in hours rather than decades. On a more positive note we ask what might it mean when AI can change the performance characteristics of whatever system it is operating

> **Chapter 6: Autonomy and Boundless Principles. Becoming an <u>Autonomous business</u> requires the seven <u>Boundless principles</u> shaping the <u>mindset</u> and business <u>operating model</u>.**

In our previous book, *Boundless*, we made the case that traditional business structures are siloed, static, and built for control, and that they're already falling short in a connected world. We introduced a new model, one rooted in flow, adaptability, and shared success. The Boundless organization, we argued, was designed not for stability, but for movement. Not for command and control, but for connection and choreography. Not for predictability, but for possibility.

At the time, we believed this model was important for businesses navigating uncertainty, complexity, and digital transformation. But we didn't yet know how fast the world would change. We didn't know that within two years, Generative AI would explode into the mainstream, creating the most powerful accelerant to organizational change since the invention of the internet.

And now, with the arrival of Agentic AI, systems that can make decisions and take actions on our behalf, the Boundless principles are no longer just helpful. They are foundational, because autonomy, true autonomy for machines *and* for humans, is not just a technical upgrade. It's an organizational redesign as we will see in our other themes, especially those covering SUDA, the seven-level AI maturity model, and RI. And without the right mindset to guide it, redesigns can become superficial embellishments on top of existing orthodoxies and conventions, not the transformations needed to achieve the nonlinear potential of AI.

In this chapter we revisit the major themes behind Boundless to demonstrate why they are more relevant than ever before. For a full treatment obviously we would recommend that you read that book as a companion to this one.

> **Chapter 7: AI Is The New UI. Taking our hands off the steering wheel:** The road to Autonomous maturity for AI, the company, and its humans requires bold leadership and a new playbook.

In this chapter we describe the journey that companies will take toward becoming autonomous. As an early example of a system that is currently evolving from being human-operated to AI-operated, we describe the well-established and accepted model of the autonomous car. The model identifies six levels of autonomy that extend from full driver control to full AI control of a car journey. We reflect on the linear progression in capabilities and on the nonlinear impact at the most advanced level, and then even beyond that.

We then apply the same approach to Autonomous work and introduce our seven-level model. We describe the technologies involved at each level and the comparative roles of human and AI. We argue that the same linear/nonlinear result happens at the most advanced levels and that there is a moment that is as dependent on the human willingness to "let go of the steering wheel" as it is on the AI to take control of it.

The seven levels progress from basic task support to AI-orchestrated ecosystems. They unfold in two distinct phases. The first is **Augmentation**, where AI enhances human capabilities and accelerates the speed of execution. The second is **Autonomy**, where AI begins to act, decide, lead, and ultimately orchestrate systems in ways no human team could match in speed or scale.

In the early levels, businesses see linear improvements, greater productivity, smoother workflows, measurable efficiency gains. But in the later levels, something different happens. The change is no longer just quantitative, it's qualitative. The transition from Level 5 to Level 6 is not unlike the moment engineers remove the steering wheel from the autonomous car. A vehicle without a driver doesn't just drive differently. It can be built differently. And the journey it makes is no longer constrained by the assumptions of human control. In the same way, a business operating at Level 6 or 7 is not just a faster, leaner version of today's firm. It's a new kind of company altogether.

Introduction xxv

As we have already highlighted, there will come a moment when the potential of AI is either enabled or choked, and the responsibility for making the right decision at that moment will stand very firmly with the leaders of the company. They need to have the courage and the willingness to let go of the steering wheel if they are to reach a new level of fitness.

Chapter 8: Summary of Key Insights. This is what defines the world's most successful companies: Autonomy.

Finally we will recap and revisit each of our seven key insights.

Chapter 9: Ten Tenets of Autonomous Businesses.

In closing, if there's anything we'd love for you to take away from the book, it would be these 10 things. We are grateful to you for investing your time in and we hope that these 10 tenets of Autonomous Businesses can be guides for you on your own journey to Autonomy.

Autonomous Company: Organization, Machine, or Organism?

As we did in *Boundless*, we use examples and analogies from living organisms and from technology systems and machines to explain certain aspects of organizations and to shed light on the potential impact of AI on those organizations. We are not saying that our businesses are living organisms or machine systems, but that they share certain characteristics, chief among them a dependence on flows of energy, matter, and information. These flows are vital to their success and yet underappreciated in business design.

As it happens, there is an ongoing debate about the difference between machines and living organisms that has been reenergized by the remarkable recent advances in AI and robotics. While the subject is fascinating in its own right, it is outside the scope of this book except for an observation that we think may be relevant as companies progress along the maturity path to Autonomy: one generally agreed difference between organisms and machines is that machines can be turned off, cut off from their energy supply, without compromising their performance once they're turned back on.

They can die, as it were, reversibly. Organisms can't. If you cut off the oxygen supply or the water supply to an organism, it deteriorates within seconds and will die irreversibly unless those supplies are restored immediately. Businesses are closer to organisms than machines in this regard. They can't survive for long without income from one source or another. But in the age of AI as organizations start to become more "machinic" on the path to Autonomy, is it possible that they'll become more resilient in that regard, better able to survive for longer without losing core function? Wouldn't it be good if they could?

Who Is This Book for?

Autonomous is for business leaders, strategists, and designers who are tasked with positioning their companies for continued success. It is also for the general business reader who likes to stay informed and who wants or needs to know how AI is going to change their world and potentially their place in it. *Autonomous* is a blueprint for the future of business. It offers leaders the insights and tools they need to succeed in the age of Agentic AI.

1

What Is a Fit Company?

In an <u>AI-powered</u> economy, the companies that are the <u>fittest</u> (best positioned to win) are <u>Autonomous</u> using <u>digital labor</u>.

Introduction

The age of Agentic artificial intelligence (AI) is suddenly upon us. There was very little advance notice of its arrival. Even the tech companies were, and still are, scrambling to position themselves and their products to exploit its current, emerging, and future capabilities. Amid all the excitement of what the technology can do *for* companies, there is little talk about what it might do *to* them. What might a company become when, and not if, Agentic AI becomes part of the workforce? Will it just be a matter of increased efficiency and productivity but otherwise business as usual, or will there be something more to it? And if there's something more, what might that be, and what do our companies need to do to prepare themselves for it?

In our book, we introduce and delve into a number of core concepts that we anticipate will greatly shape the businesses of tomorrow and the changing landscape of work. Part of the book's connective tissue, and a prerequisite for autonomy, is the concept of AI-first strategies and their profound nonlinear impact on organizations. We also address a fundamental question: what defines the most adaptable companies in an AI-driven economy? What does it mean to be fit, and what are the essential capabilities that enable the healthiest companies to thrive, compete effectively, and surpass their rivals amid growing uncertainties?

We've attempted to answer these questions by introducing and describing our vision of the Autonomous business, and to provide business leaders, strategists, and designers with stories, models, and tools to prepare their own companies to become Autonomous themselves, to survive and thrive in this new age.

The phrase "the survival of the fittest" is inextricably linked to Darwin's theories of evolution. As it happens, Darwin did not coin the phrase himself but he did adopt it in later editions of *The Origin of Species*, preferring it to "natural selection." By "fittest" Darwin meant "better adapted for the immediate, local environment," not the common modern meaning of "in the best physical shape." For example, a rabbit with light colored fur in a snowy clime is likely going to be better camouflaged than a rabbit with dark fur and so is more likely to survive predators and reproduce successfully. It's not about the rabbit being able to run faster or longer. So fitness here is not about physical fitness. It's simply about the adaptation of light fur that confers a better chance of survival than dark fur in that particular environment.

What we are saying is different. We are saying that in this particular environment a company that is physically or organizationally fit is more likely to survive than one that is not. And by "this particular environment," we mean a business world that includes AI that is developing new capabilities all the time, customers who have ever-increasing expectations, and market conditions that seem perpetually volatile.

Our definition of fitness includes being healthy, conditioned, and talented, just like a competitive athlete or team. We argue that being healthy for a company means eliminating blockages and waste and maximizing resource flows. Being conditioned means having the capacity to operate consistently, routinely at high speed and responsiveness, making the best possible use of their resource flows. Being talented means integrating AI as digital labor to assist, augment, amplify, and extend human labor

So our definition of "fittest" includes both definitions, of adaptation *and* of physical fitness. We recognize that companies really are like living organisms in some important respects and that they need to be not just adaptable but also organizationally fit to compete and collaborate effectively and survive. We are asking them to take their flows and their blockages seriously, as literally a matter of life and death, and we are asserting that integrating AI is the best way for them to become healthy, conditioned, and talented. AI makes them fit. Becoming Autonomous—which includes not only integrating AI but also handing over operational control to it, removing the steering wheel as it were—makes them the fittest.

To sum it up, the only path to fitness in this new age is Autonomy. The only path to Autonomy is AI-first strategies and design.

To understand what it might mean for a company to be Autonomous, what it might be capable of, we can use the analogy of the autonomous car. And when we say analogy, we mean something more than just a similar idea. We are at this very moment living through a time when cars are developing more and more autonomy. An increasing number of us have cars with some level of self-driving capabilities and it is clear that over the next few years these capabilities are going to continue to become ever more sophisticated. And thus the evolution of the autonomous car is not just an analogy for an Autonomous business, it is a real and important precursor for all other autonomous systems.

In its progression from being fully controlled by a human driver toward becoming autonomous or self-driving, we have the sense that the car is acquiring new capabilities incrementally, some of which are genuinely useful and some of which feel a bit more gimmicky, rather than on its way to becoming something brand new. But there comes a point in its evolution at which the car is capable of taking full control of the operations. And at that point we humans face a decision. Do we take our hands off the steering wheel or not? If we don't, because we want to be in control or we don't trust the AI, it's business as usual. We'll achieve some benefits of course. Our driving will become safer and easier. But that's all we'll achieve.

If we do cede operational control to the AI, the game changes entirely with a whole new set of possibilities. A complete physical redesign of the car itself with no instruments or interfaces for human control and no distinction between front and back. A new level of autonomy and freedom for us as passengers instead of drivers. New roles for the car in travel and transportation. A new relationship between car and human, with different options for ownership and non-ownership. Greater accessibility for people historically unable to drive or prevented from it, like kids, the elderly, the disabled. The repurposing of parking spaces and garages in cities and the redesign of streets for better pedestrian and bicycle access, and who can guess what else? Autonomy for our machines, our organizations, and ourselves has truly nonlinear impact. This is Autonomous.

The AI Boom of 2022

In November 2022, Open AI launched ChatGPT. Within 24 hours, it had attracted more than one million subscribers, the fastest adoption of any technology ever seen. Based on the transformer technology developed in 2017, ChatGPT is a large language model (LLM), meaning that it is trained on huge volumes of unstructured data, and it can perform a range of activities usually considered to require intelligence and previously only within the grasp of a human.

This was not the birth of AI itself, of course. For that, we need to go back to the 1950s when Alan Turing conceived of the Machine Intelligence test and John McCarthy coined the term *artificial intelligence* as the title of a workshop he held at Dartmouth.[1] But it stayed mostly in research labs, only episodically creating moments of newsworthy interest, like Deep Blue's defeat of Gary Kasparov in 1997 and AlphaGo's stunning defeat of Lee Sidol, the world's greatest human GO player, in 2017. And less spectacularly, but still importantly, AI has already been of great value to organizations in the form of predictive AI, the ability to predict future behavior and outcomes from a study of historic and current data.

But what suddenly grabbed the popular imagination was Generative AI, of which ChatGPT was the first example to go viral (or super-viral if that's even a thing). Generative AI marked a departure from other types of AI because it suddenly made AI available to everyone, not just technology experts, and because it had, and continues to develop, some notable capabilities that are immediately useful. First, its ability to "understand" and generate content including text, images, and even video. Second, its ability to perform tasks without human supervision, or autonomously. Third, its ability to perform tasks that require interaction with humans and therefore not just scripted interaction but also adaptive and custom responsiveness.

In other words, AI can now take action. It has the capacity to become not only a tool for us to use to get stuff done but also to use tools itself to get stuff done. Whether in disembodied format, like a ChatGPT prompt on our laptops and smartphones, or in embodied format, like an autonomous android robot, AI is becoming capable of doing increasingly more and more complex tasks. It is developing its own "agency." It's not there yet, but the current rate of progress toward it is remarkable, to the point that *Agentic AI* is now a relatively common term that hints at a nonlinear transformation of business in the not-too-distant future.

"Agentic AI is a new labor model, new productivity model, and a new economic model. The result could be a fairly significant uptick in global GDP," said Salesforce Chair and CEO Marc Benioff. In fact, Goldman Sachs predicts a 7% increase in global GDP in the next 10 years because of AI.[2]

With labor markets the tightest they've been in two decades, new labor models are sorely needed. Indeed, an estimated 85 million jobs could go unfulfilled by 2030 as populations age, birth rates decline, and worker expectations change.[3] With digital labor, companies increase output and productivity without increasing headcount. With agents, these businesses can add digital workers that require little to no supervision, taking on activities like lead management and qualification that fuel growth without adding major operational costs. This transition away from human-dependent workflows creates an opportunity for 24/7 productivity, enabling businesses to serve global markets without local teams or infrastructure.

"Digital labor is a new horizon for business … . How we architect our businesses and run our businesses and staff our businesses and think about our businesses will never be the same," says Benioff.

Business Adoption Soars

Individual adoption of Generative AI was almost immediate. Business adoption was initially less spectacular with many companies understandably nervous about data privacy and protection issues, not to mention errors and hallucinations. But it quickly heated up as the use cases for Agentic AI started to become more and more obvious. Organizations are now looking to AI to fill gaps, streamline operations, and ultimately automate a variety of business roles. The pace at which this transformation is happening is staggering, with AI capabilities advancing faster than most businesses can keep up.

Technology companies, industry analysts, and consulting firms are all now regularly reporting on the growing adoption of AI, the expectations beginning to emerge among customers, and the pressure that these place on companies to remain competitive. It may be useful to survey the picture that these sources paint of the current and near future business AI landscape.

According to Salesforce's 2024 AI report, 76% of customers now expect personalized service, and AI is uniquely positioned to meet that demand at scale.[4] With AI-driven platforms like chatbots and virtual assistants, businesses are able to provide 24/7 customer service, addressing inquiries, processing requests, and handling transactions, often without the need for human intervention. This not only enhances the customer experience but also reduces operational costs.

The speed at which AI is being integrated into business operations is increasing at an unprecedented rate. Gartner's 2024 forecast shows that 80% of businesses will have adopted AI in some capacity by 2025, up from just 30% in 2020. In a recent McKinsey report, 72% of executives cited AI as a "critical enabler" of their strategy, with 80% of global business leaders stating that AI has already helped them achieve their strategic goals in a variety of departments, including marketing, supply chain, and finance.[5] Seventy-five percent of retailers say AI agents will be essential for a competitive edge by 2026, according to the sixth edition of the Connected Shoppers 2025 report by Salesforce.[6] AI agents are poised to redefine retail, an industry that is often a fast follower of emerging technologies. AI agents greatly expand AI's impact by independently responding to customer inquiries, managing inventory, and more. Retailers view leveraging AI as their number one opportunity. As many as 84% of retailers use AI already in 2025, and only 2% have no plans for the technology. More innovation is underway as AI becomes increasingly Agentic, taking action autonomously without human involvement.

This rapid adoption reflects the urgency businesses feel to remain competitive in an increasingly digital and automated landscape. The question now is not whether to adopt AI but how to do so in a strategic and cumulatively beneficial way, leveraging its full potential at different stages of its evolution.

In data-heavy fields like finance, AI is already proving indispensable in helping analysts process vast amounts of data quickly. The ability of AI to sift through, analyze, and make predictions based on large datasets empowers businesses to make quicker, more accurate decisions. In financial trading, AI-driven platforms can process multiple data points in real time, giving traders an advantage in predicting market movements with a level of precision human analysts cannot match.

The integration of AI into the workforce is not just about replacing mundane tasks; it is about augmenting human potential. The World Economic Forum projects that by 2030, AI will create 97 million new roles, many of which will demand a different skill set than the traditional, task-oriented positions that have historically existed.[7] Whether these new roles will all be filled by humans is a matter of debate. Our view is that in the near term this may be true but in the longer term AI itself will become more than capable of filling new gaps itself. One prospect that does seem uncontroversial though is that human workers will no longer be expected to focus on repetitive tasks but will instead focus on higher-level activities such as strategy development, innovation, and relationship building, areas where AI still cannot fully replicate human capabilities.

This shift is already visible in manufacturing and logistics, where AI is enhancing human labor rather than displacing it. In companies like Amazon, robots and drones handle inventory management, picking, and sorting, while human workers oversee operations, manage systems, and handle exceptions that require creative problem-solving. According to McKinsey, 30% of tasks in manufacturing can already be automated, but this doesn't mean job loss; instead, it means that employees are transitioning to roles that require more decision-making, oversight, and cross-functional collaboration.

While AI's initial role in business was seen as a tool for enhancing productivity, it is now viewed as a core enabler of business transformation. AI's ability to optimize everything from operations to marketing to customer experience is opening up new opportunities for businesses of all sizes. For example, companies like Tesla have already begun using AI to drive automation in manufacturing processes. Tesla's AI-driven system helps reduce defects, optimize energy use, and maximize manufacturing efficiency, enabling it to scale production rapidly without the need for expanding human labor.

Salesforce 2025 research revealed that US car owners see Agentic AI as a potential game changer in the car buying and ownership experience. Consumers are bullish on Agentic AI as a solution to improve the car-buying experience. Over half (56%) of car owners and lessees believe AI agents will simplify car maintenance. Research found that 70% of car owners would use an AI agent if it meant being able to diagnose and address car issues in real time. Over one-third (37%) of car owners would use an AI agent if it meant never booking a service appointment themselves again, and 40% of car owners believe AI will make driving safer overall. The most popular Agentic AI use case involves AI systems that monitor vehicle health and decode complex information, suggesting drivers want agents to act like knowledgeable advocates in high-stakes, technically complex situations where drivers feel most vulnerable.

We are also entering the age of autonomous retail. AI agents build on earlier AI foundations and represent the technology's latest innovation. Retailers are taking notice: 43% say they are already piloting autonomous AI, with use cases spanning the business, according to Salesforce 2025 research. Customer service in retail is on a fast path to Autonomous service delivery powered by AI agents.

On a global scale, AI is also changing industries like health care. In 2019, AI-powered diagnostic tools were found to be more accurate than human doctors in diagnosing certain diseases. A study published in the *Journal of the American Medical Association* showed that an AI model could detect breast cancer in mammograms with more than 94% accuracy, outperforming radiologists in identifying tumors.[8] This type of automation is expected to dramatically reduce medical errors, lower health care costs, and provide better care to a larger population, all while freeing up human doctors to focus on complex cases and patient relationships.

Why Understanding AI's Evolution Is Crucial

AI has broken out of the research labs. It's here. Understanding its evolution, both in terms of capabilities and its integration into business practices, is crucial for any organization that aims to remain competitive in the age of automation and AI. The evolution of AI is unfolding in distinct phases, each with its own set of implications for workers, business leaders, and strategists.

As the McKinsey Global Institute reports, AI could add up to $13 trillion to the global economy by 2030.[9] This represents an enormous shift in how businesses will operate in the coming decade. However, even though data quality is widely regarded as the strongest predictor of AI readiness, only 35% of survey respondents report having a strong data culture, and over 20% report a lack of strong data culture or inconsistent leadership support, talent development, and education about data.[10] This gap in preparedness presents both a challenge and an opportunity: businesses that proactively understand and integrate AI will reap significant benefits, while those that fail to engage risk falling behind.

AI adoption requires companies to rethink everything from leadership structures to workforce training. For example, AI in supply chain management is already revolutionizing the way companies plan, forecast, and respond to demand. According to Gartner, 50% of supply chain management solutions will include Agentic AI capabilities by 2030, improving operational efficiency and enhancing customer satisfaction.[11] These kinds of shifts will be pervasive across industries, making AI literacy and strategic foresight a business necessity.

In many ways, AI is becoming the new electricity, a foundational tool that will be woven into every aspect of business operations. Satya Nadella, CEO of Microsoft, has likened AI to the advent of the personal computer and the internet, predicting that AI will be as transformative as these previous technological revolutions. The difference, however, is that AI doesn't just change how we use technology; it changes what technology can do, potentially replacing large swaths of human work while empowering others to do their jobs better, faster, and more efficiently.

Business leaders who do not embrace AI risk losing their competitive edge. According to Deloitte Digital and Salesforce 2025 Connectivity Benchmark research, 93% of information technology (IT) leaders will implement AI agents in 2025–2026.[12] Surpassing most projections for AI adoption, organizations are leveraging digital labor across all lines of business, according to the report. The report based on survey data from interviews with 1,050 IT leaders across the globe, highlighted key opportunities and challenges for adoption of Agentic AI in business, including in these ways:

- **Data is trapped across siloed enterprise apps.** The average number of apps used by respondents is 897, with 45% reporting using 1,000 applications or more—further hindering IT teams' ability to build a unified experience. Only 29% of enterprise apps are integrated and share information across the business.
- **IT workload is increasing.** With IT leaders being pushed to incorporate AI, 86% of respondents anticipate their teams' workload will rise in the next year, all while still maintaining existing systems, including 70% who report governing enterprise-wide automations.
- **Integrated user experience is elusive.** Enterprise-wide automation is on the rise; even so, 66% of respondents still don't provide an integrated user experience across their channels.
- **Integration is a challenge for accelerated adoption of AI agents.** Nearly all (95%) of IT leaders report 95% integration as a hurdle to implementing AI effectively, but Application Programming Interfaces (APIs) have helped. Fifty-five percent of IT leaders report APIs improve their IT infrastructure, while 45% recognize the ability for APIs to support enhancing user experiences.

According to Salesforce's global 2025 CIO survey, adoption of autonomous agents is a key business priority. Introducing autonomous agents within the next two years is on the road map for 93% of IT leaders; nearly half have already done so. And the key driver for AI adoption is productivity gains from the use of Agentic AI and a digital labor force. The vast majority (93%) feel that AI will increase developer productivity over the next three years, which is up seven percentage points since the 2024 report. And last, Agentic AI adoption will mean more AI models will be deployed to drive agent adoption. The average number of AI models estimated to be used doubled from 2024 (9 to 18), and IT leaders predict a further increase of 78% in the next three years to an average of 32 models.

Businesses that recognize the importance of AI early on and integrate it into their operations will have a clear competitive advantage in the future.

What Is a Fit Company?

AI adoption today is less about replacing employees and more about augmenting human potential. Leaders who understand this distinction can position themselves to be leaders in their fields. AI is already being used in sectors like health care, logistics, and finance, and its impact is growing exponentially.

According to Salesforce CIO (Chief Information Officer) 2025 research, investments in data infrastructure are 4X AI investments. To prepare for the expanded use of AI, enterprise CIOs are allocating 25% of their budgets to data infrastructure and management (compared to 5% to AI).[13] The primary obstacles to AI implementation are integration, data silos, and legacy debt. Integration remains the most significant barrier to AI implementation, with 95% of organizations facing challenges when integrating AI into their existing processes. Cybersecurity and data privacy are paramount concerns for IT leaders during AI integration. Disconnected data remains an overwhelming blocker to legacy modernization for the majority of organizations. In 2025, 83% of organizations report that integration challenges are a significant barrier to their legacy modernization efforts. And 97% of IT leaders acknowledge that their organizations struggle with integrating end-user experiences.

- **AI in health care.** In medical diagnostics, AI-powered platforms are revolutionizing the way doctors interpret imaging data. Google Health's AI system, for example, can analyze mammograms with greater than 94% accuracy, significantly outperforming radiologists in some cases.[14] This doesn't mean replacing doctors but augmenting their capabilities, enabling them to focus on patient care and complex decision-making while the AI handles routine diagnostics.
- **AI in retail.** The value of AI agents is the ability to deliver value at the speed of need. The survey found that 74% of shoppers abandon a brand after three or fewer bad experiences, this according to Salesforce's 2025 Connected Shoppers research. Shoppers say the worst retail experience is poor customer service, putting pressure on retailers to enhance support with implications for their bottom lines. Retailers are either autonomous businesses or declining businesses. The survey found that 81% of retailers trust AI to act autonomously with sufficient guardrails. Digital natives are embracing Agentic

AI—Gen Z shoppers are 2.7 times as likely as baby boomers to want product recommendations from AI agents (63% versus 23%). The top five benefits of AI in retail: increased employee productivity, improved shopper experiences, increased revenues, improved supplier relationships, and improved employee experiences. AI yields clear business results: 89% of retailers expect returns on their investments, with similar shares reporting increased online sales volumes and reduced operational costs.

- **AI in logistics.** In logistics, companies like FedEx and UPS are using AI to optimize delivery routes, predict maintenance needs, and manage warehouse operations. AI-driven predictive analytics helps reduce operational costs and improves delivery speed, benefiting both businesses and their customers. The integration of AI in these areas helps companies stay competitive by improving service levels and cutting costs.
- **AI in finance.** JP Morgan's COIN (Contract Intelligence) system uses AI to review legal documents, a task that traditionally took thousands of hours of human labor. The AI system can process these documents in seconds, enabling employees to focus on higher-value tasks such as negotiations and client interactions. This level of efficiency has enabled firms like JP Morgan to reduce operational costs by 60% while increasing the accuracy and speed of their legal processes.

The benefits of AI adoption are clear, but businesses that fail to act may find themselves in a precarious position. Complacency can lead to missed opportunities, with competitors leveraging AI to enhance customer experiences, streamline operations, and reduce costs. The gap between businesses that embrace AI and those that do not is widening, and this divide will only continue to grow.

A recent PwC survey found that more than 40% of CEOs expressed concern that their companies were not keeping up with the technological advancements required to maintain a competitive edge.[15] Moreover, 58% of companies reported that AI and automation would significantly affect their workforce by 2025, underscoring the need for strategic AI investments to ensure continued success. Failure to address this gap could result in a business losing its competitive advantage—or worse, being overtaken by more AI-savvy competitors.

Implications of AI

What should we take from these various commentators about the rise of AI? What does it all mean?

The most important lesson is that we need to change the way that we define and think about technology. Until very recently, technology was first and foremost a tool. It was something that humans built and then used to do a job. To do it better, faster, easier than we could without it. But still, we used it. What's new is that with Generative and Agentic AI we are not creating new tools to help us do a job. We are creating a new workforce to do the job for us. This is not an absolute, of course, and we can always point to older technologies that may have done part of our job for us (factory automation began at least 200 years ago) but this is clearly new in both scope and capability.

We are creating a cheaper, faster, better, scalable workforce, not a cheaper, faster, better, scalable tool set. AI is becoming like us: doers, workers, agents that get things done. In a car it is becoming the driver. In the home it is likely to become "the help." In the factory it is becoming the assembler, in the call center it is becoming the service representative. It can create and drive marketing campaigns, and it can sell to and serve customers. And more besides. We are no longer the only members of the workforce.

AI will continue to evolve in its capabilities, taking on not just single tasks and activities but entire processes and then entire groups of processes or functions. It will cross functions and integrate them, both front and back office, both customer-facing and supporting functions until it can assist and augment human resources across the organization. Eventually it will help orchestrate and choreograph a company's entire operations, and reach far beyond them, connecting with ecosystem partners as well to simplify cross-boundary flows of value and accelerate the delivery of value to the customer.

Is this just semantics, calling AI *digital labor* rather than a *digital tool*? Actually it is a critical distinction, perhaps *the* critical distinction in preparing for the future of work and the future of business. Companies that continue to view AI as a tool will miss its future, nonlinear impact when it gives us the opportunity to let go of the steering wheel, to use a metaphor from the autonomous car. They will miss the implications for its human workforce and the new relationships that will be created. They will miss the opportunities to scale and to speed up. They will miss the opportunity to learn, unlearn, and relearn. They will miss the transformation of business itself.

Enter the Autonomous Business

The logical implication of all this is the emergence of the Autonomous business. An Autonomous business is designed to be AI-first in its strategies and operations to maximize value and minimize time to value, and when it is done right it will unlock unprecedented speed, scale, and shared success. An Autonomous business will deliver nonlinear impact, but only if its leaders give up control of it.

But getting from one-off AI implementations—where most companies are at today—to autonomy will be neither easy nor obvious. Our companies are all started by humans, staffed by humans, led by humans, designed by humans to satisfy human needs. Unsurprising then that they also reflect human beliefs, values, capabilities and limitations, understanding of, and orthodoxies about how to organize ourselves to do work and how to get that work done. They are not designed, nor have they ever been designed (with some important exceptions that we will cover later), for any other type of participants for the simple reason that there haven't ever been any other types of participants or members of the workforce. But this is no longer true. The dominant logic or the paradigm of the human organization is about to be tested and replaced by a new one: that of the machine-led, AI-first organization, the Autonomous company.

Business leaders will need to challenge all these conventions, standard operating procedures, and orthodoxies underpinning businesses designed by humans for humans. They will need to build digital labor to nonlinearly scale the health, conditioning, and talent of their teams, business, and ecosystem, enabling $24 \times 7 \times 365$ continuity and responsiveness, removing blockages and waste that trap or reduce value. They will need to manage the relationships between the two types of intelligent resources: digital and human. They will need to design for AI control and teach human leaders to "let go of the steering wheel." This is truly a radical journey of transformation to achieve tomorrow's promise of Agentic AI and Autonomy. And they need to start that journey today.

The good thing is that the journey is familiar enough to begin with as Agentic AI continues to develop its capabilities. We're firmly in an initial phase right now, one that is characterized by AI in an assistive and augmentative role. But we know that there will be a fork in the road, a time when AI is mature enough to become Autonomous, to be able to take control of ever greater parts of a company's operations. And the leaders at that point need to decide whether they're willing to take their hands off the business steering wheel and let AI take over or not. Those that aren't, and there will be some, will soon find themselves on the slow road to irrelevance as they are overtaken, at great speed, by those who are.

The companies that fully embrace and exploit this emerging potential will become autonomous, with machines—in particular Agentic AI, robots, and other advanced technologies—taking operational lead (machine autonomy), and humans empowered to create and then realize their mission faster and more effectively than ever before (human autonomy).

By ceding control of the increasingly complex operations of today's businesses to AI, human leaders can assume full control of their strategies and purpose, whatever that purpose may be, and focus on it without distraction. Their evolution—and the evolution of the entire human workforce—is just as important as AI's, and it has the potential to be this: an evolution from being operators of the enterprise's systems and processes to being owners of its mission.

In Accenture's 2025 Technology Vision report,[16] AI was a declaration of Autonomy. The focus of the report was on the "Binary Big Bang" and the Agentic AI revolution in the enterprise. Accenture noted that AI will drive new levels of Autonomy throughout business, evolving the ability to reinvent with tech, data, and AI—a limitless opportunity for innovation and growth. The key disruption here is "AI cognitive digital brains."

AI "cognitive digital brains" will completely reshape the role technology plays across the enterprise and in people's lives: for individuals, the cognitive digital brain will operate as a copilot or sidekick, something that will understand their job, learn their preferences, and get to know them through its interactions, in service of helping them become an enhanced version of themselves. For businesses, it might seem more like a central nervous system—an evolution of the enterprise architecture into something that can capture the collective knowledge of the business, its unique differentiators, and its culture and persona, and become a key orchestrator (and even Autonomous operator) for parts of it.

The cognitive digital brain will become the central nervous system for enterprise decision-making and continuous learning. Used to power enterprises' future ambitions, like intention-based architectures, it is composed of four interconnected layers that together organize, process, and act on information:

- **Knowledge.** Technologies like knowledge graphs and vector databases gather, organize, and structure data from across the enterprise and beyond.
- **Models.** Large-scale Generative AI models, as well as classical machine learning and deep learning models, perform critical thinking and reasoning functions to turn data into actionable outcomes.
- **Agents.** Designed to be problem-solvers, tackle tasks with minimal human input, and learn and grow over time, AI agents bring planning, reflection, and adaptability to the mix.
- **Architecture.** A comprehensive backbone is what turns AI experiments into enterprise-grade solutions. It scales intelligence across the organization and into existing workflows, enabling repeatability so solutions can be made once and reused.

The Binary Big Bang tracks the emergence of language models coupled with Agentic systems and how they challenge conventions around building software and crafting new digital ecosystems. The trend dives into a generational transition, as leaders rethink how digital systems are designed—building the foundation for the cognitive digital brains that will become an essential part of enterprise DNA. The result will be a dramatic increase in technology diffusion touching every aspect of business, consumer, and societal interactions. It sets the stage for the emerging AI era, where we will rapidly expand digital ecosystems and increasingly trust Autonomous systems to find new ways to innovate with us.

Accenture highlights Marc Benioff's September 2024 announcement that Salesforce would "hard pivot" to Agentforce, a platform for building and deploying autonomous AI agents. "It's rare for a company of such scale to pivot like this. But Salesforce realized something groundbreaking and formidable that every company needs to recognize too: We have just entered the Binary Big Bang."

The firm emphasizes the following key takeaways: leaders must prepare today for an imminent world in which AI is everywhere and acting Autonomously on behalf of people. New Autonomy for AI also means new Autonomy for systems and people, along with a refined relationship with trust. And opportunities will be lost unless business leaders secure enough trust from employees and consumers to engage with AI's unprecedented capabilities. We view these takeaways as reinforcing evidence that the fittest companies of the future are Autonomous businesses.

Summary

The fittest companies in our rapidly evolving AI-driven economy are Autonomous, businesses that have transcended simply implementing AI tools to fundamentally redesigning themselves as AI-first in both strategy and operations. These companies are building digital labor forces powered by Agentic AI that nonlinearly scale the health, conditioning, and talent of their teams, business, and ecosystem. They enable $24 \times 7 \times 365$ continuity and responsiveness, removing blockages and waste that trap or reduce value creation.

Unlike traditional organizations designed by humans for humans, Autonomous companies recognize AI not as another tool but as a new workforce, capable of taking operational control. This represents a paradigm shift comparable to autonomous vehicles, where true transformation happens when leaders "take their hands off the steering wheel." As AI evolves from assistive to Autonomous, businesses

(continued)

(*continued*)

face a critical decision: continue using AI for incremental improvement or embrace Autonomy to unlock unprecedented possibilities.

The journey toward becoming Autonomous begins with AI in assistive roles but accelerates as AI matures into what Accenture calls "cognitive digital brains," central nervous systems for enterprise decision-making. These systems combine knowledge management, advanced AI models, Autonomous agents, and integrated architecture to transform business operations. Companies that fully embrace this evolution will become truly machine-led and human-assisted, not vice versa, with humans evolving from system operators to mission owners. This is the essence of fitness in the age of Agentic AI, a fundamental transformation that requires challenging conventions and orthodoxies to survive and thrive in tomorrow's AI-first economy.

2 | Blockages Kill Companies

Blockages are the number one cause of **death** in living organisms and businesses alike. **Autonomous** companies are **living organisms** that are **immune** to blockages.

Flow is essential to the health of most systems, from living organisms to machine systems to businesses. Blockages can be fatal in many cases, and in businesses in particular they can be hard to diagnose and even harder to remedy and cure. Autonomous businesses apply artificial intelligence (AI) to reduce and even eliminate blockages and other causes of waste and trapped value.

Introduction

A healthy living organism, from complex ones like humans to the individual cells that we're composed of, is one that optimizes flow. Optimal flows of matter, energy, and information between the organism and its environment, and flows within the organism itself, keep us all alive and healthy. For us, these flows start with breathing and blood flow. Breathing is the exchange of air between an individual and the environment. With each breath in and out we increase the oxygen levels in our lungs and reduce the carbon dioxide levels. Blood flow transports oxygen and other nutrients to the entire body and transports waste and toxins from it.

Of course these are not the only flows vital to our existence. The flow of nutrients and energy from consumption of food and drink is also essential as are the flows of information from the environment that we process as sights, sounds, smells, tastes, and physical contact (feel and touch) that enable us to navigate life safely, know what's safe and what's dangerous, enable us to find mates, and so on.

Optimal flow is also essential to the health or optimal functioning of a whole variety of machines and systems. From the flow of electricity that animates nearly all systems nowadays, to hydraulic flows, data flows, fuel flows, airflow, and so on, our constructed and built world relies on uninterrupted flow to work properly. This is as true for domestic appliances like refrigerators and washing machines as it is for large-scale circulatory and infrastructure systems like oil pipelines and logistics networks.

This same principle of optimal flow also applies to business. While people may not typically think about our companies as living organisms or as machines, it is clear that they share many characteristics, most significantly the need to exchange flows of energy—or what we would more typically describe in business terms as resources—between them and the markets and business ecosystems of which they are parts. Healthy companies have optimal flows of money, raw materials, electricity, expertise, data, and other resources coming in and flows of value to the customer coming out (product, service, information, and so on), as well as flows of money back out to providers, investors, and so on.

Blockages Cause Disease and Death

Among humans, *clinical death* is defined as the moment when breathing and/or blood flow stops. Under certain controlled conditions and for very specific medical and surgical purposes, clinical death can be induced in a person and then reversed. But in the vast majority of cases, when these flows stop, the result is irreversible and the person dies, as we all commonly understand death to mean. Per Wikipedia[1]:

> Clinical death is the medical term for cessation of blood circulation and breathing, the two criteria necessary to sustain the lives of human beings and of many other organisms. It occurs when the heart stops beating in a regular rhythm, a condition called cardiac arrest.

In other words, all deaths are ultimately associated with loss of flow. But more specifically, blockages are directly responsible for the top 3 causes of death in the United States and the world, and 6 of the top 10.[2] To take just the top two:

Coronary Heart Disease (CHD)   CHD occurs when a substance called plaque builds up that narrows the arteries in the heart. A heart attack occurs when an artery becomes completely blocked, resulting in a lack of blood flow to the heart. Heart disease is the leading cause of death for both men and women in the United States and in New York State.

Cancer   Cancer cells or tumors in organs or the bloodstream can disrupt organ function. They may destroy healthy cells in organs, block their nutrient or oxygen supply, and allow waste products to build up. If cancer becomes severe enough that it impairs or prevents vital organ function, it can result in death.

Incidentally, while not all causes of death are due to blockages, other leading causes are often due to abnormal flow, either toxic blood flow, lack of oxygen in the blood flow, and in a few cases, flow of blood outside of the body. We would call the last of these cases a spill rather than a directed flow. We view flows as always guided, for example, by veins and arteries, pipelines, banks and channels, and so on. They are never floods nor puddles nor spills nor droughts.

In addition to the flow of blood and oxygen, flows of information occur via our senses; sight, sounds, smell, taste, touch all work to keep us alive. When we are deprived of any of these, when the information coming from the world is somehow blocked and unavailable to us, our ability to navigate the world safely is diminished. And if we are unable to exchange our thoughts and our feelings with the world, perhaps because we are paralyzed or have lost our power of speech, once again our safe and healthy passage through life is threatened.

The effect of blockages is by no means limited to humans. All other living organisms depend on the optimal flow of energy and matter between themselves and their environment, and their survival is degraded when that flow is blocked or diverted and unavailable to them. And beyond individual organisms, natural systems like rivers can also experience a death of sorts when they are blocked. The good and surprising news is that when rivers are unblocked again, even after a considerable period, life often returns to them. Four dams had been built on the Klamath River in the western United States (Oregon and California) starting in 1918 and soon led to the extinction of two salmon species and the reduction by 95% of the remaining salmon populations. The first dam was demolished in 2023 and the other three in 2024. Within the first year, salmon were spotted returning to their ancestral birthing waters upstream despite having been unable to do so for over a century!

Machine Health Is Also Dependent on Flow

Those machines and systems that are dependent on flow are just as liable as humans and other living organisms to performance degradation and failure when they experience blockages:

- **Blockages in fluid systems (pumps, pipes, and hydraulics).** In machines that rely on fluid movement, such as hydraulic systems, engines, or cooling systems, blockages can cause catastrophic failures. For example, a blocked oil filter can lead to insufficient lubrication, causing overheating and wear in engine parts. Similarly, blockages in a car's cooling system can result in engine overheating and breakdown.
- **Blockages in airflow systems.** Machines such as HVAC systems, jet engines, or even basic air compressors require uninterrupted airflow to function properly. Blocked air filters or ducts can lead to reduced efficiency, overheating, or total system failure.

- **Clogs in manufacturing equipment.** In production lines, blockages in conveyor belts, 3D printers, or extrusion machines can halt manufacturing entirely. For example, a small blockage in an injection molding machine could ruin an entire batch of products and lead to significant downtime.
- **Blockages in data flow in computers.** Digital systems rely on uninterrupted data flow. Blockages like network congestion, failed processes, or clogged memory caches can slow down or halt operations. For example, in a data center, a blockage in network traffic due to a failed server can cascade into downtime for entire applications.
- **Blockages in fuel systems.** For machines like cars, planes, or generators, blockages in fuel lines can prevent the machine from functioning. For instance, clogged fuel injectors can disrupt combustion, reduce power, and ultimately damage the engine.

Blockages Slow Down and Even Threaten to Kill Companies

We have already written an entire book about one type of blockage, namely, organizational silos. Silos are not easy to get rid of, largely because—as we argue—they work, at least for those who manage them. Not only that, they are also our default way to manage our resources, our choice without even realizing that we're making a choice. In order to get rid of silos, therefore, companies need to embrace a new mindset, one that we call *Boundless*.

But there are blockages of all types in a typical organization, not all of them silos, and not all of them therefore requiring a different mindset to get rid of them. But you do need to know where to look, and then create a list of high-potential blockages, that is, those that lead to the greatest delays in getting things done *and* that can be removed or redesigned with the least effort. To help you in your search, here are the most common blockage types, and their typical impact.

Leadership Blockages

We start with a range of potential blockages associated with leadership that can have significant cumulative effects on an organization's speed and decision-making capacity:

- **Decision-maker absence.** When key decision-makers go on holiday or take extended leave, critical decisions are delayed or deferred. In some companies, executives do not allow decisions to be made in their absence, causing operational slowdowns, project delays, and missed market opportunities.
- **Insufficient delegation.** When leaders fail to empower lower-level managers or team leads to make decisions, they create delays in approvals and block project progress. This creates workflow bottlenecks, delayed product launches, and reduced innovation.
- **Priority shifting.** When leadership suddenly changes the priority of a project or reallocates budget away from a specific initiative, perhaps because it's no longer flavor of the month or the executive loses focus, teams that have invested time and resources see their work sidelined, leading to a loss of morale, wasted resources, and decreased trust in leadership.
- **Executive competition.** When senior executives compete for control over resources or influence, initiatives can be put on hold or dropped altogether due to infighting, causing project delays, strategic confusion, and decreased employee morale.
- **Leadership turnover.** Companies that experience frequent changes in leadership often see initiatives continuously reassessed, delayed, or abandoned. When a senior executive leaves, ongoing projects stall until a replacement is found or a new strategy is formed, leading initiatives to lose momentum, teams to experience uncertainty, and projects to be deprioritized.
- **New leadership syndrome.** New leadership often wants to put its own stamp on the company, deprioritizing ongoing initiatives that don't align with their vision. This causes disruption to ongoing projects, organizational whiplash, and wasted resources.
- **Leadership inertia.** When leadership is slow to react to emerging trends due to bureaucratic inertia, excessive approval processes, or personal risk aversion, companies miss opportunities and risk competitive disadvantage and loss of market share.
- **Unclear ownership.** In large organizations, projects often suffer when there's no clear ownership or leadership backing, resulting in diffused responsibility and stalled progress.

- **Organizational restructuring.** During restructuring efforts, mergers, acquisitions, or crises, companies often experience a "freeze" in decision-making while new strategies are developed and leadership is integrated, delaying innovation, creating project paralysis, and eroding customer trust.
- **Short-termism.** When leadership focuses too heavily on meeting quarterly financial targets, longer-term initiatives may be put on hold or scaled down, leading to a lack of innovation and long-term strategic disadvantage.

Operational Blockages

These blockages are embedded within day-to-day operations and often require deliberate initiatives to address:

- **Data silos.** Critical data often doesn't flow freely across departments, between employees, or between a company and its customers. This leads to poor decision-making, slower product development, and reduced customer satisfaction.
- **Technological limitations.** Outdated or incompatible technology infrastructure limits scalability, slows workflows, and impedes the development of new capabilities, reducing competitiveness while increasing customer frustration and operational costs.
- **Financial constraints.** Companies commonly encounter barriers to accessing funds or using financial resources effectively, resulting in missed investment opportunities, delayed innovation, or insufficient response to market demand.
- **Talent misalignment.** Misallocation of talent, slow hiring processes, or poor workforce communication and training create skills gaps, low productivity, and diminished capacity for innovation.
- **Untapped expertise.** Failure to leverage the full expertise of the workforce, either due to siloed departments or poor collaboration tools, causes innovation stagnation, poor product development, and weak customer service.
- **Process inefficiencies.** Inefficient processes, poor coordination between departments, or outdated systems slow down day-to-day operations, leading to higher operational costs, slow product launches, and poor customer service.

- **Supply chain disruptions.** Delays in the supply chain due to logistical inefficiencies, supplier issues, or poor demand forecasting cause production delays, stockouts, or excess inventory.
- **Legal and regulatory hurdles.** Legal issues, regulatory challenges, or compliance concerns can cause significant delays in launching products or services, putting companies at a market disadvantage while incurring mounting legal costs.
- **Customer communication gaps.** Poor communication between a company and its customers due to outdated tools, lack of customer feedback mechanisms, or misalignment of product offerings decreases customer satisfaction, leading to loss of loyalty and lower sales.

Cultural Blockages

These less visible but deeply impactful barriers are rooted in organizational culture:

- **Risk aversion.** A culture where innovation is discouraged and maintaining the status quo is rewarded leads to stagnation, missed opportunities, and eventual market irrelevance.
- **Blame culture.** When failures are met with finger-pointing rather than learning, employees hide problems, avoid risks, and fail to report issues early when they're easier to solve.
- **"Not invented here" syndrome.** Resistance to external ideas, technologies, or methods limits innovation and reinforces outdated approaches, creating blind spots and competitive vulnerabilities.
- **Status quo bias.** "We've always done it this way" thinking entrenches inefficient processes and prevents adaptation to changing market conditions.
- **Siloed thinking.** Departments operating as independent entities with minimal cross-functional collaboration create redundancy, communication gaps, and inconsistent customer experiences.
- **Perfectionism.** Excessive focus on flawless execution delays launches and prevents the iterative improvement that drives success in fast-moving markets.

Knowledge Management Blockages

Ineffective knowledge sharing creates significant organizational drag:

- **Concentrated expertise.** When institutional knowledge is concentrated in a few individuals, organizations become vulnerable to their departure and dependent on their availability.
- **Poor documentation.** Inadequate documentation of processes, decisions, and rationales forces repeated "reinvention of the wheel" and slows onboarding of new team members.
- **Ineffective knowledge transfer.** When knowledge isn't effectively transferred during role transitions or organizational changes, valuable insights are lost and mistakes are repeated.
- **Knowledge hoarding.** When employees hoard information as job security, organizations experience duplicate work, inconsistent approaches, and slower problem-solving.
- **Fragmented information systems.** Multiple disconnected repositories for information make finding relevant knowledge time-consuming and frustrating, reducing productivity and innovation.

Decision-Making Process Blockages

How decisions are made often determines organizational speed:

- **Analysis paralysis.** Excessive research and data collection without action thresholds leads to missed opportunities and delayed responses to market changes.
- **Consensus requirements.** Cultures requiring unanimous agreement for decisions create watered-down compromises or permanent stalemates, slowing progress dramatically.
- **Unclear decision rights.** When it's unclear who has authority to make specific decisions, initiatives stall while teams seek clarification or approval.
- **Framework deficiency.** Lack of consistent evaluation frameworks for opportunities leads to subjective, inconsistent decision-making that frustrates teams and stakeholders.

- **Meeting overload.** Excessive meetings for routine decisions consume valuable time that could be spent on execution or higher-value strategic thinking.
- **Decision reversals.** Frequent reversal of decisions creates whiplash, wastes resources, and undermines confidence in leadership.

External Relationship Blockages

Relationships with external entities can create significant constraints:

- **Vendor lock-in.** Excessive dependence on specific vendors limits flexibility, innovation options, and negotiating power.
- **Partner ecosystem challenges.** Ineffective integration with partners creates friction in joint offerings, slowing time to market and limiting collaboration benefits.
- **Extended regulatory timelines.** Regulatory delays beyond standard compliance requirements create unpredictable product launch timelines and increased costs.
- **Broken customer feedback loops.** When customer feedback doesn't reach decision-makers effectively, product development becomes disconnected from market needs.
- **Supplier communication gaps.** Poor information flow between companies and suppliers leads to misaligned expectations, quality issues, and delivery problems.

Technical Debt Blockages

Past technical decisions often constrain future options:

- **Legacy system constraints.** Outdated systems requiring significant maintenance resources divert attention from innovation and limit new capabilities.
- **Architecture limitations.** Structural technology decisions that made sense historically can prevent scalability and integration with modern systems.
- **Security constraints.** Necessary security measures can sometimes create friction in processes, slowing down development and deployment.

- **Technical skills gaps.** When organizations lack expertise in emerging technologies, adoption lags and implementation quality suffers.
- **Integration challenges.** Difficulty connecting disparate systems creates manual workarounds, data inconsistencies, and workflow inefficiencies.

Change Management Blockages

Even necessary changes can encounter resistance inside the company:

- **Implementation resistance.** Employee resistance to new systems or processes slows adoption and reduces realized benefits from investments.
- **Inadequate training.** Insufficient skill development for new initiatives creates frustration, errors, and reversion to old methods.
- **Change fatigue.** Too many simultaneous initiatives overwhelm employees' capacity to adapt, resulting in superficial compliance rather than genuine adoption.
- **Poor change communication.** When employees don't understand the why behind changes, they lack motivation to embrace new approaches.
- **Insufficient transition support.** Lack of resources during critical transition periods creates temporary performance dips that can derail change initiatives.

Resource Allocation Blockages

How organizations distribute limited resources can affect performance:

- **Team over-allocation.** Assigning teams to too many concurrent projects creates context-switching costs and prevents deep focus on priority initiatives.
- **Portfolio mismanagement.** Failure to regularly prune the project portfolio leads to resources being spread too thinly across too many initiatives.
- **Budget cycle misalignment.** Annual budget processes that don't align with opportunity timing create artificial delays for time-sensitive initiatives.

- **Zero-sum resource competition.** When departments compete for fixed resources without consideration of enterprise-wide priorities, suboptimal allocation decisions result.
- **Rigid resource allocation.** Inability to quickly reallocate resources in response to changing conditions creates organizational inflexibility.

Innovation Blockages

Barriers to developing new approaches limit future competitiveness:

- **Exploration time deficit.** No dedicated time for exploration (e.g., no "20% time") prevents discovery of new solutions and approaches.
- **Bureaucratic idea evaluation.** Overly complex processes for evaluating new ideas discourage submission and delay implementation of promising innovations.
- **Innovation measurement gaps.** Lack of appropriate metrics for innovation activities leads to underinvestment in future-focused initiatives.
- **Missing innovation infrastructure.** Absence of labs, sandboxes, or other spaces for experimentation increases the cost and risk of trying new approaches.
- **Incremental bias.** Preference for small, safe improvements over transformative innovation limits growth potential and increases vulnerability to disruption.

Psychological Blockages

Individual and collective mindsets create powerful constraints:

- **Fear of failure.** When mistake avoidance is prioritized over learning, experimentation is stifled and organizations become risk averse.
- **Executive ego.** Leaders' unwillingness to admit mistakes or change course prevents timely correction of failing initiatives.
- **Sunk cost fallacy.** Continued investment in failing projects due to previous resource commitment wastes resources and attention.

- **Misaligned incentives.** When rewards and recognition don't align with stated priorities, behavior follows incentives rather than strategic goals.
- **Cognitive biases.** Confirmation bias, recency bias, and other thinking errors distort decision-making in predictable but harmful ways.

Crisis and Resilience Blockages

How organizations handle disruption affects continuity:

- **Continuity planning gaps.** Inadequate business continuity planning creates vulnerability to disruptions and slower recovery times.
- **Single points of failure.** Lack of redundancy in critical processes or roles creates vulnerability to individual absences or departures.
- **Scaling constraints.** Inability to rapidly scale resources during demand spikes leads to missed opportunities and customer dissatisfaction.
- **Crisis tunnel vision.** When crises occur, all-hands response approaches divert resources from innovation and future-focused work.
- **Reactive posture.** Organizations without proactive risk management and scenario planning spend more time responding to preventable issues.

Moving Forward: From Identification to Action

That was obviously a very long list, and we are not suggesting that they all apply equally to all companies and situations. So the first step is to identify which blockages are relevant and which are not, which are benign or even beneficial (e.g., taking time to ensure that all stakeholders are on board with important and strategic decisions), and which are most severely affecting your organization's performance. Having done that, it can be useful to set a baseline and estimate the cost of each blockage in terms of time, money, and missed opportunities. Then focus first on high-impact blockages that can be addressed with relatively low effort and, as the practice of blockage removal starts to become more accepted, look to move beyond treating symptoms to addressing root causes. And as you go, track improvements to demonstrate value and maintain momentum.

By systematically addressing these organizational blockages, companies can dramatically improve their ability to execute, innovate, and adapt to changing conditions, creating significant competitive advantage in increasingly dynamic markets.

There are, in short, lots of ways, big and small, in which company operations can be slowed down or even brought to standstill. Most remarkable is the fact that many of them are treated as "just the way things are." It is an all too common belief that the status quo has no cost associated with it and little to no risk. That has never actually been true, and in this new age of AI it is going to be an increasingly costly and risky point of view.

All blockages are wasteful. They're a waste of time and they're a waste of value. In an AI economy where speed and intelligence are the new drivers of value, this needs further discussion and attention drawn to it as a matter of urgency.

Waste Versus Cost

As we disseminate the main findings of our book *Boundless* through conference keynotes and speaking engagements we're finding that CEOs resonate strongly with our message that "silos kill." Many of them have voiced their determination to smash their own particular silos, and we applaud and support this all the way. But this support comes with a word of warning: understand that when you smash your silos and you don't have an alternative way to manage your resources, you risk creating a spill instead of a flow. A spill is a waste of resources that can even become a pollutant or a hazard. A Boundless organization, by contrast, creates and then directs flows of resources to wherever most needs them. Our message, therefore, is that Boundless can, and should, become the alternative for any organization looking for continued success in this increasingly turbulent world.

This focus on waste is an important point that is worth reemphasizing especially in light of the more demanding market conditions that have visited us over the last few years. Both the goal and the outcomes of a Boundless mindset is shared success among key stakeholders. But that does not make it a free for all. There is a risk with the name *Boundless* that it may be misunderstood to stand for unfettered growth and that it signifies a lack of discipline and an insensitivity to issues like cost and productivity demands. But nothing could be further from the truth. The real question is: how are these issues handled in the Boundless model compared to the silo model?

The most common business response to softening demand and/or deteriorating market conditions is to focus on cost cutting.[3] This seems to be true more or less regardless of industry and company status. In other words, big or small, incumbent or new entrant, mature or fast growth, traditional or cutting edge, when things are not going as well as they were and pressure to respond is being felt at the executive level, cost cutting is the go-to strategy.

The problem with this from a Boundless perspective at least is that cost cutting is a silo-based strategy. By that we mean that it is resource management oriented rather than value creation oriented. Even in these market conditions or in business cycles that favor margin growth over revenue or customer growth, we believe that a focus on reducing waste is a better strategy than cutting costs. There are four main reasons why:

- First, all waste is costly, but not all costs are wasteful. Cost cutting—especially when it is carried out "across the board" to appear impartial or fair (also known as "peanut buttering")—risks harming value, quality, effectiveness, employee satisfaction, customer experience, and reputation.[4] But all efforts to reduce or even eliminate waste will cut the right kinds of costs, costs that generate no value. At a minimum this means that they will not cut into the "muscle" of the organization and make it less fit. More likely they will actually improve its fitness and responsiveness. In other words, waste reduction is a path to becoming Boundless, one we would recommend in any cycle and is thus more disciplined and more constructive than pure cost cutting.
- Second, and of particular interest to us from a Boundless perspective, cost cutting by itself does nothing to improve the flow of data, decision-making and action taking across the organization, and may well actually make it worse. As we argue in the book, silos can literally kill. All forms of silos, blockages, friction, bottlenecks, and roadblocks slow or stop people, projects, and processes in their tracks and threaten responsiveness and resilience.
- Third, waste has a negative impact on value to the customer, quality, and/or sustainability. Reducing waste therefore has a positive impact

on value, quality, and/or sustainability. This means that reducing waste is always a good strategy regardless of business or market cycle.
- Fourth, some waste bears a cost not just for the company but also the world beyond it. This type of waste is known in economics as an externality, a by-product that is borne unwittingly by a third party. Reducing or eliminating externalities is rarely addressed in business books but it has particular relevance in terms of sustainability and helps achieve shared success and so is worthy of a slight detour.

Externalities

Wine growers everywhere fear spring frosts. New vine buds emerge in the spring and are highly susceptible to freezing temperatures that can kill them and result in significant crop loss for the year. If the primary buds are destroyed by frost, secondary buds may grow, but they typically produce lower yields and lesser-quality grapes.

Severe frosts can lead to substantial economic losses for vineyards due to reduced grape production and potential long-term damage to the vines. To mitigate this risk, wine growers employ various strategies, such as deploying heaters or frost pots throughout the vineyard, using wind machines to mix warmer air from above with the colder air at ground level, applying water via sprinklers to the vines, and covering vines with special materials. Others plan proactively and plant vineyards on slopes or in locations less prone to frost accumulation, or they delay pruning to postpone bud break until after the risk of frost has decreased.

At the Kit's Coty vineyard in Kent, England, owned by wine producer Chapel Down, the winemakers are less concerned than most in the industry about the frost—for a surprising reason. And that is the passing by, every hour or two, of the Eurostar train on its journey between London and Paris.

The effect of the train, moving at high speed and whooshing in and out of the North Downs Tunnel just the other side of the A229 road from the vineyard, is to mix up the air in the local environment just as wind machines do, creating a movement of warmer air that acts against the settling and accumulation of frost. This effect has a direct and clear benefit for the winemakers who have a safeguard against the risk of frost on their vines and the financial viability of their entire enterprise.

This unexpected benefit is a prime example of what economists call an externality; a by-product of a company's operations that has an indirect cost or benefit to an entirely separate entity. Many externalities are negative, the most common being the costs to communities and ecosystems of industrial pollution, costs not borne by the polluting entities themselves. But this particular case is a happy example of a positive externality. Chapel Down and the Eurostar are entirely separate entities, but the winemaker benefits indirectly from the activities of the train operator, rather than incurring costs from them.

Of course, this externality is unplanned. This interaction is not an example of industrial or commercial symbiosis. And yet it can inspire company leaders, strategists, and designers as we think about the impact of our products, services, and operations. This relationship should remind us our organizations are never really separate entities. We are all connected in one way or another and influence each other in one way or another. So how can we ensure we design for the greatest good and least possible harm while designing for our financial success?

The most important thing is to develop a mindset attuned to the impact that we can have on the world, unintended as well as intended, and to become familiar with design principles that can help put that mindset into practice. Mindset, principles, and action are all as important as each other. One well-recognized model is the circular economy.

Another model is the one that we developed and that we have already introduced, namely the Boundless model. To recap briefly, this model is a mindset and set of principles for having the greatest possible awareness, both situational and horizontal, of one's impact and designing that impact to be overwhelmingly positive. We can design for synergy and symbiosis and do our best to ensure our externalities are mutually successful.

Once you have chosen your model and have deeply assimilated it into your daily decisions and actions, some tools can help you minimize the risk of negative externalities and increase the possibility of positive ones. As seen next, AI can be a useful tool for both.

Identifying and Mitigating Negative Externalities

- **Predictive analytics for environmental impact.** AI can analyze data from various sources, such as satellite imagery and weather patterns, to predict how a company's operations might affect the

environment. For example, AI models can predict the impact of emissions on local air quality and help companies take preemptive measures to reduce their carbon footprint.
- **Supply chain optimization.** AI can optimize supply chains by analyzing data to find the most sustainable and efficient routes and methods for transporting goods. This effort can reduce fuel consumption and emissions, minimizing the environmental impact.
- **Social media sentiment analysis.** By using AI to analyze social media and other online platforms, companies can gauge public sentiment and identify potential negative reactions to their products or services. This effort helps them address issues proactively before they escalate.
- **Risk management and compliance.** AI can help companies comply with environmental and social regulations by continuously monitoring their operations and flagging potential violations. This work reduces the risk of legal penalties and reputational damage.
- **Water use and waste management.** AI can optimize water use in manufacturing processes and manage waste more effectively by predicting waste generation patterns and suggesting more efficient waste disposal methods.

Designing for Positive Externalities

- **Product life cycle assessment.** AI can evaluate the entire life cycle of a product from raw material extraction to disposal and suggest design changes that minimize environmental impact and maximize positive contributions to communities and ecosystems.
- **Energy management systems.** AI can optimize energy use in buildings and industrial processes, reducing costs and environmental impact. For example, smart grids and energy management systems use AI to balance energy loads and integrate renewable energy sources.
- **Community impact analysis.** AI can analyze demographic and economic data to predict how a new business or product will affect local communities. This effort can help companies design initiatives that support local development, such as job creation or community services.
- **Customer behavior prediction.** AI can predict customer behavior and preferences, enabling companies to design products and services that meet societal needs more effectively. This work can lead to positive social outcomes, such as improved health or education.

- **Agricultural optimization.** AI can be used in precision agriculture to optimize water use, fertilizers, and pesticides, reducing environmental impact while increasing crop yields. This effort benefits both farmers and the broader ecosystem.

Examples in Practice
- **Salesforce Trailhead and its AI-focused curriculum.** The demand for AI-skilled employees has skyrocketed. Salesforce's Trailhead program can supercharge your career and help you learn the latest AI skills. With over 21 million active learners on the platform, analyst IDC forecasts the Salesforce community will create 11.6 million new jobs and $2 trillion in incremental business revenues by 2028.[5]
- **IBM's Environmental Intelligence Suite.** This suite uses AI to predict and mitigate the impact of climate events on supply chains, helping companies reduce their environmental footprint.
- **Google's DeepMind for energy efficiency.** Google has used its AI subsidiary, DeepMind, to reduce the energy used for cooling its data centers by 40%, demonstrating significant operational efficiency and environmental benefits.
- **Microsoft's AI for earth.** This initiative provides AI tools to organizations working on sustainability challenges, such as biodiversity conservation and climate change, enabling them to have a greater positive impact.
- **Unilever's sustainable living plan.** Unilever uses AI to analyze and improve its supply chain, ensuring sustainable sourcing of raw materials and reducing the overall environmental impact.
- **Patagonia's use of AI for environmental monitoring.** Patagonia employs AI to monitor and mitigate the environmental impact of its production processes, aiming for sustainability and positive community impact.

In summary, AI has the potential to significantly enhance a company's ability to design for positive externalities and mitigate negative ones. By leveraging AI's predictive and analytical capabilities, companies can make more informed decisions that benefit their bottom line and the environment.

We may not be able to replicate the happy accident of Eurostar's impact on frost mitigation and Kit's Coty's efforts to make some of the best sparkling wines in the world, but we can be inspired by it and set out to design intentionally for positive impact and shared success.

Of course, this makes it sound easier than it really is. It's standard accounting practice to identify, measure, and report on an organization's costs. But not all forms of waste are so easily identifiable or measurable. In particular, outside of the manufacturing industry—which focuses deeply on waste, as typified by the Toyota Production System and *muda*, or seven forms of waste—business processes are rarely scrutinized in any formal way for waste even with the increase in disciplines and certifications like Lean Six Sigma. And business complexity has grown to the point where it can be difficult to trace activities back to customer or stakeholder value. To compound matters further, people naturally favor their own ways of completing tasks and solving problems, even when those ways may be objectively more complicated and more time-consuming than consistent, standardized, or shared approaches. So waste can be difficult to pinpoint and even more difficult to eliminate.

Despite these challenges, removing waste from all aspects of a company's operations focuses the organization on creating value for the customer and itself, as well as for other stakeholders. It prioritizes the flow of resources including data and decisions, and increases responsiveness to both new challenges and opportunities. It is a key tool in sustainability as well as profitability. Continuous waste elimination is always a good practice and goal regardless of economic cycle. And maybe, surprisingly, it is always Boundless.

One final thought on waste versus costs, which is a reassessment of "cost centers," a mainstay of conventional business but one that is perhaps due for an AI-led overhaul.

From Cost Center to Service Engine: The Rise of the Minimum Viable Cost Center

In traditional business logic, cost centers are an uncomfortable necessity. They don't generate revenue directly, so their primary mandate has often been austerity: keep them cheap, lean, and out of the way. But in the age of Agentic AI, that framing is not only outdated, it's counterproductive. What matters now is not cutting cost, but cutting waste. And that shift begins with transforming the cost center into something far more dynamic: the minimum viable cost center (MVCC).

The MVCC is not a downsized, weaker version of a traditional support function. It's a reimagined, intelligent core powered by AI agents operating autonomously, continuously learning, and executing across the mSUDA (machine-scale Sense, Understand, Decide, Act) chain. These cost centers don't require large teams of humans to perform repetitive, rule-bound tasks. Instead, they run on machine power: 24/7 responsiveness, real-time analysis, and adaptive decision-making.

And, most important, they cut waste, not just cost.

A payroll department that runs on Agentic AI doesn't just eliminate headcount; it eliminates delays, errors, bottlenecks, and opaque processes. An AI-led HR function doesn't just automate onboarding; it senses morale issues early, optimizes team configurations, and enhances cultural fit. This is the essence of the MVCC: not doing the same work for less money, but doing better work for less waste.

That distinction matters. Because, as we have already written, not all costs are wasteful, and not all cuts are wise. Some cost centers provide essential connective tissue in a business, the ones that hold the fabric of employee experience, customer trust, and operational resilience together. What Agentic AI makes possible is a shift from the legacy view of cost centers as overhead, to a new vision: the high-value service center (HVSC).

The MVCC is the first step, an efficient, intelligent baseline. But the real opportunity is in the evolution toward HVSCs, where AI doesn't just eliminate inefficiency but also amplifies value. These functions become strategic engines of service, insight, and differentiation. The finance center becomes a simulation lab for strategic modeling. The legal center becomes a real-time risk analyst and deal optimizer. The support center becomes a trust-building, relationship-deepening engine.

In short: waste is eliminated, cost is optimized, and value is made visible.

Agentic AI unlocks this transformation. With SUDA operating at machine speed, the business no longer has to choose between excellence and efficiency. The old trade-off dissolves. The stigma attached to cost centers, as places to trim rather than invest, disappears.

In the Autonomous business, every function must justify its existence not by cost alone but by flow, intelligence, and contribution. And when designed correctly, even a cost center can become a source of advantage.

To Become Healthy, Remove Your Blockages

Speed is one of the currencies of the information—and now AI—age, and companies that can process all the signals coming in from the market, make decisions, and take action at speed will outperform those that can't and render them irrelevant. Some companies achieve speed in the short term by piling pressure on their employees and, where necessary, bypassing standard processes and controls. But speed cannot be sustained by a dependence on heroics and shortcuts. For this, a company needs instead to focus on creating flow—of information, expertise, finance, and other resources—across the entire organization to ensure that the right resources get to the parts that need them most. And the first step to creating flow is to get rid of anything that prevents flow, in a word, the types of blockages that we listed previously.

As we mentioned, the process of removing blockages other than silos can be started without needing a new mindset. But leaders must have a sense of urgency about it. Blockages in the human body cause up to 50% of all deaths, and all death is ultimately determined by the cessation of flows: the flow of breath and the flow of blood. While companies are not the same as bodies in the literal sense, they are nevertheless alive and they are just as dependent on flows to stay healthy. Blockages—of information, money, expertise, decision-making, HR, and so on—cause them to slow down and become less effective. Ultimately, we believe that blockages have a similar impact on company success as they do on individual human health and life (although to our knowledge no one has ever done a deep dive to measure their impact).

Using AI to Help

AI today can identify blockages in the coronary arteries based on angiogram images with 90% accuracy, based on research that shows this innovation could significantly reduce the need for pressure wire testing, saving health care providers time and reducing patients' discomfort.[6] More research on AI's ability to identify people at risk of a heart attack in the next 10 years has been hailed as "game changing" by scientists.[7] The AI model detects inflammation in the heart that does not show up on CT scans. Early detection of blockages in humans is hard, and in business, it is incredibly difficult.

Fortunately, AI can also be a powerful resource for identifying and removing various types of blockages across different aspects of business operations. Here are some examples:

- When faced with decision-making delays due to lack of actionable insights or slow analysis, companies can use AI-driven analytics platforms to process large datasets in real time, offering predictive insights that empower faster decision-making.
- When information and expertise is trapped in silos or made difficult to access across departments, AI-powered knowledge management systems using natural language processing and machine learning to categorize and make information searchable help employees quickly find and share the knowledge they need.
- When delays occur in customer support, leading to low customer satisfaction and lost sales opportunities, AI agents can handle customer queries instantly, route more complex inquiries to the right human agent, and provide 24/7 support, ensuring faster response times and reducing customer wait times.
- When poor allocation of skills or slow recruitment processes cause inefficiencies in HR, AI can predict staffing needs and allocate resources dynamically, helping ensure that the right talent is available for each project and that skill gaps are proactively addressed.
- When supply chain delays arise due to inefficient inventory management, forecasting inaccuracies, or unexpected demand shifts, companies can use AI-driven demand forecasting and supply chain automation to help them predict inventory needs, adjust order levels in real time, and mitigate risks in supply chain operations.

These examples show how AI can remove bottlenecks, accelerate workflows, and increase a company's agility, enabling it to respond quickly to both internal and external demands.

In an AI economy, where speed is more important than ever before, companies have to be able to remove blockages and optimize flow across the entire organization and beyond to be healthy, to function well, and thrive.

They have to go beyond the internal flows, and maximize the flow of data that is coming at them from all angles, all customer touchpoints, product data, market, and so on. To use two of Alibaba's principles for building a smart company, it's necessary to "datafy" every customer exchange, and to "software every activity." When every exchange is datafied the maximal flow of valuable, accurate, and timely data is enabled. To stress this point again, data is the lifeblood of AI. AI thrives on the maximal flow of live data. It does not get overwhelmed by data in the way that we commonly do. There is no need to throttle it back or to divert it.

Summary

In summary, there's a wealth of low-hanging fruit as well as more resource-intensive opportunities for any company wanting to move fast, outperform their competitors, and survive as one of the fittest in this time of unprecedented change. AI demands speed and, fortunately, offers solutions to enable it.

Chapter 3 introduces the Autonomous operating model, the mSUDA model, whose entire goal is to enable routine speed of decision-making and action taking based on these flows of data and other resources throughout the organization.

3

A New Autonomous Operating Model

Autonomous companies have <u>operating models</u> for <u>decision dominance</u> and action at <u>machine speed and scale</u> (mSUDA).

Autonomous businesses are not just healthy; they are conditioned for high performance. This demands an operating model that enables routine, systemic speed to action. And in an age of Agentic artificial intelligence (AI), this means an operating system that supports both humans and machines but is tuned for the scale and speed that only AI and other advanced technologies can achieve.

Introduction

Autonomous companies transcend the limits of traditional organizations. They are designed to achieve shared success, generating value for their customers, business partners, and communities as well as for themselves and their employees. This success is realized by resources that are individually empowered to be autonomous, connected, and mobile and that are collectively organized to be integrated, distributed, and continuous.

Pursuing autonomy calls for reimagining an organization's operating model, especially in how it enables the business to be in a state of constant flow and connectedness. The operating model reflects the idea of the company being more like a modern technological system: technological, but also living. The Autonomous operating model supports and enables continuity and enables the organization to focus on reducing waste of all types, including delays in responding to signals from customers, from the market itself, from technological advances and other external sources as well as internally from colleagues and connected systems across the enterprise. This chapter will focus on this new business operating model.

Introducing the Autonomous Operating Model

The traditional operating model is based on the idea that a company is a thing, an entity, a structure. But Autonomous organizations are differentiated in their responsiveness to both current and future customer needs and market conditions, and in their associated decision-making and action taking.

In this book, we introduce the Autonomous operating model, our update to other contemporary sense-and-respond or situational awareness models, as a guide to help organizations design and develop the necessary processes and capabilities for amplifying and accelerating their responsiveness.

How do companies make themselves aware of what's going on around them, and how do they respond to those inputs? As we started to think about how companies can develop these capabilities, we looked at other situational awareness models to see what we could learn from them.

From OODA to mSUDA

One of the models that we have used is known as the Observe-Orient-Decide-Act loop, also known as the OODA loop, which was designed by military strategist John Boyd. His goal was to explain how fighter pilots can excel in a combat setting. His insight was that the ability to sense and respond to rapidly changing conditions more quickly than an adversary gives the pilot a competitive advantage.

The OODA loop describes the processes required to sense and respond and enables the military to design the most streamlined ways of doing so. This model has been broadly adopted by the military and by businesses who can use it as a conceptual framework for designing and developing business management processes. The goal, as in the military setting, is to enable faster strategic decision-making processes and innovations through effective process management.

As we did our research, we realized that the OODA loop is very similar to the Sense-Perceive-Decide-Actuate model that is used to describe how autonomous vehicles work. In this model, the vehicle performs the following functions in real time and continuously:

- **Sense.** The vehicle uses its sensors to gather real-time data about its immediate environment or situation, primarily the road and nearby vehicles. *Sense* is a broader word than *observe* and reflects (1) the fact that not all sensors are based on sight and (2) that they're not assessing the meaning of the data they're gathering and sharing.
- **Perceive.** The vehicle interprets the data that the sensors are sharing and makes sense of them, using machine learning and AI to do so. Tesla has developed its own supercomputer, Dojo, to train the on-vehicle intelligence with data from across its fleet to improve the accuracy of its perception and decision-making.
- **Decide.** The vehicle then selects from among the options available to it and decides on the safest course of action, again using its AI to do so.
- **Actuate.** The vehicle initiates the actions that it has decided to take. The three primary (but not only) actuators in a vehicle are the accelerator or "gas" pedal for speed, the steering wheel for direction, and the brake for stopping. Of course there are many other actuators in a modern vehicle, but these are the three primary ones that help the vehicle achieve its mission and reach its destination safely.

In the case of the vehicle, the Sense-Perceive-Decide-Actuate model describes how a single autonomous system can operate effectively in and with the world around it. How, then, do these models of autonomous systems apply to Autonomous businesses, and how might we adapt them to create an Autonomous operating model? The short answer is they work very well, but we think the following tweaks are worth making to make them the most useful.

First, Autonomous companies live as part of markets and ecosystems and communities, not apart from them. The idea of a company going it alone is no longer tenable. Identity is not defined in terms of isolation and exclusion, but in terms of connectedness and inclusion. From an operating model perspective, we want to be able to show that an Autonomous company is connected to a larger ecosystem and that everything it does happens within the context of that ecosystem.

Second, the models described tend to focus on sensing immediate and/or local conditions, what is sometimes described as situational awareness. This is critical to effective decision-making, but nowadays situational awareness by itself is no longer enough. Today's company needs to be horizontally aware as well. Horizontal awareness means being connected to the larger world beyond the immediate here and now.

Companies need to be able to see "further down the road" in exactly the same way that an autonomous car can be aware of conditions anywhere along its journey and can take active steps to anticipate and avoid problems, all because of its global as well as local connectedness.

Third, as may have become clear from the discussion of the same model applying to one Autonomous system as well as to a "family" of them, Autonomous systems are self-similar at various levels (also known as fractal). Individual resources within an Autonomous company are themselves Autonomous, have the same responsibility as the company to be responsive to the immediate needs of their customers and to current market conditions and to be attuned to and prepared for future ones. And just like the company as a whole, when individual employees and teams take action, they do so in the world, not in a vacuum.

Sense, Understand, Decide, Act (SUDA)

So let's take this operating model discussion out of the realm of the vehicle and focus on its applicability to the business world. How can a company assess faster and more effectively than its competitors?

In our 2023 book *Boundless*, we introduced the Sense-Understand-Decide-Act (SUDA) model as the operating model for business in the age of AI. Any company's ability to sense, understand, decide, and act is enhanced by AI, and that translates to a competitive advantage. These companies will be able to make more informed decisions more quickly and gain what the military calls decision dominance and overmatch.

Of critical importance here is that a company's success will depend on reducing the time between each stage of the SUDA model in order to shrink the delta between Sensing and Acting as close to zero as possible.

In this new world of the Autonomous company, which still rests on the Boundless mindset and principles but is driven by AI-first strategies and designs, we need to double down on SUDA model as Agentic AI will be the most effective way to reduce the time from Sensing to Acting given their ability to act on your behalf at all times.

The seven levels of Autonomous work, which we will cover in Chapter 7, show that each level of the model represents an increase in AI's capacity in one of four SUDA stages as well as a general acceleration across the entire model at different scales of decision-making and action taking—from the minute-to-minute activities of individual employees to end-to-end business processes to strategic, enterprise-wide initiatives.

AI will accelerate and amplify both stage and scale. Companies that are not able to reduce their own sense to act delta will be overmatched by those that can. So what is decision dominance, and why does it matter for how businesses will operate in the age of AI-powered economies?

"Decision dominance," according to US Army Futures Command chief General John "Mike" Murray, "is the ability for a commander to sense, understand, decide, act, and assess faster and more effectively than any adversary." The US military highlights why decision dominance matters and the key components are necessary, including speed, range, and convergence.[1]

Speed refers to the physical speed of weapons and also to the cognitive speed of an AI offering a commander options, enabling a commander to make faster and better-informed decision as result, leaving the enemy commander a fatal step behind.

Range refers to physically outreaching the enemy and prepositioning the right forces, gear, and supplies. "The quickest way to get from Point A to Point B is to already be at point B," said General Murray.

"Convergence refers to connecting different Army and even non-Army systems on a common data-sharing network, as at the Project Convergence wargames last fall," Murray said. But it also refers to bringing together different institutions, whether across the Army or between the Army and private industry.

Achieving a SUDA model operating at the machine level is not just about technology and advanced uses of AI. "It is much more than technology," Murray said. "It's about what we will fight with but it's also just as much about how we will fight, and how we are organized for that fight. It's about scaling."

Our model must place action and reaction in its context, local or global, and it must be able to work at the individual, the team, and the company levels. The outcome of these considerations is the Autonomous operating model, which separates the four functions discussed into a figure eight, or infinity loop model.

On the left side of the model we have the Sense and Act functions that happen in, and in connection with, the larger world of which the system is a part. The point here is that these systems don't act in a vacuum. They act in and on the world and the world acts on them. There are two loops on this side. The smaller loop (solid line) describes the local and immediate world in which the system acts. This is the same as the "situation" in situational awareness. The fighter pilot, the autonomous car, the company, and the team, sales rep, or project team all have to be enabled and equipped to sense and respond to the situation they find themselves in, to react to a car slowing down in front of them, to have the information available to them to respond effectively to a customer call, and so on. The larger loop (dotted line) describes the global and near future or emerging world in which the system also has to act.

The autonomous car is not only connected to the other cars around it and knows through its sensors its real-time position relative to them and the other entities on the road, it is also connected to the larger world and knows the emerging conditions further on down the road. As a result, it can predict the likely impact on its own "mission" and take preemptive actions to avoid it. All companies now have access to predictive and prescriptive data analytics, and the successful ones will be those that use these tools to make informed decisions and take anticipatory action, either to avoid knowable challenges or to seize knowable opportunities or both. We call the dotted loop *horizonal* to express this broader context in both time and space that all companies must be connected to in order to succeed.

On the right side of the model we have the Understand and Decide functions. Of immediate importance here is that in a post-pandemic, do-anything-from-anywhere world, a company's teams and employees are all increasingly distributed and remote from the center and must therefore be given the autonomy to make timely and accurate decisions about how to fulfill their missions. The company will need to revamp its management and supervision processes in the form of resource orchestration in order to deal with this decentralized and Autonomous workforce.

Meanwhile, the company itself must also be Autonomous in the sense of having a unique identity and mission, despite its connection and its Autonomous nature.

As previously mentioned, the Autonomous operating model is designed not only to support the requirement for all companies to have situational and horizonal awareness but also to work at both individual and collective levels. Companies can use the model to design and develop processes for individual employees, teams of employees, and organization-wide business management processes.

Among the various different versions of the SUDA and OODA loops that exist, here's broad consensus about the names of each function with only a few minor differences. We believe Sense is more appropriate than Observe given that this model can apply as well to technology systems like autonomous vehicles as it can to human organizations. We prefer Understand to Perceive or Orient because it has more general use. All models agree on Decide. We prefer Act to Actuate again because it has more general use, although we also recognize that this function may involve both actuation (putting into action) by the orchestrator component of the overall system and action by the executor component, where those components are decoupled from one another. This leaves us with the acronym SUDA (Sense, Understand, Decide, Act) for the Autonomous operating model.

In short, SUDA is an evolution of other situational awareness or sense-and-respond models that are designed to reflect dynamically changing conditions, unlike for instance the PDCA or Deming cycle, which was designed for continuous improvement in stable conditions or relatively controlled environments.

We did not invent the SUDA model. We have extended the Sense and Act portion of the "connection" logic for both internal and external factors. It places an autonomous entity, be that an employee, a team, or a company, in the context of a connected world both locally and globally, and it can be used by companies as a conceptual model to identify, define, and develop processes that will enable it to act decisively, learn and improve continuously, and respond at the speed of need in that world.

As Agentic AI adoption increases in business, and actions can be taken 24/7 on behalf of human workers, we will see the emergence of a new measure of productivity, "machine power" or something similar, not simply in terms of GPUs/CPUs or transactions per second but probably as some function of complexity, accuracy, and speed.

This measure will be needed to represent how machines will no longer just do "human" jobs faster, more accurately, and cheaply. They'll also be doing jobs that we can't do, jobs far more complex, with more inputs to handle, more moving parts to orchestrate, and less time to solve.

Decision dominance, achieved through machine-scale SUDA operating models and powered by Agentic AI capabilities, will enable businesses to massively shrink the time between each stage of Sensing, Understanding, Deciding, and Acting to nearly zero. And so we've updated our SUDA model for this age, for the Autonomous business. We call it mSUDA: Sense-Understand-Decide-Act at machine scale and speed.

Introducing mSUDA: Machine-Scale SUDA for the Autonomous Business

Let's explore the mSUDA framework in some detail since it is such a critical part of becoming Autonomous. We have chosen to do this deep dive to demonstrate that the framework is not just a concept but is something that can help leaders think deeply through their core operations and see where AI can help them in every step of the way. An important goal of every business leader in the AI economy should be to minimize time to action, and the mSUDA framework shows how to do that (see Figure 3.1).

For years leaders have been advised to develop a digital operating model for their businesses but it has not always been clear what that should look like other than technology governance. Our view goes far beyond that. We believe that the entire organization should be viewed as an intelligent system that achieves decision and action dominance by having those capabilities intentionally designed into it. mSUDA is the digital operating model for that intelligent system, the conditioned company that is consistently and routinely ready to respond, compete, collaborate, and win.

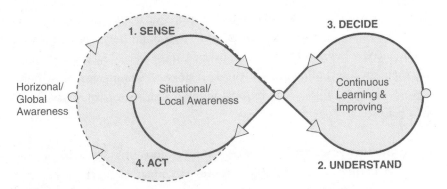

Figure 3.1 The mSUDA operating model for Autonomous business: ΔtSUDA ≈ 0.

In this deep dive, we include a discussion of the scope of each stage as well as the core technologies involved. The scope is important because we want to show that mSUDA is for the entire organization. It is not an IT function. It is not just for front office functions that support and enable the customer relationship. It provides an operating mode for both digital and human resources to perform at the highest level. And we include the technologies simply because they will provide the infrastructure for the model as well as important users of it.

We begin with Sensing, the first and arguably most critical stage of mSUDA. Without a robust Sensing capability, subsequent decisions are made with incomplete or outdated information, significantly reducing the effectiveness of AI-driven operations.

AI-Powered Sensing

The sensing stage of mSUDA is responsible for gathering raw data in real time. Organizations must capture as many relevant data points as possible, including customer behaviors, market trends, competitive intelligence, regulatory changes, product performance, and emerging technologies. By transitioning from human-observed inputs to fully automated, AI-driven data collection, organizations can eliminate lag, improve precision, and expand decision-context awareness.

The Scope of Sensing   Sensing is not just about monitoring customer touchpoints, although those are perhaps the most important category. It is about capturing every possible data point or signal relevant to the business. Organizations that excel in Sensing will build decision and action dominance by being fully aware of internal and external factors influencing their success. Following are the key areas of Sensing for most businesses, although of course individual industries or sectors may have their own priorities:

- **Customer Sensing.** Understanding customer behavior is the backbone of market responsiveness. Companies must track direct and indirect interactions, from customer support calls and online orders to product reviews and social media mentions. AI-driven natural language processing (NLP) and sentiment analysis can assess consumer sentiment in real time, providing businesses with actionable insights.
- **Competitive intelligence.** Organizations must continuously monitor competitor activities, including pricing strategies, product launches, marketing campaigns, and partnerships. AI-powered analytics platforms can scrape competitor websites, analyze social media engagement, and track industry reports to detect emerging trends.
- **Market and industry trends.** Macroeconomic conditions, technological breakthroughs, and industry trends must be closely monitored to anticipate disruptions. AI-driven predictive analytics can process millions of data points, economic indicators, patents, and funding rounds to signal upcoming shifts.
- **Regulatory and policy changes.** Industries such as finance, health care, and manufacturing are heavily regulated, requiring businesses to track legislative updates continuously. AI-based regulatory monitoring systems can assess new policies in real time and alert companies about necessary compliance adjustments.
- **Social and cultural trends.** Consumer preferences evolve based on societal changes, generational behavior shifts, and cultural movements. AI-powered social listening tools enable businesses to understand evolving sentiment before trends peak.
- **Product and service performance monitoring.** Smart products embedded with Internet of Things (IoT) sensors enable companies to track real-time performance metrics, user engagement, and failure rates.

This enables businesses to offer proactive maintenance, software updates, and personalized recommendations.
- **Workforce and employee Sensing.** Monitoring employee engagement and workplace productivity can enhance retention and optimize performance. AI-driven HR analytics track patterns of productivity, burnout signals, and team sentiment.
- **Supplier and logistics tracking.** Real-time visibility into supply chain efficiency, transportation routes, and inventory levels is critical to minimizing operational disruptions. AI-powered logistics platforms predict delays and optimize shipment routes dynamically.
- **Emerging technology monitoring.** AI-powered research and development intelligence platforms track scientific research, patents, and startup activity to identify disruptive innovations early. By integrating this intelligence, businesses can strategically pivot before a competitor capitalizes on new technology.
- **Environmental and sustainability awareness.** Tracking carbon emissions, sustainable sourcing, and waste reduction is no longer optional. AI-powered environmental monitoring enables businesses to meet regulatory requirements and corporate social responsibility goals.
- **Economic and financial Sensing.** Monitoring interest rates, inflation, exchange rates, and global investment flows enables businesses to anticipate economic shifts and adjust their financial strategies accordingly. AI-powered economic modeling provides real-time insights into financial risks and opportunities.
- **Geopolitical and risk Sensing.** For global enterprises, tracking geopolitical events, trade policies, regional conflicts, and diplomatic shifts is essential. AI-driven geopolitical intelligence platforms analyze news reports, social sentiment, and government policies to help businesses anticipate risks and navigate regulatory landscapes.

Technological Components of AI-Powered Sensing For businesses to master AI-powered sensing, they must leverage cutting-edge technologies capable of collecting, processing, and analyzing vast amounts of data in real time. These technologies enable companies to detect critical patterns, anticipate shifts, and make faster, more accurate decisions. Following are the foundational technologies that support AI-powered sensing across each of the data categories described previously, although it should be noted that not all companies will need all of these technologies:

- **Edge computing an IoT-enabled sensor.** Edge computing enables data processing to be closer to the source, reducing latency and dependence on centralized cloud processing. IoT sensors, embedded in devices, vehicles, infrastructure, and even clothing, provide real-time streams of environmental, operational, and consumer data.
- **Multimodal AI for data fusion.** Multimodal AI integrates multiple data sources, including video, text, audio, and sensor data, into a unified analysis model, forming a holistic picture of the situation or environment and improving decision-making accuracy as a result. For example, autonomous vehicles combine light detection and ranging (LiDAR), cameras, radar, and global positioning system (GPS) data to create comprehensive situational awareness.
- **Real-time data streaming and processing.** Real-time data streaming platforms process high-velocity data from various inputs, ensuring instant analysis and actionability. For instance, financial institutions use real-time market data ingestion to execute algorithmic trading with near-zero latency. This capability, to operate in real-time decision loops, is at the heart of mSUDA and routine high performance.
- **NLP for unstructured data (sensing and understanding).** NLP enables AI systems to interpret, classify, and derive insights from text-based data sources such as customer feedback, regulatory documents, and competitor announcements. Sentiment can be assessed in real time, enabling urgent issues to be automatically and immediately escalated.
- **AI-driven predictive analytics and digital twins (Sensing and Understanding).** Predictive analytics, powered by AI, uses historical data to forecast trends, behaviors, and outcomes. Digital twins, virtual models of real-world systems, simulate environments to optimize decision-making. This enhances strategic agility, enabling organizations to test different operational models before real-world execution (more on digital twins is discussed in Chapter 5).
- **Blockchain for data integrity in Sensing.** Blockchain enhances data security and traceability, ensuring that sensing data remains tamper-proof and enabling companies to verify product authenticity and prevent counterfeits or scams or knock-offs.

- **Computer vision for advanced Sensing.** Computer vision enables machines to extract insights from images and videos, making it a core component in retail, manufacturing, and security applications. AI-powered surveillance systems can detect and act on security threats by analyzing real-time camera feeds, improving safety, and enhancing operational efficiency.
- **Cloud AI and scalable machine learning infrastructure.** Cloud AI solutions offer businesses scalable access to AI models that enhance sensing capabilities without requiring in-house infrastructure. This reduces the costs and other barriers to mSUDA and other AI implementations.
- **Geospatial AI and satellite data processing.** Geospatial AI processes satellite and aerial imagery, detecting environmental, economic, and security patterns and empowering businesses to make sustainability-driven decisions using large-scale environmental data.

These technologies collectively support all of the sensing categories described. While edge computing, IoT, and computer vision primarily drive sensing, technologies like NLP and predictive analytics also play key roles in understanding. Businesses that integrate these technologies holistically will have a future-proof sensing capability, driving real-time intelligence across their operations.

Sensing Examples Amazon employs AI-driven IoT sensors and real-time analytics to track inventory movements across its vast network of fulfillment centers, warehouses, and last-mile delivery routes. By combining edge computing, AI-powered forecasting models, and dynamic rerouting algorithms, Amazon has reduced delivery times to as little as two hours in some regions.

Meanwhile, Walmart uses AI-driven demand forecasting to optimize inventory levels in thousands of stores worldwide. By analyzing consumer behavior, weather patterns, and geopolitical events, Walmart's AI-powered sensing systems anticipate changes in demand, enabling them to adjust stock levels before shortages occur, leading to 50% reduction in stockouts and improved profitability.

Alibaba, as we have already discussed, has pioneered the practice of "datafying" and "softwaring" everything," which involves embedding real-time AI tracking mechanisms across all customer touchpoints, including mobile apps, websites, and physical stores. By processing billions of transactions, Alibaba's AI can detect shifts in customer sentiment, predict purchasing patterns, and personalize recommendations at an unprecedented scale.

The US Department of Defense has integrated AI-driven sensing into multi-domain warfare strategies, where real-time situational awareness is critical. Using AI-powered drones, satellite surveillance systems, and battlefield IoT sensors, military leaders can now gather, analyze, and act on intelligence data in minutes rather than hours.

Without robust sensing capabilities, the ability of a company to stay competitive will soon collapse. AI-driven sensing enables organizations to collect, interpret, and act on data with minimal human intervention, ensuring decisions are informed by real-time, high-fidelity intelligence. Organizations should evaluate their current sensing strategies and assess where AI-driven sensing can close gaps. A structured approach to Sensing enables businesses to achieve decision dominance by ensuring that no critical market, operational, or customer data point is missed.

While Sensing provides a steady stream of data, its true value is unlocked in the next stage, Understanding. Raw data alone is insufficient without context, analysis, and predictive modeling. The ability to transform massive amounts of sensed data into meaningful intelligence is the key to achieving machine-speed decision-making and is only possible with robust AI and other advanced technology infrastructure. A consistent theme throughout this book is that the only path to unlocking the nonlinear potential of an Autonomous business is by applying AI-first strategies and designs and removing the constraints of human capabilities (even though it sounds harsh to say it!). At the risk of repetition, the model here is Alibaba's strategy of datafying and softwaring everything. Companies must look to increase their data input volumes and sources, not reduce or throttle them back.

In the next section, we will explore the Understanding phase of mSUDA, where AI converts raw data into actionable insights and predictive intelligence.

AI-Powered Understanding

As organizations refine their ability to sense vast amounts of data through AI-powered sensing, the next crucial step in the mSUDA framework is

Understanding. Without this stage, raw data remains unstructured, overwhelming, and often meaningless. The ability to extract context, patterns, and meaning from data is what distinguishes truly intelligent AI-driven enterprises from those merely collecting information.

AI-powered Understanding enables businesses to transform raw inputs into actionable intelligence, allowing for strategic decision-making at machine speed. This section explores the role of AI-driven analytics, context modeling, knowledge extraction, and continuous learning, ensuring that businesses do not just react to data but also anticipate future developments.

The Scope of Understanding Just as sensing required a structured approach to capturing key data points, Understanding necessitates a framework for analyzing, contextualizing, and making sense of vast datasets. Trying to do this without AI-first capabilities will quite simply fail when the volume of data coming into the business gets to a certain point, as even the most skilled and qualified humans will not be able to keep up with it.

Here are the key analytical areas that enterprises must master for true AI-powered Understanding:

- **Contextual data analysis.** Contextual AI ensures that data is interpreted within its relevant environment rather than in isolation. It looks beyond raw numbers and evaluates historical, environmental, and behavioral factors. This approach helps organizations uncover hidden patterns that simple data aggregation would miss. For example, a sudden increase in customer complaints might not be a reflection of poor service but could be influenced by external factors like supply chain disruptions or seasonal fluctuations. This does not mean, of course, that they can be ignored, only that additional factors should be taken into account when dealing with them.
- **Predictive and prescriptive analytics.** Predictive analytics forecasts future trends based on historical data, identifying potential outcomes with a probability score. Prescriptive analytics, however, suggests optimal actions based on AI-driven simulation models and reinforcement learning. These insights enable companies to shift from reactive decision-making to proactive strategies, mitigating risks before they materialize. For example, predictive maintenance in manufacturing

can prevent costly breakdowns by detecting wear patterns in machinery before failure occurs. While not particularly glamorous, this kind of capability is vital to business continuity and to the minimization or elimination of waste arising from delayed production.

- **Knowledge graphs and semantic AI.** Knowledge graphs help AI systems establish connections among concepts, entities, and behaviors to enhance decision-making. Semantic AI improves comprehension by enabling machines to interpret intent, meaning, and relationships rather than just keywords. These technologies power everything from enterprise search engines to fraud detection systems, enabling businesses to retrieve insights more efficiently.
- **Causal inference and decision modeling.** Unlike predictive analytics, which focuses on correlation, causal inference AI seeks to determine actual cause-and-effect relationships. This is essential for high-stakes decision-making where understanding the true drivers of a trend or anomaly is crucial. For instance, in medical research, causal AI can distinguish whether a particular drug genuinely improves recovery rates or if external variables are influencing the results.
- **Real-time sentiment and behavioral analysis.** AI-powered sentiment analysis evaluates emotions in customer feedback, social media discussions, and employee interactions. Behavioral analytics tracks actions over time to identify engagement patterns. This enables businesses to react in real-time to customer dissatisfaction, emerging PR crises, or employee burnout indicators before they escalate.
- **Risk and anomaly detection.** Advanced anomaly detection algorithms establish a baseline for normal activity and flag deviations as potential risks. In cybersecurity, for example, AI detects irregular user behaviors, such as logins from unfamiliar locations or unexpected data transfers, that may indicate hacking attempts. By continuously learning from new threats, these systems stay ahead of evolving risks.
- **Personalized AI recommendations.** AI-powered recommendation engines analyze vast amounts of user data to deliver highly personalized content, product suggestions, or service offerings. By factoring in real-time preferences, behavioral data, and situational context, businesses can enhance customer engagement and retention.

This is particularly useful in e-commerce, where personalized product suggestions can significantly increase conversion rates.

- **Adaptive learning systems and AutoML.** AI models must be able to evolve through continuous learning. AutoML automates the process of selecting, training, and optimizing machine learning models, reducing the need for human intervention. These adaptive systems improve over time, refining their accuracy with each new dataset, making them indispensable in dynamic industries like health care and finance.
- **AI-powered market intelligence.** Market intelligence AI scans multiple sources, including news reports, financial statements, and competitor activities, to generate actionable insights about industry trends and market shifts. This enables companies to make data-driven strategic decisions, from launching new products to adjusting pricing strategies in response to economic changes.
- **Policy and regulatory interpretation.** AI-powered systems analyze regulatory documents, legal precedents, and compliance frameworks to keep businesses updated on changing laws. Automated compliance monitoring ensures that organizations remain aligned with evolving regulations, reducing legal risks and fines. This is particularly crucial in heavily regulated industries such as finance and pharmaceuticals.
- **AI-augmented decision intelligence.** Decision intelligence uses AI to weigh different decision paths, considering multiple variables to recommend optimal choices with the least risk. This is widely applied in manufacturing, logistics, and financial planning, where AI dynamically adjusts production schedules, supply chain operations, and investment strategies based on current conditions.
- **Cross-domain intelligence fusion.** AI-driven cross-domain intelligence integrates insights from multiple disciplines to provide holistic decision-making frameworks. By combining data from customer behavior, supply chain analytics, and financial forecasting, businesses can operate with a unified strategic vision rather than in silos. This approach is vital in industries such as autonomous driving, where data from traffic conditions, sensor inputs, and vehicle performance must be synthesized in real time.

Technological Components of AI-Powered Understanding For businesses to achieve AI-driven Understanding, they must deploy advanced computational models that extract intelligence beyond simple pattern recognition. These technologies form the foundation of AI-powered understanding, allowing for deep contextualization, reasoning, and strategic intelligence across industries. Following are the core technologies powering AI-driven Understanding:

- **Large language models (LLMs) and transformer AI.** LLMs and transformer-based AI architectures, such as GPT models (OpenAI) and Claude (Anthropic), have revolutionized AI comprehension of human language. These models enable machines to interpret, summarize, generate, and analyze text at near-human proficiency (as of July 2025), and they're capable of processing massive knowledge repositories, distilling insights and accelerating the Understanding phase in legal, financial, and research sectors.
- **Deep reinforcement learning (DRL).** DRL models enable AI to learn optimal decision pathways in complex, uncertain environments. Unlike traditional machine learning, DRL continuously improves through feedback loops, enabling AI to adjust strategies dynamically and refining its ability to predict and then act in fast moving conditions like high-frequency trading, industrial automation, and real-time logistics optimization.
- **Causal AI models.** Causal AI moves beyond correlation-based machine learning models to understand true cause-and-effect relationships. This technology is critical for industries where identifying why something happens is more important than simply predicting what will happen, for instance, in pharmaceuticals where it can help determine which drug ingredients lead to patient recovery, reducing reliance on correlation-driven studies.
- **Neurosymbolic AI.** Neurosymbolic AI merges symbolic logic and neural networks, combining the interpretability of rule-based AI with the pattern recognition strengths of deep learning. This enables AI to perform reasoning tasks that require logical deduction, rather than just data-driven insights and makes them suitable, for instance, in highly regulated industries where transparency is crucial.

- **Federated learning.** Federated learning enables AI models to train on distributed datasets without centralizing sensitive data, preserving privacy and regulatory compliance. This ensures that AI models learn from diverse datasets while maintaining data privacy and security compliance (GDPR, HIPAA, etc.).
- **Hybrid AI (machine learning and expert systems).** Hybrid AI blends traditional expert systems (rule-based reasoning) with machine learning models, creating AI that is both knowledge-driven and data-driven. This means that businesses benefit from explainable AI decisions while still leveraging the power of deep learning.
- **Real-time data pipelines and decision automation.** Real-time AI decision pipelines process, analyze, and act on live data streams, ensuring businesses operate in true real time. This clearly helps transition toward fully mSUDA-operated businesses, enabling them to move from batched (or blocked!) to continuous decision intelligence.
- **Ethical AI and explainable AI (XAI).** Explainable AI (XAI) ensures that AI-driven insights and decisions are transparent, interpretable, and bias-mitigated. It builds trust in AI decision-making, making adoption easier in health care, law, financial services, as well as in business processes like hiring where AI-powered applicant screening must comply with anti-discrimination laws, ensuring fair and explainable decision-making.

These eight core technologies form the backbone of AI-powered Understanding, ensuring that raw data transitions into context-rich, actionable insights. By integrating these AI systems, businesses can accelerate Decision-Making, improve reasoning accuracy, and anticipate future developments with unprecedented precision.

Understanding Examples AI-powered health care diagnostics have revolutionized early disease detection, predictive treatment planning, and personalized medicine. With the integration of deep learning, causal inference, and knowledge graphs, modern AI models can process massive medical datasets, identifying patterns that would otherwise go unnoticed.

For example, Google's DeepMind Health has developed AI systems that analyze retinal scans to detect signs of diabetic retinopathy and macular degeneration before human ophthalmologists can. AI-driven diagnostic tools are now being used in oncology, where they evaluate MRI scans to predict tumor growth progression and recommend personalized treatment options.

The financial sector relies heavily on AI-powered understanding to detect market patterns, assess risk exposure, and automate high-frequency trading. Hedge funds and investment firms employ real-time AI pipelines that process millions of financial transactions and market events per second. JPMorgan Chase, for example, uses AI-powered market intelligence to conduct fraud detection, algorithmic trading, and credit risk analysis.

By combining LLMs, reinforcement learning, and contextual AI, modern retail platforms can anticipate trends, detect emerging consumer preferences, and enhance supply chain efficiency, ensuring that customers receive seamless, hyper-personalized experiences both online and in-store.

While Sensing ensures that organizations collect data, Understanding ensures that the right insights are extracted, contextualized, and acted on. Without AI-powered Understanding, organizations risk drowning in data with no strategic advantage. The ability to turn raw information into real-time, contextual intelligence is a key capability of the Autonomous business.

In the next section, we will explore Decision-Making in mSUDA, where AI models transition from analysis to selecting the optimal course of action at machine speed.

AI-Powered Decision-Making

With AI-powered Sensing and Understanding providing an unparalleled depth of real-time intelligence, the next crucial phase in mSUDA is Deciding, or Decision-Making. This stage determines how well an organization can convert insights into action, ensuring that the choices they make are optimized, timely, and scalable.

Traditional decision-making processes rely heavily on human intuition, historical-precedent, and static data models. By contrast, AI-powered decision-making leverages machine learning, game theory, probabilistic models, and real-time scenario analysis to enhance accuracy, speed, and strategic advantage. As we did with Sensing and Understanding, we'll explore key decision-making strategies, the technological foundations of AI-driven decisions, and examples of AI-first Decision-Making in practice.

The Scope of Decision-Making For businesses to fully leverage mSUDA, they must integrate AI into their Decision-Making frameworks. The AI-powered decision strategies that they should consider using include the following:

- **Automated decision engines.** AI-driven decision engines automate routine, rules-based decisions, freeing human expertise for more complex strategic analysis. These systems rely on machine learning algorithms, business logic frameworks, and predictive analytics and drive increased efficiency, accuracy, and scalability while reducing human error and bias in high-volume Decision-Making processes.
- **Probabilistic decision-making.** AI evaluates potential outcomes using probability distributions, helping organizations make decisions under uncertainty. This approach is particularly useful in industries where multiple variables influence outcomes, such as weather-dependent logistics, dynamic pricing models, and supply chain management.
- **Reinforcement learning (RL) for strategic planning.** RL enables AI to learn and optimize decisions over time based on past outcomes. By continuously evaluating the success of previous actions, RL-driven AI can develop adaptive, self-improving decision models, ensuring that business strategies remain effective even as conditions change dynamically.
- **Multi-agent AI decision systems.** Organizations leverage AI-driven agents that interact and collaborate to simulate, negotiate, and optimize decision paths. These systems are crucial for complex environments where multiple independent entities must coordinate for optimal Decision-Making. This will become increasingly important as Autonomy spreads. For example traffic management systems will need AI-first decision systems like these to coordinate autonomous traffic and reduce congestion by optimizing routes and adjusting real-time traffic signals.
- **Game-theoretic decision models.** AI applies game theory to assess competitive environments, ensuring optimal choices in adversarial settings. This offers strategic foresight and the potential for decision dominance in highly competitive or adversarial situations, helping businesses anticipate competitor moves and adjust strategies accordingly.

- **Scenario-based decision modeling.** AI systems analyze "what-if" scenarios to prepare for multiple contingencies, ensuring robust Decision frameworks. These models leverage simulated environments, Monte Carlo simulations, and decision trees to empower organizations to proactively prepare for disruptions, policy changes, and operational shifts.
- **Prescriptive analytics and optimization.** Unlike predictive analytics, prescriptive models recommend specific actions for achieving the best outcome. These AI systems use constraint-based optimization, mathematical modeling, and decision theory to generate actionable recommendations, thereby increasing efficiency and effectiveness.
- **Human–AI hybrid decision systems.** AI assists humans by providing recommendations, while human oversight ensures alignment with business goals and ethics. These systems balance automation and human expertise, ensuring that AI-driven decisions are contextually aware and ethically sound.
- **Context-aware decision-making.** AI considers real-time contextual factors, ensuring decisions adapt dynamically to environmental changes and enabling organizations to respond to real-time market conditions like demand fluctuations, competitor activity, and economic condition rather than relying on static, outdated decision models. This approach integrates situational data, behavioral analytics, and real-time event processing.
- **Explainable AI (XAI) in decision systems.** Explainable AI ensures that AI-powered decisions can be audited and understood, building stakeholder trust, improving accountability, and ensuring AI decisions remain transparent.
- **Federated decision-making across organizations.** AI models enable secure, decentralized decision collaboration without sharing raw data, preserving privacy. These models encourage collaborative Decision-Making across business ecosystems and industry sectors, leveraging federated learning, distributed AI networks, and secure multiparty computation.
- **Real-time AI-driven decision loops.** AI operates in continuous feedback loops, updating decisions dynamically as new data arrives and so enabling businesses to adapt in the moment. These systems integrate real-time monitoring, AI inference, and automated execution.

Technological Components of AI-Powered Decision-Making For businesses to implement AI-powered Decision-Making effectively, they must deploy advanced AI architectures that enable real-time, high-precision choices. Following are the key technologies driving AI-based Decision-Making:

- **DRL.** DRL enables AI systems to learn and refine Decision-Making by trial and error in dynamic environments. By leveraging reward-based feedback loops, DRL can optimize long-term decision pathways, making it invaluable for complex and evolving scenarios.
- **Bayesian decision networks.** Bayesian decision networks introduce probabilistic reasoning into AI-driven decisions, ensuring that uncertainty is accounted for in complex problem-solving scenarios. For instance, AI in medical diagnostics leverages Bayesian networks to assess patient conditions based on symptoms and medical history. These models use conditional probability distributions to weigh different outcomes based on available data.
- **Hybrid AI (neural networks and rule-based logic).** Hybrid AI combines deep learning with rule-based logic, creating decision frameworks that merge human expertise with AI-driven adaptability.
- **Multi-agent AI simulations.** Multi-agent AI involves multiple AI systems interacting to negotiate, collaborate, and optimize outcomes in large-scale environments. This enhances collective intelligence, enabling AI agents to self-coordinate and optimize Decision-Making, and is particularly valuable for supply chains, autonomous vehicles, and game theoretic applications.
- **Quantum AI for decision optimization.** The promise of quantum AI is to leverage quantum computing principles to solve highly complex decision-making problems at speeds unattainable by classical computers. It is expected that quantum computing will offer an exponential leap in AI decision processing, enabling businesses to compute previously unsolvable optimization problems.
- **Federated learning for distributed decision intelligence.** Federated learning enables multiple organizations to train AI models collaboratively without sharing raw data, ensuring privacy while benefiting from collective decision intelligence.

- **Real-time AI inference and decision execution.** Real-time AI inference systems ensure that decisions are executed instantly, based on continuously incoming data. This technology is critical in industries that require millisecond-fast decision-making, which we believe will apply to all businesses regardless of industry in the very near future.

These eight core technologies provide the backbone for AI-powered Decision-Making, ensuring that organizations can make the transition from insight to action with maximum efficiency.

Deciding/Decision-Making Examples Autonomous vehicles rely on AI-powered decision models that integrate sensor fusion, reinforcement learning, and real-time risk assessment to navigate safely. Waymo's AI models leverage deep reinforcement learning to improve driving performance over millions of miles of real-world and simulated driving data. AI continuously refines decision-making strategies based on real-time data from LiDAR, radar, cameras, and GPS sensors, ensuring adaptive responses to unpredictable road conditions.

Financial institutions use AI-powered fraud detection systems that operate in real time, analyzing millions of transactions per second. AI models detect anomalous spending patterns, flag suspicious activity, and prevent fraudulent transactions before they occur.

For example, Mastercard and Visa leverage machine learning–based fraud detection algorithms that identify high-risk transactions within milliseconds. AI-powered risk assessment tools analyze consumer behaviors, device fingerprints, and transaction locations to detect fraud attempts, reducing false positives and enhancing security.

AI-powered grid management platforms dynamically allocate energy resources based on demand fluctuations, reducing waste and improving energy efficiency. By leveraging AI for decision-making in infrastructure planning, emergency response, and environmental sustainability, cities are becoming more adaptive and resilient.

Organizations that master AI-powered Decision-Making will outperform competitors, optimize resource allocation, and mitigate risks faster than ever before. In the next section, we explore how AI executes these decisions at scale, transitioning from planning to real-world impact in the Act phase of mSUDA.

AI-Powered Action

The final phase of the mSUDA framework is Action, where AI-driven insights and decisions translate into tangible outcomes. In this stage, AI-powered systems execute decisions autonomously or augment human-led initiatives, ensuring that responses are instantaneous, optimized, and adaptive to changing conditions.

Historically, organizations have relied on manual execution, delayed response cycles, and fragmented automation to carry out decisions. Blockages and waste have nearly always manifested. However, AI-driven action systems eliminate inefficiencies, reduce errors, and ensure continuous operational refinement through Autonomous execution, robotic automation, and real-time AI-driven intervention.

The strategies and technologies that we set out here will probably feel more commonplace than those in the other stages. That's because the world of action is where companies have always focused. This is by no means a criticism but simply a reminder that in the age of AI, business can be far more intentional about the decisions they make and the actions they take based on a far greater volume of data coming into the organization at much higher velocity and on a far higher level of sophistication and accuracy when it comes to analyzing and synthesizing that data for those decisions and actions.

The Scope of AI-Powered Action For businesses to fully implement AI-powered action, they must adopt execution models that ensure seamless, intelligent, and adaptable responses. Following are key AI-driven action strategies for organizations to incorporate into their operations. As mentioned, these will probably be more familiar than the scope of Sensing and Understanding capabilities and the technologies driving and enabling those capabilities:

- **Autonomous process automation.** AI-driven RPA and AI-driven workflow automation systems handle repetitive, high-volume tasks with minimal human intervention. These systems leverage machine learning and rule-based AI to streamline data entry, invoice processing, compliance verification, and HR workflows, increasing speed, accuracy, and scalability while reducing operational costs and freeing human workers for high-value tasks.

- **AI-powered robotics and smart factories.** AI-driven robots operate in manufacturing, logistics, and warehouse environments, executing actions with real-time precision and adaptability. These robots can adapt to changing production demands, self-correct errors, and optimize throughput dynamically. As the first, obvious members of the digital workforce, they enhance production speed, quality control, and operational efficiency, minimizing downtime and increasing overall productivity.
- **Intelligent supply chain execution.** AI-powered supply chain execution platforms dynamically reroute shipments, adjust inventory levels, and predict logistics disruptions in real time. These systems integrate demand forecasting, route optimization, and warehouse automation to reduce or even remove blockages, improve efficiency, lower cost, and enhance service levels.
- **Autonomous AI agents for customer service.** AI-powered virtual agents handle customer interactions, troubleshoot issues, and escalate cases when necessary. These systems leverage NLP, sentiment analysis, and reinforcement learning to provide human-like customer support at scale, reducing response times, increasing customer satisfaction, and scaling support services.
- **AI-guided field operations.** AI-driven field management systems dynamically deploy workforce and resources based on demand, location, and priority levels. These platforms integrate real-time geospatial data, workforce scheduling AI, and predictive maintenance models to provide faster service delivery in dynamic environments.
- **AI-driven personalized marketing execution.** AI systems autonomously adjust marketing campaigns, ad targeting, and promotions in real time based on consumer behavior. By analyzing customer intent, purchasing patterns, and engagement data, AI optimizes advertising bids, content placement, and email marketing personalization.
- **AI-orchestrated IT operations (AIOps).** AI-driven IT operations predict and resolve system failures before they occur, ensuring uninterrupted services. These platforms integrate machine learning–driven anomaly detection, automated root cause analysis, and proactive system maintenance to reduce downtime, improve IT resilience, and enhance security, ensuring continuous digital operations.

- **Smart infrastructure and IoT execution.** AI systems integrate with IoT networks to control smart buildings, traffic systems, and city infrastructure dynamically, enhancing sustainability and optimizing energy efficiency. These AI-powered platforms adjust HVAC settings, optimize energy grids, and improve urban planning.
- **AI-powered health care intervention.** AI-driven medical robotics and digital health platforms assist in surgical procedures, monitor patients, and provide personalized treatments. These systems analyze patient data, predict complications, and assist in diagnosis with unparalleled accuracy to improve patient outcomes, reduce medical errors, and make health care more proactive and efficient.
- **AI-enabled real-time business decision execution.** AI continuously evaluates business key performance indicators and automatically triggers strategic interventions. These AI-driven execution models adjust corporate policies, budget allocations, and operational workflows dynamically, enabling businesses to adapt dynamically to real-time market conditions and maintain or even increase their competitiveness.

Technological Components of AI-Powered Action For organizations to achieve seamless and intelligent execution, they must integrate cutting-edge AI technologies that enable real-time, automated, and adaptive responses. Following are the key technological pillars powering AI-driven Action:

- **Intelligent RPA 2.0.** Traditional RPA is evolving into AI-enhanced intelligent automation, enabling systems to self-learn, adapt, and handle exceptions autonomously.
- **AI-driven edge computing for real-time execution.** Edge AI moves computational power closer to data sources, enabling ultra-low latency decision execution in real-time environments.
- **Autonomous decision execution systems.** AI-powered decision execution platforms enables businesses to trigger automated workflows based on real-time analytics, facilitating autonomous business operations and reducing dependency on manual (which is to say, human) interventions.

- **AI-enabled digital twins for Action optimization.** Digital twins create real-time virtual replicas of physical systems, enabling organizations to simulate, test, and optimize actions before real-world implementation. mSUDA itself enables a digital twin of the entire company's operations, not just single processes, that can potentially simulate the impact of large scale strategic changes before implementing them (see Chapter 5 for more on digital twins).
- **Real-time AI inference and response mechanisms.** AI inference engines process streaming data in real time, enabling immediate action based on new insights.
- **Adaptive AI workflow orchestration.** AI orchestrates complex workflows by dynamically adjusting execution sequences based on external conditions. Orchestration, like its peer-based cousin choreography, ensures fluid, adaptive execution across dynamic environments, optimizing efficiency and effectiveness.
- **AI-powered autonomous robotics.** AI-driven robots perform autonomous task execution, process optimization, and operational assistance in industrial and commercial settings like warehouses where they automate inventory restocking and order fulfillment with near-zero error rates.
- **AI-integrated IoT execution networks.** AI-enabled IoT devices operate as execution nodes, ensuring that AI-driven decisions translate into real-world actions.
- **Continuous learning AI execution systems.** AI-powered execution models continuously refine decision-making strategies based on feedback loops and real-world performance monitoring. Continuous learning will bring an unprecedented level of responsiveness to business operations, making them paradoxically feel more human, or at least more "alive."

Action Examples AI-powered manufacturing plants leverage RPA, AI-driven predictive analytics, and adaptive scheduling algorithms to optimize production efficiency. Companies like Siemens and General Electric use AI-powered digital twins to simulate production workflows and identify inefficiencies before real-world execution.

Leading e-commerce and logistics firms such as DHL have deployed AI-powered execution systems that dynamically optimize delivery routes, warehouse inventory, and last-mile fulfillment. AI-driven supply chain orchestration platforms integrate real-time demand forecasting, route optimization, and autonomous delivery drones to minimize delays and maximize cost efficiency.

Smart cities leverage AI-powered traffic management systems, autonomous energy distribution networks, and AI-optimized urban planning to improve infrastructure efficiency. Cities like Singapore and Dubai use AI-driven IoT networks to control traffic lights, reduce congestion, and manage public transportation schedules dynamically.

For example, AI-driven traffic control systems integrate real-time traffic monitoring, weather prediction, and commuter demand data to optimize vehicle movement dynamically. These AI-powered systems reduce congestion by adjusting traffic light sequences and rerouting vehicles to less congested paths. Similarly, AI-driven smart grids automatically balance power distribution by analyzing energy consumption patterns and adjusting supply levels to reduce energy waste.

AI-first Action represents the culmination of intelligence-driven business execution. While Sensing, Understanding, and Decision-Making provide the foundation for AI-driven strategies, the true impact is realized when organizations translate insights into tangible results through seamless execution.

Companies that master AI-powered action will achieve unparalleled efficiency, scalability, and adaptability in their operations. Whether through autonomous manufacturing, self-optimizing supply chains, or smart infrastructure execution, AI-driven Action ensures that businesses remain resilient and future-proof in an era of constant change.

With the completion of the Action phase, the mSUDA framework is fully realized, enabling enterprises to operate at machine speed, with precision, intelligence, and adaptability. But as we hope we've emphasized, once Action has been taken, the cycle starts all over again as the employee, team, function, leadership, or even entire organization needs to sense what difference their Action has made. Have they succeeded in their goals or in moving them forward? How has their customer responded, or their partner(s), competitors, or the market? And is the impact of their response fully understood? The mSUDA loop is fractal as we discussed in *Boundless*, meaning that it applies to all levels of company operations, from actions that individual agents or other employees take from minute to minute all the way to large scale, strategic shift that are made at the enterprise level. mSUDA is fractal and continuous, enabling operational speed to value routinely and at scale.

Summary

In the coming years, decision-making will be the core differentiator between successful and struggling enterprises. Companies that remain reliant on slow, human-dependent decision frameworks will be increasingly outmaneuvered by those that have fully embraced AI-powered execution.

mSUDA is not just about speed. It's about ensuring that speed translates into strategic advantage. Decision dominance is about owning the competitive landscape by ensuring that your organization is always steps ahead of the market, the customer, and the competition.

The future belongs to companies that do not just respond to change but drive it through real-time intelligence and execution. Those who implement mSUDA fully will not just keep up with the competition, they will redefine the game itself and its rules.

4
Relational Intelligence for Digital Labor

Autonomous companies are <u>hyper-talented</u>, integrating <u>human and digital resources</u> and building deep <u>relational intelligence</u>.

Artificial intelligence (AI) capabilities, such as Generative AI, robotic process automation, and digital assistants, are becoming integral to enterprise operations. Digital labor is enabling 24/7 productivity and scalability. What used to be science fiction is fast becoming a reality. Within the next few years there will be no doubt that this technology has crossed the cognitive border from being part of the tool set to being part of the workforce. Being talented demands the integration of that digital workforce that assists, augments, and amplifies the capabilities and outcomes of their human colleagues.

In this chapter we first want to convince you that this is not just the product of our fevered imaginations but is well documented and researched by leading firms. We will share some of their research findings into Agentic AI to leave no doubt that this is happening and happening fast. Next we want to stress that even as this becomes true, relationships, which we believe are the heart of all business, will retain their importance and perhaps become even more so. While this is not the place to unveil a new discipline for relational intelligence and design, we will certainly advocate for one, as well as for the development of a few human qualities that we think will shine in our new relationships with AI. Finally, we will discuss the impact of all these digital and human workforce changes on the human resources (HR) department.

Introduction

The most important strategic technology for 2025 and beyond is Agentic AI, according to the latest forecast by tech analyst Gartner.[1] Spending on AI will help drive a healthy increase in information technology (IT) expenditure. Worldwide IT spending is expected to total $5.74 trillion in 2025, an increase of 9.3% from 2024. The target spending for Agentic AI is aimed at creating a digital labor force, where humans and AI agents collaborate to create customer value.

According to the 2025 Connectivity Benchmark Report by MuleSoft and Deloitte Digital, 93% of IT leaders report intentions to introduce autonomous AI agents within the next two years, and nearly half have already done so.[2]

Spending on software is predicted to increase 14% to reach $1.23 trillion in 2025, up from 11.7% growth in 2024. Meanwhile, spending on IT services is expected to grow 9.4% to $1.73 trillion in 2025, up from 5.6% in 2024. Agentic AI systems autonomously plan and take actions to meet user-defined goals. Agentic AI offers a virtual workforce that can offload and augment human work. By 2028, at least 15% of day-to-day work decisions will be taken autonomously through Agentic AI, up from 0% in 2024. The goal-driven capabilities of this technology will deliver more adaptable software systems, capable of completing a wide variety of tasks.

By 2029, Agentic AI will autonomously resolve 80% of common customer service issues without human intervention, leading to a 30% reduction in operational costs. Unlike traditional AI systems that require explicit instructions from users, Agentic AI operates independently, enabling it to quickly analyze complex datasets, identify patterns, and take action. This capability is expected to significantly enhance decision-making processes across industries. Some of the opportunities Agentic AI brings to businesses include the following:

- Agentic AI enhances decision-making by autonomously selecting actions for desired outcomes, improving performance over time.
- It quickly analyzes complex data, reducing manual modeling and enabling scalable solutions.
- This technology upskills teams to manage projects through natural language, though it requires robust governance and orchestration tools.
- Effective implementation necessitates clear guidelines on autonomy, security, and data privacy.

By 2028, 33% of enterprise software applications will incorporate Agentic AI, a substantial increase from less than 1% in 2024. This shift will enable organizations to automate various tasks and workflows, thereby improving overall efficiency. Gartner projects global spending on AI software will grow to $297 billion by 2027, with Generative AI leading this growth. Worldwide IT spending is expected to reach $5.74 trillion in 2025, driven by investments in AI and cloud technologies. The beauty of AI agents lies in their limitless applicability. They can be tailored to handle a diverse range of tasks:

- **Personalize customer experiences.** Dynamically adjust to real-time customer needs and preferences.
- **Accelerate research and development (R&D).** Sift through massive datasets to identify trends and insights, accelerating scientific discovery and innovation.
- **Optimize logistics and supply chains.** Predict demand fluctuations, proactively manage inventory, and streamline delivery routes.
- **Automate complex decision-making.** Analyze risk factors and potential outcomes to guide strategic business decisions.

While digital labor creates efficiency, it raises concerns about job losses in traditional roles. However, it also generates opportunities in tech-driven fields like cybersecurity and AI development. Organizations like Salesforce are leveraging platforms like Agentforce 2 to integrate human–AI collaboration effectively. Marc Benioff, CEO of Salesforce, envisions digital labor as a trillion-dollar market opportunity. The rise of digital labor represents both opportunities and challenges for enterprises as they navigate this transformative era. AI tools are automating administrative tasks, reducing the need for traditional middle management roles focused on oversight and coordination. Middle managers will shift their focus to strategic decision-making and areas where human judgment adds higher value. Self-organizing teams supported by AI may replace hierarchical structures, creating flatter organizational models.

Traditional human-centric key performance indicators, such as response times, will evolve to include AI-driven metrics like automation success rates and collaboration efficiency between humans and AI agents. This hybrid approach reflects the integration of digital labor into workflows. Management will increasingly involve overseeing human–AI collaboration, ensuring ethical AI use, compliance, and alignment with business goals. Managers will act as governance layers to synthesize AI outputs and fine-tune automation. Resistance to change and skill gaps may arise as traditional management models adapt to AI integration. Companies will need to invest in training and upskilling managers for new roles. AI-driven digital labor is reshaping management structures by enhancing efficiency, enabling flatter organizations, and redefining leadership roles.

What is the impact of adopting Agentic AI and a digital labor force for chief information officers (CIOs) and IT? Here are 2025 IDC forecasts on the impact of Agentic AI for CIOs:[3]

- By 2025, 70% of organizations will be formalizing policies and oversight to address AI risks (e.g., ethical, brand, and personally identifiable information), aligning AI governance with strategic business goals.
- Responding to the drag of technical debt, 40% of CIOs in 2025 will drive enterprise initiatives in high-impact areas to remediate technical debt for competitive advantage.
- In 2026, over one-third of organizations will be stuck in the experimental, point solution phase of AI experimentation, requiring a shift of focus to enterprise use cases to deliver return on investment. This stagnation hinders competitiveness and slows growth.

- By 2026, 70% of CIOs will lead the creation of a strategic road map to rapidly implement responsible AI solutions, maximizing benefits while mitigating risks across their operations.
- In 2026, 50% of CIOs will diversify and broaden security strategies across their organization's IT and security teams to address new/fast-evolving threats to their technology and supply chain ecosystem.
- By 2027, 50% of CIOs will be accountable for embedding sustainability goals into every technology project, measuring outcomes to refine investments and align with environmental objectives.
- By 2028, 50% of A1000 will adopt cutting-edge tools to close the digital and AI skills gap, easing reliance on specialized talent, boosting the workforce, and bridging the expertise gap for innovation.

"The CIO role is evolving rapidly, with AI at its core. CIOs must move beyond technology facilitation and take the lead in AI governance, cybersecurity, skills development, sustainability, regulatory compliance, and technical debt management."

—*IDC president Crawford Del Prete*

The following are predictions from Gartner on Agentic AI adoption in business[4]:

- By 2029, Agentic AI is predicted to autonomously resolve 80% of common customer service issues without human intervention, reducing operational costs by 30%.
- By 2028, 33% of enterprise software applications will include Agentic AI.
- By 2028, 15% of day-to-day work decisions will be made by Agentic AI.
- By 2028, 75% of enterprise software engineers will use AI code assistants, up from less than 10% in early 2023.
- By 2029, 10% of global boards will use AI guidance to challenge executive decisions that are material to their business.
- By 2028, 40% of CIOs will demand "guardian agents" be available to autonomously track, oversee, or contain the results of AI agent actions.

What Is Digital Labor?

Salesforce is focusing on "digital labor" with its Agentforce platform, which enables businesses to build and manage AI agents to perform complex tasks, creating a "limitless workforce" that complements human employees. Salesforce views digital labor as the rise of AI agents capable of performing tasks once limited to human agents or employees, offering unprecedented scalability, efficiency, and reach. Digital labor refers to technologies (such as AI automation and AI agents) that mimic human decision-making and cognitive abilities. It extends human capacity to complete tasks at speeds and scales that a human-only workforce cannot match.

The benefits of digital labor include the following:

- **Increased productivity.** AI agents can handle routine tasks, freeing up human employees for more strategic work.
- **Scalability.** Digital labor enables businesses to scale their operations quickly and efficiently without increasing head count.
- **24/7 availability.** AI agents can work around the clock, providing support and completing tasks even when human employees are off-duty.
- **Cost savings.** By automating tasks, businesses can reduce operational costs.

The following are some examples of digital labor use cases. They are not all line of business, and all functions across any company size, in any industry or geography, will have numerous use cases for Agentic AI adoption and creation of digital labor:

- **Customer support.** AI agents can handle basic customer inquiries and resolve simple issues, freeing up human agents for more complex cases.
- **Lead management.** AI agents can qualify leads, assign them to the appropriate sales representatives, and track their progress.
- **Data entry.** AI agents can automate data entry tasks, reducing errors and saving time.

- **Order processing.** AI agents can process orders, track shipments, and provide updates to customers.

Today's CEOs are the final generation of executives who will lead exclusively human workforces, a gentle reminder from Marc Benioff. In a *Wall Street Journal* article, Benioff noted the following:

> "While much of the AI conversation is about large language models, the real revolution is happening in AI-driven digital labor: autonomous, intelligent agents. Because such agents act on their own, collaborate and continuously learn and improve, companies of any size can scale beyond human limits. Today's CEOs are the final generation of executives leading exclusively human workforces. Going forward, we'll need to learn how to manage human workers and digital labor to work together to deliver efficiency and productivity. Integrating AI agents into daily operations will become a leadership skill that separates companies that thrive from those that fall behind."

The healthiest companies in the AI-first economy are Autonomous companies. Autonomous companies have adopted a hybrid workforce—humans and AI agents—to create digital labor, enabling them to deliver value at the speed of need. Autonomous businesses have Boundless labor, powered by AI, scaling how they distribute, connect, engage, and serve all stakeholders unlike any time in history.

The Importance of Relationships

Why are we elevating and drawing attention to the role of relationships in business, especially in the middle of an evidence-heavy discussion of AI? What is it about relationships that we find so compelling that it is worth our time imagining their future?

The first and most simple answer is that business is nothing without them, that in some ways relationships are all that exist in business. This is most obvious when we recognize that words like *customer* and *employee* actually define relationships between people rather than individual people per se. A person only becomes a customer through interacting with a company in a particular kind of way, namely, purchasing a service or product from it. And even then the label *customer* only applies to that individual person in their relationship with that specific company. Similarly, a person becomes an employee only through engaging with a company in a particular kind of mutual commitment and contractual obligation. It is less immediately obvious that the products and services a company provides are also relationships. But even then we can understand those services as interactions that help define, shape, and nurture those relationships. And we can understand those products—digital or physical or hybrid—as outcomes of relationships between people who need to get a job done and those who want to provide a way to get it done. Products simply do not exist independently of the maker/provider and the user/consumer and the connections between them.

Given this fact, it might become more of a surprise to learn that relationship design simply does not exist in the business language! No one is focused on their primary relationships enough to build their company around them. We think that as AI transforms businesses, it will become even more evident that successful relationships are the difference between a company that is fit for this new AI economy and one that is not.

The second answer is that AI is going to create some brand new relationships, and it is useful to be forewarned so we can then be intentional about them. The key relationships here are the ones that will emerge between digital and human employees as the former become an everyday part of any company's workforce and, after a time, a dominant part.

Beyond, or underpinning, this view of the world of business lies a deeper perspective on the nature of the world writ large. This is a perspective that the world and everything and everyone in it is connected to one another. A perspective that these connections are primary and that they are always in flux. Meaning that, as in the business world, relationships between entities are more important than the entities themselves, that they are responsible for the continuous evolution of the entities, and that they too are in a state of constant change.

This way of seeing the world feels new to us largely because we live in a predominantly Western tradition that gives primacy to the idea of the individual entity. We tend to hold that the entity owns its relationships and that it maintains its essential, unchanging nature even as those relationships change (or not). And yet the relationship-first perspective is not new by any means, and it pervades a broad set of worldviews that we are only recently coming to recognize including those of Asian, Indian, African, and Indigenous cultures. It feels like time, as we contemplate "the future," to be inspired and guided by these other wisdoms.

In short, our focus on relationships is a way not only to differentiate and enhance our company that has always stood for relationships anyway but also to embrace ways of thinking that have been long overlooked and that deserve our attention as we seek to build a more inclusive future for all.

One of our insights as we did research for this book was that the introduction of a digital workforce into our businesses will give us the opportunity to revisit many of the ways we conventionally go about designing them. We think we will find that certain human capabilities, virtues, and qualities turn out to be less relevant in a world of Autonomous Agentic AI. They will turn out to be orthodoxies, beliefs that no one questions because they are thought to be "just the way things are," that are in need of a refresh. In Chapter 5, we discuss the human qualities of effort and experience and also our need for stability and structure that is woven into our organizational designs almost universally. Here, in our discussion about relationships we want to briefly consider one more.

Our People Are the Difference

One of the most common orthodoxies in business is characterized by the phrase "Our people are the difference." A simple Google search can attest to its popularity. Some companies use it as their official or unofficial tagline, a tribute to their employees that they hope "sends the right message" both internally and externally. They hope their employees feel special and that their customers take it as proof of their human goodness. Others just use it as part of their explanation of what makes the company as a whole different. It's part of their corporate story. It sounds nice; it sounds caring and positive. The only problem is it's simply not true.

The most obvious way in which it's not true is that most employees of nearly all companies have worked somewhere else before joining their current one. And most of them have worked at one or more competitors. We know this because perhaps the most common phrase in all of recruiting history is the one in job postings that says, "relevant industry experience mandatory." All HR managers in all HR departments in all companies just about everywhere appear to think that prior experience in their industry is an essential quality for a prospective employee. A deal breaker even. It's another orthodoxy that should, by the way, also be closely scrutinized for its value, but the outcome of it is that everyone moves within their industry. They just do. So, in fact it is more true to assert that "our people are reassuringly familiar."

But there is another, less obvious, way in which it's not true, a way that may even be a more significant blocker to innovative thinking. And that is the fact that what makes the difference is not the individual employee but the conditions that are set for them by the company culture and the relationships that they are encouraged and allowed to make with each other, their customers, their bosses, and so on. The truth is that individuals can thrive in one environment and struggle in another. We see this most clearly in professional sports teams where trades can result in surprising performance changes. Some players flourish in new surroundings and become highly valued members of the team after failing to differentiate themselves in their former club, while others fail to live up to expectations. In either case, the player themself is not the difference, though they certainly have the capacity to bloom or to wilt. It is the conditions they are put in and the relationships they make, or do not make, that enable them to do so.

Another way to put this is that individual employees are not fixed assets. They do not behave the same way in all conditions. They are, in most cases, adaptable, capable of absorbing and responding to change. But it is the environment, the conditions, and the potential for relationships that cause this capacity to express itself.

On the one hand, one company's employees are the same as any other company's employees in the same industry. They move from company to company, they read the same magazines, they attend the same conventions, they learn the same strategies and processes. But on the other hand, one employee can perform in one way at one company and very differently at another. They can be stars at one and struggle to shine at another. They can love working at one company and hate the same job at a different company.

The lesson here is that performance, the "difference" that companies seek from their people, is not an attribute that is owned or embodied solely by the individual employees themselves. Rather, it is a shared attribute that emerges from the coming together of the employee and the conditions, the culture, and the other people with whom they interact, including but not limited to their managers. Performance is emergent and it is relational. Companies who leave it up to their people to be the difference or to make the difference because, well, that's what the orthodoxy tells us are at risk of missing a bigger truth (actually a truer truth!). It's the relationships between people that are more important to business success than the people themselves. Our relationships make the difference.

And yet, we don't design for the relationships we want to have. There is simply no business practice for relationship design. We leave the kinds of relationships we get, with our employees, our customers, our business partners, somewhat to chance, hoping that we'll just get along. Even developing genuinely compelling experiences is no guarantee that the underlying relationship will be mutually valuable over the long term.

We introduced relational intelligence (RI) previously in the book. It is the ability to design, cultivate, nurture, and enhance successful relationships in the age of AI and smart machines. RI integrates human individuality, creativity, and empathy with the efficiencies, contextual awareness, and data-driven insights of AI agents at machine scale and speed to deepen the connections that matter most, with customers, employees, and with other valued stakeholders.

Relational design is the intentional practice of developing organizational relational intelligence: designing for strong, meaningful, and productive relationships in business, focusing both on the relationships themselves and on the conditions, structures, and interactions that enable them to emerge and thrive.

It includes designing individual relationships between employees, customers, partners, and teams, but goes further. It addresses the underlying patterns, environments, expectations, and shared rituals that determine *how* people relate, not just *what* they do together.

One of the implicit strengths of relationships is that they are, by nature, boundary crossing. A relationship only exists when an individual or a department or an organization is able to reach out beyond itself to connect with another. Relationships are inherently silo breaking. And yet, we must be careful here. When relationships within a department become close, there is always the danger of ignoring new relationships outside the department or even actively discouraging them. When a leader seeks to foster camaraderie and a sense of belonging, they might have their team create a vision for itself, a set of values, even a mission statement that unwittingly begins to supersede the vision, values, or mission of the larger organization.

Designing for successful relationships requires, of course, that they take into account what makes a business relationship successful in the first place. While there are some qualities that may be industry or brand specific, there are a few characteristics that are the underpinning to all successful relationships at least in business. The most widely researched and discussed of all characteristics is trust. We explored trust in *Boundless* and so will not cover it here other than to say that we fully agree with the consensus that trust is the most important of them all. Other characteristics that we believe are important and yet comparatively unsung are delight (an emotional and evocative characteristic pursued mostly by experience and brand designers) and mutual value, or shared success. This characteristic is the animating principle behind *Boundless*, and so we won't dwell on it here other than to note that it is sprinkled throughout this book, too.

One other characteristic that gets some attention but certainly not as much as trust is commitment. Commitment is usually studied as an individual attribute, one's persistence or determination or grit. But what we're particularly interested in is the fact that commitment is nearly always pointed toward something outside of the self. We are committed *to* something. And this facet of commitment differentiates it from other individual qualities like intelligence or financial status or appearance or even trustworthiness.

Commitment

A major research study into relationship success, reviewed in a 2022 article in *Psychology Today*,[5] shows that high quality, successful relationships are defined more by the effort their members put into them than by the characteristics of the members themselves.

More specifically, the one single factor that stood out among all others as critical to the success of a relationship was the perception, by one member of the relationship, of *the level of commitment to the relationship* by their partner.

This is noteworthy because we tend to pay more attention to the individuals within relationships, to their qualities and their needs, than we do to the relationships of which they are a part. Commitment fosters and maintains the relationship over the longer term, and it is a *commitment to the relationship itself*, not to the other person directly. *Commitment* is the one word that recognizes the relationship itself before the person or people with whom a relationship is desired or built.

So, what is commitment exactly, why is it important, and how might we build committed relationships in the business world? When it is applied to a pursuit (sport, music, skill, craft, or trade), commitment is the consistent and continuous practice and performance of that pursuit, usually fueled by the expressed desire and goal to achieve and maintain expertise or even mastery of it, and perhaps even to be able to contribute something to its own continued success or popularity. In this application, commitment is recognized as the single factor that is most likely to result in success in that pursuit. Commitment is a mix of passion and persistence, devotion and dedication, will and grit. It is a single mindedness that often rejects commonsense ("you're too short," "you'll never make a living at it," "the odds are too great," etc.). Of course, it does not guarantee "objective" success at the pursuit, but even without that it usually brings its own intrinsic satisfaction. As they say, "the journey is the reward," and while practice never makes perfect, it is a key to success and is the only key to success in a skills-based pursuit.

When it is applied to a relationship, commitment is the consistent and continuous engagement with that relationship, usually fueled by the express desire for the relationship itself to be successful and achieve its goals. In the personal world, the success and the goals of a relationship are usually measured by its duration and by the satisfaction of its members. In other words, the relationship has its own continued existence as its primary rationale and goal. In the business world, a relationship or partnership usually has goals other than its own existence and therefore other ways of measuring success. We have already discussed the goals and purpose of business relationships previously, but the point here is that commitment to business relationships is as important a factor in achieving their success—and the most powerful indicator of their likely success—as in personal relationships and pursuits.

In short, commitment in both pursuits and in relationships denotes a continuous, consistent practice, and performance and it is the number one factor in predicting success in both.

Commitment doesn't just suddenly appear, fully formed. Even personal commitment, to a sport or to a career, isn't always a sudden epiphany, an aha moment in which life's purpose suddenly becomes clear, followed by a full mind and body dedication and devotion to that new purpose. Oftentimes it comes more gradually, sometimes even after an initial dislike of a job or a reluctance to engage. And when it comes to a business relationship in which one is tasked to join forces with a colleague or channel partner or vendor to achieve a specific business goal, commitment can easily start at zero, so to speak. And so, commitment needs to be built intentionally and methodically to a point where the relationship can be thought to stand a realistic chance of success.

To do this, there are three phases of commitment building for relationships: Design, Declaration, and Demonstration.

Design is about understanding the nature of the commitment that is being requested of the prospective partners: who and/or what am I making it to? and what are the parameters of the commitment? What is expected of me? How long will it last? What is the goal and the purpose of the partnership that I am committing myself to?

Declaration is about making our commitment real through being voiced. Abraham Lincoln called commitment the thing that turns promise into reality, and it is true that the real proof of commitment is demonstration (as detailed next). But the act of declaring one's commitment externalizes that commitment and shares it with those who are listening. One's commitment is now a thing of record, with its own identity or existence that others can point to.

Demonstration is putting that commitment into continuous and consistent practice. You demonstrate commitment through action—doing things that clearly and directly help achieve the partnership's purpose—and through inaction—not doing things that are not aligned with the purpose even if they could help you personally.

You demonstrate commitment through focus, which is related to action. Focus is knowing what to spend time and resources on and what not to in order to achieve the partnership purpose.

You demonstrate commitment through accountability: being accountable and holding your partner accountable to your joint goals (the things that you jointly decide and plan to do to fulfill the partnership's Purpose).

You demonstrate commitment through your consistent and voiced support for your partner.

You demonstrate commitment through tenacity, grit, stick-with-it-ness, persistence, courage, call it what you like, but it is the quality of seeing the partnership through, not giving up on yourself, your partner, or the purpose and goals of the partnership ('til death do us part!).

What does this mean in practice? How do you demonstrate your commitment to your partner or your customer? By taking the perspective of *standing next to them*. Buyers, and especially senior leaders, are being sold to all the time. They know that they're seen as keepers of the corporate purse strings. The more senior they are, the more budget authority they hold and the fewer hoops they have to jump through to make a procurement decision. And so they have a steady stream of people wanting to sit across the table from them trying to convince them that their company's offer is just what they need.

It can be a lonely place, knowing that your popularity is based only on the size of your budget. But standing next to them is a different proposition. It forces the seller to see the world from the leader's perspective, to see all the challenges and opportunities that are in front of them. And it tells the buyer that the seller is on their side and is ready to go into battle with them.

This is obviously similar to the advice to "walk a mile in their shoes" and to "see the world through their eyes." The difference, and what makes this stronger, is that standing next to your customer goes further than demonstrating empathy with them. It goes further than showing that you are a "trusted advisor." It demonstrates not only that you empathize but that you're right there with them.

It is easy and natural to extend this idea to your partner in an internal partnership. Stand next to them. Show them that you're committed to the partnership with them, seeing the same picture and fighting the same fight.

With the word *committed* we add the preposition *to*, and what that preposition shows is that the effort we're making is being directed away from ourselves and toward our partner or our customer and toward the partnership itself. Making this effort toward the other and toward the "in-between-ness" is what counts in making the partnership as successful as possible.

Finally, in this discussion of human qualities, there are two that stand out to us as being important for our success as humans in our interactions with our digital colleagues: curiosity and imagination.

The Human Edge: Curiosity and Imagination in the Age of AI

As AI continues to progress from the assistive stages of the Autonomous maturity framework into the Autonomous ones, the question of how its human colleagues can best position themselves for success is one that will continue to be one of the most pressing concerns of the age. The most successful organizations of the future will be those that encourage, enable, and elevate those human capabilities that best complement AI's strengths.

We think that two distinctly human characteristics emerge as particularly valuable in this new paradigm: curiosity and imagination. These traits represent the essence of human inquiry and creative vision, our ability to ask the questions that AI cannot formulate on its own. While AI can provide increasingly sophisticated answers and execute fast solutions, it cannot independently wonder about possibilities beyond its current scope or envision entirely new paradigms. This creates an unprecedented opportunity for humans to leverage their natural capacity for curiosity-driven exploration and imaginative leaps as the driving force behind AI-powered innovation.

The relationship between human inquiry and AI capability is symbiotic rather than competitive. This partnership transforms traditional business models from execution-focused to inquiry-focused, placing premium value on the human ability to generate meaningful questions and envision transformative possibilities.

Curiosity: The Art of Open Inquiry Curiosity represents one of humanity's most distinctive cognitive traits, the intrinsic drive to explore, understand, and discover. In the context of AI partnership, curiosity becomes the engine that drives exploration beyond predetermined parameters.

While AI systems can process vast amounts of information and identify patterns within existing datasets, they cannot independently develop the wonder that leads to breakthrough questions.

The curious mind approaches AI as a powerful investigative partner, using it to explore lines of inquiry that might never have been pursued through traditional means. This goes far beyond simple information retrieval. Curious professionals learn to engage with AI in iterative conversations, where each answer generates new questions, and each insight opens pathways to deeper exploration. They ask not just "what does the data show?" but "what patterns might we be missing?" and "what would happen if we examined this from a completely different angle?"

This type of open inquiry proves particularly valuable in business contexts where traditional analytical approaches may miss emerging opportunities or fail to identify underlying assumptions that need questioning. The curious mind doesn't accept AI outputs as final answers but treats them as starting points for deeper investigation. When an AI system identifies a correlation, curiosity asks about causation. When it suggests an optimization, curiosity wonders about unintended consequences. When it provides a solution, curiosity questions whether the problem has been correctly defined.

The business value of curiosity manifests in several critical ways. First, it drives continuous learning and adaptation. In rapidly changing markets, the ability to ask probing questions about evolving customer needs, emerging technologies, and shifting competitive landscapes becomes essential for maintaining relevance. AI can process signals from these changes, but curiosity determines which signals warrant investigation and what questions should guide that investigation.

Second, curiosity enables deeper customer understanding. While AI can analyze customer behavior patterns and predict preferences, curious minds ask why those patterns exist and what underlying needs they represent. This leads to insights that go beyond optimization of existing offerings to the identification of entirely new value propositions. The curious approach to customer research involves using AI to explore not just what customers do, but what drives their behavior, what frustrates them about current solutions, and what possibilities they might not even realize they want.

Third, curiosity drives innovation by questioning fundamental assumptions about how business should be conducted. Instead of using AI merely to improve existing processes, curious organizations use it to explore whether those processes are necessary at all. They ask whether traditional industry boundaries make sense, whether established value chains could be reimagined, and whether current business models address the most important problems.

The cultivation of organizational curiosity requires intentional effort. It means creating cultures where questioning is rewarded over quick answers, where exploration is valued alongside execution, and where AI is positioned as a tool for investigation rather than just optimization. Leaders must model curious behavior by asking open-ended questions, encouraging experimentation, and demonstrating that the best questions often lead to unexpected discoveries.

Curious professionals also develop specific skills for maximizing their AI partnerships. They learn to frame questions in ways that help AI systems provide more useful responses. They understand how to structure iterative inquiries that build on previous insights. They become adept at recognizing when AI responses reveal new avenues for exploration and are skilled at translating their wonderings into prompts that generate meaningful investigation.

Imagination: Envisioning the Possible While curiosity drives open exploration, imagination represents the uniquely human ability to envision possibilities that don't yet exist. Imagination in the business context isn't simply about creativity or artistic expression, it's about the cognitive capacity to synthesize information, extrapolate from current conditions, and construct visions of what could be. This imaginative capability becomes particularly powerful when combined with AI's analytical and Generative abilities.

Imagination asks fundamentally different questions than curiosity. Where curiosity wonders "what if we explored this further?" imagination asks "what if this were completely different?" When curiosity seeks to understand existing patterns, imagination envisions entirely new patterns. This visionary quality enables humans to guide AI toward possibilities that wouldn't emerge from data analysis alone.

The imaginative mind approaches AI as a partner in possibility exploration. Rather than simply asking AI to solve existing problems, imagination frames challenges in terms of desired futures and asks AI to help map pathways toward those visions. This creates a dynamic where human imagination sets the direction while AI provides the analytical power to evaluate feasibility, identify obstacles, and suggest implementation approaches.

In business applications, imagination manifests as the ability to envision new market opportunities, revolutionary product concepts, and transformative business models. While AI can analyze market trends and identify optimization opportunities within existing frameworks, imagination questions whether those frameworks should exist at all. It asks whether entire industries could be reimagined, whether customer needs could be met in radically different ways, and whether emerging technologies could enable previously impossible solutions.

The imaginative approach to AI partnership involves using these systems to stress-test visionary ideas rather than simply validate existing assumptions. When imagination conceives of a new business model, AI can help model its economic implications, identify potential challenges, and suggest refinements. When imagination envisions a revolutionary product, AI can help analyze market receptivity, competitive responses, and technical feasibility. This partnership enables rapid iteration between vision and analysis, enabling imaginative ideas to be refined and developed with unprecedented speed and rigor.

Imagination also proves essential for navigating uncertainty and disruption. While AI can model various scenarios based on historical data, imagination helps organizations prepare for possibilities that fall outside historical patterns. It enables leaders to envision how emerging technologies might reshape their industries, how changing social values might create new market opportunities, and how global events might require entirely new approaches to business.

The business value of imagination extends beyond product and service innovation to organizational transformation. Imaginative leaders use AI to explore how work itself might be reimagined, how organizational structures could evolve, and how human–AI collaboration might create entirely new forms of competitive advantage. They don't simply automate existing processes but envision how AI partnership could enable fundamentally different ways of creating value.

Developing organizational imagination requires creating environments where visionary thinking is encouraged and supported. This means establishing processes for capturing and evaluating imaginative ideas, creating safe spaces for exploring seemingly impossible concepts, and developing capabilities for translating visions into actionable strategies. It also requires leaders who can balance imaginative thinking with practical execution, ensuring that visionary ideas lead to real-world impact.

Imaginative professionals learn to leverage AI as a thinking partner rather than just a tool. They understand how to use AI to explore the implications of their visions, test assumptions underlying their imaginative leaps, and identify pathways for bringing possibilities into reality. They become skilled at translating abstract concepts into concrete prompts that help AI systems contribute meaningfully to the visioning process.

The combination of curiosity and imagination creates a powerful foundation for human–AI collaboration. Curiosity ensures continuous exploration and questioning of assumptions, while imagination provides the visionary framework for directing that exploration toward transformative possibilities. Together, these human characteristics complement AI's analytical and Generative capabilities, creating partnerships that can navigate complexity, drive innovation, and adapt to rapidly changing business environments.

Organizations that recognize and cultivate these human capabilities position themselves to thrive in an AI-driven future. They understand that while technology provides the tools, human curiosity and imagination provide the direction, ensuring that AI serves not just efficiency but also discovery, not just optimization but also transformation.

Cognitive Downloads Versus Cognitive Upgrades: A Deliberate Balancing Act

While we're still on the subject of talent, and some of the ways that humans and AI can work together most effectively and harmoniously, let's explore the concepts of "cognitive download" and "cognitive upgrade" as they relate to AI and its increasing role in both assistive and Autonomous work environments.

Essentially, *cognitive download* occurs when we offload our mental tasks to AI systems. This might look like relying on AI for simple calculations or for recalling information, and it carries the potential to reduce our own active cognitive engagement and, over time, hinder our personal skill development in those areas. For example, if we constantly depend on GPS navigation, our innate sense of direction and ability to navigate independently might weaken. Similarly, an overreliance on AI for writing tasks could diminish our fundamental understanding of grammar, syntax, and effective communication. Notably, some studies have indicated a correlation between the frequent use of AI tools and a noticeable decline in critical thinking abilities, particularly among younger individuals who are growing up with these technologies readily available.

However, *cognitive upgrade* involves strategically using AI to augment and enhance our inherent cognitive abilities. In this paradigm, AI serves as a valuable partner, assisting us in thinking more effectively, accelerating our learning processes, and enabling us to tackle more complex problems than we could manage independently. Consider AI tools that can process vast datasets and provide insightful data visualizations, or those that can facilitate brainstorming sessions by offering diverse perspectives and connections. These applications of AI free up our limited mental capacity, enabling us to focus on higher-level cognitive functions such as creativity, strategic planning, and nuanced decision-making. The concept of neural synergy strongly supports this idea, envisioning a powerful collaboration where human ingenuity and intuition are seamlessly combined with AI's unparalleled processing power and analytical capabilities.

In the realm of assistive technology, the primary objective is typically cognitive upgrade. Here, AI is specifically designed to help individuals overcome specific cognitive or physical limitations and enhance their existing abilities. Examples include sophisticated AI-powered prosthetic limbs that can learn and adapt to a user's movements, or AI-driven memory aids that can assist individuals with recall and organization. Even in the context of fully autonomous systems, where AI takes over the execution of specific tasks without direct human intervention, the underlying goal is often to free up valuable human resources and intellectual capital for more strategic and innovative endeavors, effectively representing a cognitive upgrade at a broader organizational or societal level.

To illustrate the difference more concretely, consider a student using an AI-powered writing tool. If the tool simply rewrites sentences or generates text without providing any explanation or rationale, it represents a cognitive download, potentially preventing the student from actively learning and improving their own writing skills. However, if the AI tool is designed to provide detailed feedback on grammar, style, and clarity, along with explanations for its suggestions, it transforms into a cognitive upgrade, actively helping the student to understand and improve their writing abilities over time. Similarly, in the context of navigation, a GPS system that not only provides turn-by-turn directions but also explains the reasoning behind suggested routes, such as real-time traffic patterns or potential hazards, promotes a deeper understanding of the environment. By contrast, a GPS that solely gives directions without context can foster overreliance and diminish the user's own navigational skills.

It's important to recognize that the distinction between cognitive download and cognitive upgrade isn't always immediately clear-cut, and the ultimate impact of a specific AI tool can heavily depend on the specific context of its use and the intentions of the user. For instance, a language translation application could, in some situations, hinder the process of actively learning a new language (representing a download of cognitive effort), while in other scenarios, it could serve as a valuable aid in understanding complex texts and accelerating the learning process (acting as a cognitive upgrade).

At Salesforce, for example, the company is actively exploring and implementing AI in ways that strive for cognitive upgrade (high-value work) and cognitive download (low-value work) for our employees and our customers. For example, our AI-powered sales agents are designed to provide coaching and insights to sales professionals, helping them to improve their strategies and close more effectively. Furthermore, we have a company-wide initiative focused on proactively reskilling our employees in the age of AI, recognizing the importance of adapting to these technological shifts. As part of this initiative, we are providing quarterly AI learning days and have set an ambitious goal of ensuring that 80% of our entire workforce gains fundamental AI skills by the year 2025.

It's important to note that the line between cognitive download and upgrade isn't always sharp, and a single AI tool can potentially lead to either outcome depending on how it's used and the user's mindset. For example, a language translation app could lead to a cognitive download if someone solely relies on it without attempting to learn the other language. However, it could be a cognitive upgrade if used as a tool to aid in language learning and communication.

In the Context of Assistive and Autonomous Work Assistive AI aiming for cognitive upgrade. Think of AI-powered tools for individuals with learning disabilities that personalize the learning experience based on their specific needs and provide tailored feedback to help them understand concepts more effectively. This isn't just giving them the answer (download) but helping them learn *how* to arrive at the answer (upgrade).

Autonomous AI facilitating a cognitive upgrade at a higher level. Consider an Autonomous manufacturing plant managed by AI. While the AI handles the intricate details of production (which might seem like a cognitive download of those specific tasks), it frees up human engineers and managers to focus on strategic planning, innovation, and overall system optimization—a cognitive upgrade at a management level.

The goal should often be to design and use AI in ways that foster cognitive upgrade, empowering humans to achieve more and develop their abilities further, rather than simply becoming reliant on AI to think for them. Low-value work should benefit from cognitive download and be performed Autonomously via digital labor (AI agents). High-value tasks should be targeted for cognitive upgrade, ensuring our people's labor-force are working on meaningful work that delivers real value to our stakeholders.

Ultimately, our collective goal should be to thoughtfully leverage the power of AI in ways that actively foster cognitive upgrade for high-value nonrepetitive and creative work, empowering individuals to enhance their abilities, expand their knowledge, and realize our collective potential, rather than inadvertently creating overdependence on technology and contributing to the degradation of essential human skills.

Values Need to Be Exercised and Developed Too It's not just cognitive capabilities that need to be exercised and upgraded; business values do, too. In corporate environments, values are typically represented as foundational pillars: architectural elements that support the entire organizational structure. These visual metaphors communicate stability and permanence, suggesting that once established, values stand firm regardless of circumstance. However, this conceptualization fundamentally misrepresents how values actually function within organizations.

Values are not static constructs carved in stone. Unlike the enduring Roman pillars that still stand despite the collapse of surrounding structures, organizational values exist only through consistent practice and application. They are more accurately understood as muscles, living tissues that strengthen with use and atrophy without exercise.

The muscle metaphor provides critical insight into how values operate. When regularly exercised through daily decisions and actions, values develop strength and resilience. They become more integrated into the organization's identity and more natural to express. Conversely, when values remain theoretical concepts—admired but unpracticed, they weaken and eventually lose their influence on organizational behavior.

As Mahatma Gandhi observed, "Your thoughts become your words. Your words become your behavior. Your behavior becomes your habits. Your habits become your values. Your values become your destiny."[6] This progression illustrates the living, dynamic nature of values development. Values emerge through consistent practice rather than through declaration alone.

This understanding has significant implications for how organizations should approach values integration. First, values must be exercised in everyday operations in customer interactions, stakeholder communications, team collaborations, and product development. Whether an organization values trust, innovation, or community impact, these principles must manifest in daily activities to remain viable.

Second, organizations should develop specific training initiatives focused directly on values strengthening. Just as targeted exercises develop particular muscle groups, dedicated programs can reinforce specific values. These initiatives should themselves embody the values they aim to strengthen. For instance, training on innovation should employ innovative methodologies; programs on trust should demonstrate trustworthiness in their design and delivery.

Complementary approaches include developing policies and systems that reinforce values practice. For organizations valuing trust, this might involve creating guidelines that empower individual decision-making rather than imposing rigid controls. Such systems encourage values exercise throughout the organization's operations.

When understood as muscles rather than pillars, values become integral components of a living organizational system. They enable effective operation, facilitate movement toward objectives, and establish distinctive identity. By embracing this dynamic conception of values, as elements requiring consistent exercise rather than static structural components, organizations can build authentic cultures where values truly drive behavior and outcomes.

This perspective transformation provides a pathway to exceptional organizational performance and sustainable success. Values, properly exercised and strengthened over time, don't merely support the organization, they become the very means through which it moves forward and evolves.

CHROs Forecast for Adoption of Digital Labor

AI agent deployments will grow 327% from now to 2027. HR chiefs recognize the transformative power of agents. Organizations must focus on strategy, skills, and teamwork to create successful hybrid workplaces.

Chief human resources officers (CHROs) plan to expand their digital labor in the next two years, investing in AI agents to increase productivity, according to the latest Salesforce global research. The research surveyed 200 global human resource executives to gather their perspectives on integrating AI into the workplace. The findings indicate a strong consensus among CHROs about the transformative potential of AI agents.

Most (77%) respondents believe agents will become a fundamental part of the workforce, transforming the organizational makeup. This result signals that digital labor is not merely a peripheral development but a central pillar of future business strategy that demands serious consideration.

The research also points to a rapid adoption trajectory for AI agents. Over the next two years, HR executives anticipate a 327% increase in their deployment. This widespread integration of agents is expected to yield a 30% gain in overall productivity, underscoring the compelling business case for embracing AI in operational processes.

This projected integration of AI agents is expected to drive considerable changes in workforce skill sets and the overall structural design of businesses. Regarding structure, CHROs foresee a significant need to redeploy nearly a quarter of their global workforce (24%) to accommodate new roles and responsibilities due to implementing digital labor. This trend highlights the proactive measures HR leaders must take to adapt to this evolving landscape.

These findings collectively underscore AI's profound transformative potential to reshape the future of work. The findings also emphasize the critical role that HR leaders will play in strategically navigating these significant changes to ensure a smooth and effective transition into a new era of digital labor.

Here are the key findings from Salesforce's CHRO and digital labor research.

The Future of Work Is Hybrid

The research suggests people and AI agents will co-create value at the speed of need. By 2030, 80% of CHROs believe most companies will have humans and AI agents working together. Almost 9 of every 10 CHROs will focus on integrating AI agents into the workforce. So, what will be the most appropriate name for HR, as most labor will be a blend of humans and machines? The answer, perhaps, is *talent resources*.

By 2027, CHROs anticipate 327% growth in agent AI adoption, from 15% in 2025 to 64% in 2027. Surprisingly, 36% of respondents have no plans for AI agent adoption. The healthiest companies of the future will be Autonomous and use digital labor. Sadly, almost 4 in every 10 companies of the future will be unable to successfully compete and win in an AI-first powered economy, where digital labor will be the main competitive differentiator.

CHROs expect an average employee productivity gain of 30% and a 19% reduction in labor costs using agents. Productivity gains will be immediate, but the overall potential of efficiency and effectiveness based on AI agent deployments requires additional analysis.

Reskilling and Redeploying Talent

CHROs will have several strategic priorities that focus on new capabilities, organizational structures, and fresh opportunities. More than four in five HR chiefs plan to reskill their workers to be more competitive in a market shaped by AI agents. How we measure success will change with the greater adoption of digital labor. Concepts about effort and experience will be less important in the age of Boundless possibilities and talent abundance. AI agents will quickly learn, improve, and scale their abilities to create an impact for stakeholders. Data and AI literacy will rise in the reskilling priority lists.

Most CHROs also agree that soft skills, like relationship building and collaboration, will be even more critical as humans work alongside agents.

Adoption of AI agents will reshape organizational structures. Over three-quarters (77%) of CHROs believe AI agents will transform organizational structures.

Integrating AI agents is anticipated to create significant opportunities for human talent. Most CHROs (89%) believe AI and digital labor will enable them to transition employees into new and more impactful positions. This shift involves delegating routine tasks to AI agents, enabling human employees to concentrate on more intricate and critical responsibilities. While HR executives predict that a substantial portion of their workforce (61%) will maintain their current roles while collaborating with digital labor, they anticipate a considerable redeployment of approximately 23% of the workforce to different roles or teams by 2027. They consider this strategy of redeploying existing talent highly advantageous, with 88% of CHROs finding it more cost-effective than external hiring for new roles.

Furthermore, a large percentage of CHROs (81%) are already engaged in (20%) reskilling or planning (61%) to reskill their employees to prepare them for roles with enhanced prospects. Salesforce has also embraced this approach. This evolution signifies a cognitive upgrade rather than a simple knowledge transfer from humans to AI. By leveraging AI as trusted assistants, human employees can perform their work with greater speed, intelligence, and scale.

Taking a Team Approach to Agents

The research suggests autonomous businesses will need teams with a blend of capabilities. The CHRO survey found that 85% of businesses haven't embraced Agentic AI. CHROs must adopt a greater sense of urgency and partner with IT and R&D to accelerate their adoption of digital labor. With greater adoption of AI agents, CHROs anticipate that IT, R&D, and sales teams will grow as their businesses adopt AI agents. In the near term, more technical roles that require higher data and AI literacy will attract employee reassignments. CHROs believe AI literacy is the number one skill workers need as businesses move into the Agentic economy.

The most important skills are soft, and they're also the hardest to codify and teach. Building long-lasting relationships, earning trust, showing empathy, and creating a safe space to foster a greater sense of belonging will require the large-scale reskilling of employees. The survey found that 75% of CHROs say AI agents will increase their organization's need for soft skills.

CHROs plan to reassign employees to relationship-building roles, where collaboration and adaptability skills are most valued, anticipating that teams, such as customer service, operations, and finance, will decrease in size and see some redeployment with the augmentation and efficiencies of agents.

What Happens Next

Integrating digital labor, particularly AI agents, into business operations is still in its infancy, with widespread adoption being less than two years old. This novelty has generated significant excitement and a sense of urgency among HR executives. However, despite this enthusiasm, many CHROs are still in the initial planning stages as they prepare their workforces for this shift. Only 15% report that their organizations have fully implemented Agentic AI.

Interestingly, three out of four employees are still unaware of the potential impact of AI agents on their daily tasks and roles. This result highlights a crucial need for managers to craft the transformation narrative. Our primary focus should be on the cognitive upgrade of our human employees, empowering them to work alongside AI, rather than viewing AI as a mere cognitive download or a replacement for our existing talent.

We stand at a unique juncture as the last generation of business leaders to manage a purely human workforce. The future of work is undeniably hybrid and increasingly Autonomous, where human expertise and AI capabilities converge. People and AI agents will function as trusted partners, forming a combined human and digital labor force that will revolutionize nearly every facet of business.

However, amid this technological evolution, one fundamental aspect of the human experience will remain constant: the innate desire to belong and feel valued, to pursue career growth, and to experience trust, respect, and care within the workplace.

This moment presents an unprecedented opportunity for CHROs and HR (or talent resources) leaders to actively shape the future of work in a meaningful way that fosters a positive and engaging environment for our people. This effort isn't simply about HR gaining a seat at the boardroom table. Rather, if approached thoughtfully and strategically, HR will host this crucial discussion, with all other business leaders recognizing the imperative of earning a place at this HR-led table.

Summary

The rise of "digital labor" through the integration of AI agents leads to the concept of Autonomous companies that blend human and AI workforces. Analysts predict significant growth in AI adoption and spending, highlighting the potential for increased productivity, automation of tasks, and new roles focused on AI management.

The role of AI will vary, from assistive to Autonomous, which differentiates between cognitive download (offloading mental tasks to AI, potentially hindering skill development) and cognitive upgrade (using AI to enhance human cognitive abilities). The goal should be to leverage AI for cognitive upgrades in high-value work and cognitive downloads for low-value, repetitive tasks.

Furthermore, the importance of actively practicing and strengthening organizational values (compared to them being static pillars) is key to ensuring successful adoption of digital labor.

Finally, the findings from a Salesforce survey of CHROs indicates a strong belief in the transformative power of AI agents, a projected 327% growth in their deployment, and the need for reskilling and redeployment of the human workforce to adapt to this hybrid future. CHROs see AI agents as fundamental to the workforce, leading to productivity gains and cost reductions, while also creating opportunities for employees in more impactful roles. The transition requires a focus on AI literacy and soft skills, with HR playing a crucial role in navigating this evolution.

The number one factor for happiness and a sense of belonging and mattering is relationships, not fame or fortune. Relational intelligence will be a critical success factor for building Autonomous business powered by digital labor.

5

AI-First Design and Nonlinearity

> Adopting an <u>AI-first</u> strategy is the <u>only</u> path from assistive to <u>Autonomous</u> capabilities, producing <u>nonlinear</u>, exponential outcomes.

Design is about to become a lot more exciting. We have made inroads into ensuring that products and services are considered from a human-centered perspective, that they do the job users need them to do, and that they are designed in both form and function to be beautiful and useful. And we have expanded that into service design and increasingly into user experience. By *users*, we mean customers and employees and other members of the business ecosystem. Now we have to consider a brand-new participant: the intelligent digital agent. The design of work itself—the way it is organized and executed; the ways in which the workforce is enabled, supervised, measured, and rewarded; the ways in which decisions are made—all of this needs to be revisited for artificial intelligence (AI).

Introduction

As we saw in Chapter 4, designing our companies to become Autonomous will have a similarly profound effect to the revolution in travel and transportation and the redesign of cities that we anticipate when autonomous cars are mainstream. The lessons we can take from the evolution of the car are numerous, but chief among them is the lesson that this effect, on the companies themselves and on the market as a whole and likely on society too, will only happen if we identify and enumerate all the ways in which our companies are designed for humans and then are ready to replace them or at least augment them with designs for AI. Our leaders have to be ready and willing to take their hands off the steering wheel. They are the ones that need, more than anyone else in the organization, to take a leap of faith as they are the ones that are used to having control. They may perceive this leap as a loss of control, but in truth it is a loss that unlocks a greater gain, the gain of mission control, of true autonomy in directing the company toward realizing their ultimate goals, whatever those goals may be.

The goal of this chapter is to identify some of the main orthodoxies, compromises, and biases that come from human-first designs and describe some of the ways in which they can be replaced by AI-first strategies and designs. The first of these is the compromise between performance and stability.

Performance and Stability

The Lockheed F-117 was the world's first stealth aircraft. Its unconventional appearance is still intimidating 50 years after the project to design it began. But the plane was not designed to be intimidating. In fact it was designed to be invisible, at least to radar. The flat, triangular surfaces, rather than rounded ones, minimized radar detection. But they also caused the plane to be unstable in all three dimensions of yaw, pitch, and roll.

Without getting into details, all planes in flight are free to rotate in these three dimensions, and controlling the degree of rotation in each, individually and in combination, is what enables a pilot to fly their plane from point A to point B. In most cases, the plane is also designed to be stable in each dimension, meaning that once airborne it will tend to fly straight and level and at a constant altitude unless the pilot manipulates its control surfaces (the rudder, ailerons, and elevators) in order to change course. Even after being buffeted by winds or turbulent air, the plane will tend to come back to its original position and will seek out stability.

AI-First Design and Nonlinearity

Stability makes a plane safe and easy (at least relatively speaking) for a trained pilot to fly it. Instability makes it harder, and instability in all three dimensions makes it extremely dangerous and difficult. And at speed it becomes basically impossible for a human, even the most highly trained, to do so. There are so many inputs to respond to coming in so fast and so continuously that it becomes simply overwhelming, and any lag in response time can amplify, rather than dampen, potential problems and cause the entire system to fail catastrophically and for the plane to fall out of the sky.

So you would be forgiven for thinking that stability should be a fundamental design goal or principle for aircraft. And in many cases it is. The most successful airplane of all time, with over 44,000 being made since initial production began in 1956, is the Cessna 172 Skyhawk. More novice pilots have been trained to fly using the Skyhawk than any other trainer plane. And the principal reason for this is its stability. It is forgiving of pilot error, it is easy to control, and it is so stable that it can recover from stalls and spins, as long as it has sufficient altitude, and return to level flying even without pilot intervention. For an inexperienced pilot, this is an incredible safety mechanism. If they lose control for whatever reason or they panic and nothing they do seems to be working, they can simply let go of the yoke and let the plane itself regain stability and return to straight and level flight.

But in some circumstances, other performance characteristics take precedence over stability. Fighter jets, for instance, require speed and maneuverability over stability. In a combat situation, a stable plane with low maneuverability is a sitting duck. But the higher the maneuverability, the lower the stability. So conventionally, there has always been a trade-off, a compromise, that limits the performance objectives of any given plane to enable the pilot to keep it flying.

In the case of the F-117, the performance objective was radar invisibility, stealth. But to achieve that the plane had to be built using triangular, flat surfaces that rendered it inherently unstable in all three dimensions. Before the late 1970s that meant it would have been basically unflyable and therefore a nonstarter. Even the most highly qualified and experienced human pilots would have been unable to keep it in the air at speed. But about that time new technology was being developed that allowed computer systems on board planes to assist the human pilot in flying them. These systems were known as fly-by-wire to differentiate them from the mechanical systems that pilots previously used to activate the rudder, ailerons, and elevators.

Fly-by-wire changed the game. It enabled aeronautical engineers to start designing planes for very specific performance characteristics, whether that was maneuverability, or stealth, or fuel efficiency, without compromising the safety of the pilot or the plane itself. The new system took care of keeping the plane in the air, enabling the human pilot to take care of the mission goal or directive.

Fly-by-wire is common in aircraft of all types now. It preceded AI, of course, but now AI is being developed that takes the possibilities of fly-by-wire still further. These new systems, known as Intelligent Flight Control Systems (IFCSs), no longer just keep the planes in the air; they work to understand the outcome that the pilot is trying to realize and help them do so. They are increasingly able to predict and prevent failures, and to keep a plane flying even when engines and/or other parts of the plane fail that would otherwise cause the plane to crash. They are learning systems that can change a plane's flight characteristics if necessary and optimize its performance in flight.

The lesson here is that we used to make trade-offs or compromises in aircraft design to account for human capabilities. But now we no longer need to do that and we can design for specific outcomes without those constraints. Thanks to the fly-by-wire and IFCS technologies, aircraft can be optimized for their mission or goals, whether that is getting passengers home safe and sound, bypassing enemy radar, winning in combat, or improving fuel consumption, or presumably other goals we haven't yet considered. When we take the need for human operational control out of the mix, we remove constraints and compromises we didn't always know we were making.

As it turns out, this compromise between stability and performance is by no means limited to aircraft design. It is relevant in the design of many different products and systems, and it has to do with the kind of control that we want from them. What do we mean by that?

Control is an interesting word. It broadly means the ability to direct, determine, or influence behavior, to get something (or somebody) to do what you want them to do within a given domain (e.g., a sport or a practice or a discipline). But that is achieved in two quite different, actually opposite, ways. The first way of achieving control is by dampening, absorbing, cushioning, or stabilizing that thing's current behavior in order to make it easier to change it into what you want. This is the kind of control that we want to achieve when we're nonexpert in our domain. The second way is by amplifying its behavior in order to make the change and its desired behavior have more impact. And this is the kind of control we want when we are experts in our domain.

This sounds complicated. But let's say I'm a beginner tennis player. When I go to return a shot from my opponent, I want to maximize the likelihood of getting the ball back over the net. If I have the right tennis racket for my skill level, it will tend to dampen down the speed and spin that my opponent imparts to the ball and make it easier for me to keep the ball in play, even if I have less say exactly where the ball lands and at what speed and spin. With the right equipment, I can "control" the ball and at least stay in the game even if the chances of me winning it are slight.

If, however, I'm a skilled player, I will want to use the ball's spin and speed to my own advantage. I may want to impart even more spin or speed, or I may want to surprise my opponent with a dropshot or a lob, and I know exactly where on the court I want the ball to land. To do this I need a racket that gives me that "feel" of the ball and use it against my opponent. Now, if I get it wrong the ball may go straight into the net or off the court entirely, but if I get it right I increase my chances of winning the point.

This distinction occurs in just about every domain. If I'm a casual runner, I want to have high stability and high cushioning in my shoes to make my running easier and less painful. If I'm an experienced runner looking to set a personal best, I want shoes that give me speed at the expense, if necessary, of comfort. Beginner skiers use skis that have a high degree of stability and make it easier for them to enjoy the slopes. Experts use skis that maximize speed and precision. Casual cooks at home tend to use general-purpose knives that are reasonably priced, can be used in a variety of ways, and tend to keep their edge. Professional chefs tend to use knives that are purpose built (e.g., the fuguhiki knife specifically designed to prepare blowfish sashimi), with the capacity to be extremely sharp but that require significant effort and care to keep them that way, and are very expensive. An everyday photographer will use their phone to take pictures and have annoyances like the shakes or the glare of the sun dealt with for them. A professional photographer will use a camera and other equipment (lenses, tripods, lighting, etc.) built specifically for the type of picture they want to take and will set aperture, focal length, shutter speed manually and will wait patiently for the right conditions in order to get the exact effect they want.

The point here is that if you're looking for ease of use in order to participate or engage in a domain, you'll want a system or tool or piece of equipment that absorbs, dampens, stabilizes conditions and that is forgiving. You want what we call *down-control*, which in an airplane is stability at the cost of performance.

If, however, you want a specific performance characteristic like speed, precision, maneuverability in order to compete successfully and win in a domain, you need a system, tool, or piece of equipment that amplifies those conditions. You want *up-control*, which in an airplane is performance at the cost of stability.

The key point to understand here is that this compromise between stability and performance is obliterated with the inclusion of AI. AI takes care of the stability so the user can focus on the performance. And because this is true, the designer can design for maximum performance, not just high performance and create entirely new classes of system.

It turns out that this all applies just as much to business as it does to any other domain. We are accustomed to think that a stable business is a good business, especially if the surrounding conditions are turbulent or tumultuous or challenging. But what if the pursuit of stability is holding our businesses back from high performance? What if stability is a crutch we lean on because we are ill-equipped to operate at higher levels?

To explore this further, we've created the Control Matrix, a 2 × 2 that demonstrates the traditional trade-off that different systems including businesses make and the impact that AI can have (see Figure 5.1). The two axes are Performance and Stability, with High and Low for both. At top left, we have the Up-Control Systems quadrant for those systems that prioritize performance over stability. At the bottom right, we have the Down-Control Systems quadrant for those systems that prioritize stability over performance. The top right quadrant, AI-First Systems, shows this new possibility that simply didn't exist in the past—the possibility of having high performance *and* high stability. The bottom right quadrant is the place where you really don't want to be: the Risky/Failing Systems.

AI-First Design and Nonlinearity 109

	Low Stability	High Stability
High Performance	**Up-Control Systems:** Maximize output and capability Require expert handling Specialist and Precision oriented Examples: Professional level tools and equipment (e.g., F1 cars), Start-Ups	**AI-first Systems** Achieve both performance and stability AI handles stability while humans focus on performance Creates new value propositions Examples: F-117 with fly-by-wire, Autonomous Businesses
Low Performance	**Risky/Failing Systems** Neither stable nor high-performing Often transitional or degrading systems Unsustainable long-term Examples: Poorly designed products, organizations in crisis	**Down-Control Systems** Prioritize reliability and consistency Forgive mistakes and dampen variation Generalist and broad scope oriented Examples: Training aircraft, consumer products, highly regulated businesses

Figure 5.1 The Control Matrix.

Let's look at the business implications of this matrix in more detail. We'll focus here on five core aspects of business: organizational designs, business models, leadership approaches, product and service designs, and competitive strategies.

Reimagining Organizational Design

Traditional organizational structures have long reflected the fundamental trade-off between stability and performance. The hierarchical, process-driven organization, with its clear reporting lines, detailed standard operating procedures, and multiple approval layers, exemplifies the down-control approach. These organizations excel at consistency and risk management but often struggle with innovation and responsiveness. We see this model in established financial institutions, government agencies, and regulated utilities, where reliability takes precedence over speed and adaptability.

At the opposite end, we find the flat, networked organization, with minimal management layers, empowered teams, and limited formal processes, embodying the up-control approach. These organizations can innovate rapidly and respond quickly to market changes but often face challenges with consistency and coordination as they scale. Early-stage startups, creative agencies, and specialized consulting firms typically operate in this mode, accepting instability as the price of exceptional performance.

AI creates the possibility of a fundamentally new organizational archetype that transcends this traditional trade-off, one in which an organization maintains the adaptability and innovation speed of a startup while simultaneously achieving the reliability and coordination of a mature enterprise. Such organizations would feature network-based structures where teams form and dissolve dynamically around specific challenges, with AI systems handling the complex coordination that would overwhelm traditional management hierarchies.

Rather than detailed procedures that constrain innovation, these organizations would establish clear outcome expectations and boundaries, using AI to monitor activities and provide early warning of potential issues. Decision authority would be pushed to the edges of the organization where market contact occurs, but supported by AI systems that provide relevant data and recommendations to inform those decisions. The result would be both the speed and creativity of decentralization and the consistency and alignment of centralized control.

Transforming Business Models

The Control Matrix reveals how business models themselves embody different approaches to the stability-performance trade-off. Down-control business models prioritize predictability and scale, like subscription services with consistent offerings, franchise systems with strict operational requirements, or mass-market products with limited customization. These models create value through reliability and efficiency, capturing that value through volume-based pricing and long-term contracts.

Up-control business models, by contrast, prioritize customization and exceptional experiences, bespoke professional services, limited-production luxury goods, or cutting-edge technology with frequent innovation cycles. These models create value through superior performance and perfect fit for specific needs, capturing that value through premium pricing and exclusivity.

AI enables a new generation of business models that deliver personalization at scale, the seemingly impossible combination of individualized experiences with the economics of standardization. Amazon's recommendation engine, Netflix's content personalization, and Spotify's custom playlists offer early glimpses of this potential, but they merely scratch the surface.

Future AI-enhanced business models will feature offerings that adapt continuously to individual needs and preferences while maintaining consistent quality and reliability. They will implement dynamic pricing systems that optimize for both provider and customer value in real time. They will anticipate individual needs through predictive analytics as well as responding to expressed demands. And they will create self-optimizing product ecosystems that become more valuable to each specific user over time.

The result will be businesses that can say yes to the seemingly contradictory customer demands for both perfect fit and consistent reliability, creating entirely new sources of value in the process.

Evolving Leadership Approaches

Leadership styles have traditionally aligned with either down-control or up-control philosophies. Down-control leaders emphasize process adherence, detailed planning, and risk mitigation. They create stability through clear rules and structured feedback, making decisions based on established precedent and comprehensive data. While effective at ensuring consistent execution, this approach often struggles with innovation and adaptation to rapidly changing conditions.

Up-control leaders, by contrast, set ambitious visions and challenging goals, empowering teams with significant autonomy and accepting productive failure as a natural part of pushing boundaries. They focus on outcomes rather than processes and make intuitive decisions based on limited information. While effective at driving innovation and growth, this approach can lead to inconsistency and coordination challenges as organizations scale.

AI enables a new leadership model that combines the best elements of both approaches. Leaders in AI-enhanced organizations will establish clear directional intent and outcome expectations while designing systems that enable autonomy within monitored boundaries. They will use algorithmic insights to inform both strategy and execution decisions, balancing human judgment with data-driven support.

Rather than spending their time monitoring process compliance or making all key decisions themselves, these leaders will focus on capability building and system design. They will create learning processes that capture and apply insights across the organization at scale. They will define what success looks like and establish guardrails rather than detailing every step of execution.

The result will be leadership that simultaneously provides the clarity and consistency of traditional management and the empowerment and innovation of entrepreneurial leadership, setting ambitious performance targets while using algorithmic guardrails to prevent catastrophic outcomes.

Reimagining Product and Service Design

Product and service design has long reflected the Control Matrix trade-offs. Consumer products typically employ down-control approaches, simplified interfaces, limited features, and extensive error prevention to ensure reliable performance for average users. Professional tools, by contrast, employ up-control approaches, extensive features, complex interfaces, and significant customization to deliver maximum capability for expert users.

This trade-off creates natural performance ceilings for mass-market products. Add too many features or capabilities, and the product becomes confusing and error-prone for most users. Simplify too much, and the product fails to meet the needs of advanced users. Companies have traditionally addressed this challenge by creating product lines with different models for different user segments, but this approach forces users into predetermined categories and creates significant development and support costs.

AI enables a fundamentally different approach to product design, one that adapts to individual users rather than forcing them into predefined user categories. Adaptive interfaces can evolve as users develop expertise, presenting new capabilities at the moment they become relevant. Intelligent assistance can provide guidance without limiting options, helping users navigate complexity without removing it. Self-optimizing systems can learn individual preferences and use patterns, creating experiences that feel custom designed for each user.

The result will be products that are simultaneously accessible to beginners and powerful for experts, that prevent critical errors while enabling advanced capabilities, and that feel intuitive to each specific user rather than to an abstract "average user."

Redefining Competitive Strategy

Organizations have traditionally positioned themselves competitively along the control spectrum, emphasizing either reliability or performance as their primary value proposition.

Down-control positioning emphasizes trustworthiness, dependability, and peace of mind. Organizations competing on these dimensions build brands centered on never letting customers down, develop operational excellence capabilities that deliver consistent experiences, and often use regulatory compliance as a competitive differentiator. Traditional banks, established insurance companies, and family-oriented brands typically adopt this positioning.

Up-control positioning emphasizes exceptional outcomes, innovation, and customization. Organizations competing on these dimensions build brands centered on leading-edge capabilities, develop innovation processes that deliver continuous advancement, and leverage specialized expertise to provide unique solutions. Luxury brands, specialized consultancies, and technology pioneers typically adopt this positioning, competing on the promise of "the best possible experience."

AI enables a new competitive positioning that combines the appeals of both approaches. Organizations can leverage data assets and AI capabilities to deliver personalization without compromising quality and innovation without sacrificing reliability. They can build ecosystems where products and services become more valuable through integration and learning systems that continuously improve performance based on individual use.

The most successful future competitors will be those who recognize that customers shouldn't have to choose between reliability and performance, and who deploy AI strategically to deliver both simultaneously. They will develop data advantage strategies, building unique information assets that enable superior AI performance. They will create distinctive experiences through proprietary AI capabilities that competitors cannot easily replicate. They will build interconnected systems that increase in value as customers engage across their portfolio.

In doing so, they will transcend the traditional stability-performance trade-off that has constrained competitive positioning for generations, creating entirely new sources of competitive advantage in the process.

Why Planes and Automobiles?

Why is there such a focus on autonomous cars and fly-by-wire planes in our book? Because they represent the first complex systems in our everyday experience that are undergoing the process of becoming Autonomous before our very eyes. While they are obviously very different entities from our companies in all sorts of ways, they have an important similarity. They are all systems that have evolved from being designed by humans for operation by humans to being designed by humans and computers for operation by AI.

The other purpose is to show that our conventional designs for complex systems like cars and planes assume human operators and as a result place certain unrecognized limitations on both the systems and the humans. Designing systems to be AI-first requires recognizing the constraints and removing them. Who knew that aerodynamic stability could be a design choice, not a guiding principle?

The lessons are nonobvious but clear nonetheless: humans thrive when they have autonomy, but autonomy and control are not the same. To reach the next level in autonomy, they have to be willing to let go of the current level of control. Leaders need to let go of the steering wheel.

An Autonomous company then is designed for machines first, and in the future will likely be designed by them, too. It is no longer designed for humans. The dominant logic of the human goes away. We've already discussed the need for stability, or rather our need for stability. But we need to reexamine the ongoing value of qualities or even virtues like effort and experience, virtues that turn out to be important among humans and perhaps even other animals that work or have worked alongside us, but not necessarily for this new digital addition to the workforce.

The Culture of Effort

For centuries, our cultures have lauded hard work as a cornerstone of human achievement. Our success stories often highlight individuals who, through sheer effort, overcome significant obstacles. Thomas Edison's famous quote about genius being "one percent inspiration and ninety-nine percent perspiration" has deeply influenced our understanding of success, permeating everything from factories to boardrooms.

In the business world, figures like Elon Musk exemplify extreme dedication, with his well-known long work weeks and reported periods of sleeping on the factory floor during critical production phases at Tesla. Similarly, NVIDIA CEO Jensen Huang has stated that "the most important part of work is suffering," reinforcing the idea that hardship is integral to great accomplishments. This narrative, equating sacrifice with progress, is widespread.

This emphasis on effort extends beyond the tech industry. Health care professionals routinely work very long shifts, often affecting their own well-being, a demanding schedule often seen as inherent to the profession. We also see this in sports, where athletes are celebrated for intense training, and students for relentless studying, sometimes fueled by unhealthy means. Phrases like "Hard work beats talent when talent doesn't work hard" are commonplace, reflecting a belief that effort equates to virtue and achievement is earned through sheer hard work.

In this view, those who consistently work harder are believed to be more likely to succeed, with research suggesting "grit" as a primary predictor of success, even more so than talent or socioeconomic status. However, it's important to acknowledge that for many globally, hard work is not a choice but a necessity for survival, often without recognition or the chance to truly thrive.

The relentless pursuit of effort also has its downsides, leading to fatigue, burnout, and impaired decision-making. Research indicates that long hours and insufficient rest negatively affect cognitive performance and increase errors, particularly in critical situations. The very qualities we admire, like grit and endurance, can become detrimental. Furthermore, our focus on effort can blind us to the potential of intelligence-driven success.

As the 21st century progresses, the limitations of effort as the primary driver of success are becoming increasingly clear, especially in fields requiring speed, precision, and complexity beyond human capabilities. Examples include fly-by-wire systems in aviation and high-frequency trading in finance, where intelligent systems outperform humans through rapid data processing and decision-making.

The 2016 victory of AlphaGo, an AI system, over a top human Go player, Lee Sedol, marked a significant turning point. Initially, experts doubted AI's ability to master the intricate game. While both AI and the human grandmaster displayed moments of brilliance during the match, the subsequent achievement of AlphaGo Zero was even more remarkable. This successor learned to play Go solely by playing against itself, reaching a superhuman level of skill within just four days and defeating AlphaGo 100–0.

AlphaGo Zero's success signifies a paradigm shift, where intelligence, learning, and adaptation, rather than sheer effort, led to unprecedented mastery. While some might argue that the vast number of games played by AlphaGo Zero diminishes the demonstration of "intelligence," the undeniable outcome is that AI achieved a superior level of competence in a specific domain far more rapidly than humans, at least in terms of accumulated learning over time. This compels us to rethink our understanding of learning, experience, and effort in the context of business capabilities.

As the business world increasingly relies on rules-based and algorithmic processes, we can anticipate the growing application of such intelligence and learning capabilities. As we analyze our human-driven processes, we may find them less complex than they appear.

This leads to a crucial point: we need to move away from measuring value solely by the number of hours worked. In fact, we should consider excessive effort wasteful if AI can achieve the same results more efficiently. Process optimization, aided by AI, should be a priority across all business functions. Leaders should embrace AI as an advisor and encourage their teams to do the same, focusing on minimizing the time between identifying a need and taking action. In an era where intelligent alternatives exist, simply putting in long hours is no longer a badge of honor.

We are entering the Age of Intelligence. We see the beginnings of this in health care, where AI enhances diagnostic accuracy, and in supply chains that intelligently adapt to disruptions. Even creative fields are exploring the synergistic potential of AI and human artistry. The primary challenge lies not in developing these intelligent systems but in accepting the fundamental shift they represent. These systems operate without the limitations of human fatigue or emotion, capable of processing vast amounts of data and making rapid decisions in complex environments. This has profound implications for how we define work, measure success, and allocate resources. While a culture of effort has historically been valuable, it is no longer sufficient in the Age of Intelligence. Success will increasingly favor those who effectively leverage the power of intelligence.

Experience: The Diminishing Requirement of Time

Closely related to effort in the traditional business paradigm, experience has always been considered the irreplaceable foundation of expertise. We pay a premium for it, promote based on it, and build entire organizational hierarchies on it. The underlying assumption is simple yet powerful: mastery comes only through time, the gradual accumulation of knowledge, skills, and judgment that cannot be accelerated or bypassed.

The examples that drive our cultural understanding of experience and expertise are all around us. Lee Sedol invested decades to develop his understanding of Go, climbing to become one of the greatest players in history. Traditional sushi chefs spend up to 10 years in apprenticeship, often devoting the first two years solely to perfecting rice preparation before ever handling fish. Symphony conductors typically don't reach their prime until their fifties or sixties. Even the most brilliant software engineers need years to develop the pattern recognition that distinguishes exceptional from merely competent code. We all learn from experience. Or at least we should!

This time-based model of expertise acquisition has been so fundamental that we've built entire economic and social structures on it. Compensation systems reward years of service. Leadership positions require "sufficient experience." Job postings routinely specify "minimum 7–10 years industry experience mandatory." We've accepted as universal truth that there are no shortcuts to mastery.

And yet, AI systems are now fundamentally challenging this premise. The AI behind AlphaGo Zero didn't just learn faster, it learned differently, unconstrained by human cognitive limitations or preconceptions about optimal strategy.

This phenomenon extends far beyond games. AI systems can now diagnose certain medical conditions with greater accuracy than experienced physicians and generate legal documents with precision that rivals senior attorneys. They can design engineering solutions that outperform those created by veteran engineers and can create marketing campaigns that outperform those developed by seasoned professionals

What does this mean for businesses built on the foundation of human experience?

First, it suggests a decoupling of expertise from time. If an AI system can develop domain mastery in days rather than decades, the premium we place on years of human experience may require fundamental recalibration. Organizations will need to reassess compensation structures, promotion criteria, and hiring practices that have traditionally been anchored to experience metrics.

Second, it points toward a transformation in how we understand learning and development. Traditional apprenticeship and mentoring models assume a gradual transfer of knowledge from expert to novice, from senior to junior, from manager to employee. AI systems offer the possibility of radically accelerated learning paths, where newcomers can access not just information but contextualized expertise on demand.

We're already witnessing early signals of this shift. Tech companies began relaxing college degree requirements years ago, recognizing that formal credentials were often poor proxies for capability. Now, we can expect businesses to deploy AI-enabled training programs that rapidly upskill employees regardless of their background experience. The AI becomes a real-time guide, mentor, and teacher, creating a cognitive upgrade that enables individuals to apply whatever experience they do have more effectively to new domains.

This doesn't mean human experience becomes irrelevant but its value will shift from accumulated knowledge to adaptability, from memorized procedures to creative problem-solving, from past solutions to novel approaches. The most valuable human experience may become meta-experience: knowing how to learn, adapt, and collaborate with AI systems that possess deep domain expertise.

Organizations at the forefront of this transition are already reimagining their approach to talent. Rather than seeking candidates with linear career progressions in a single domain, they value cognitive flexibility, learning agility, and collaboration skills. They're creating systems where AI handles the aspects of expertise that can be digitized and accelerated, while humans focus on the dimensions that remain uniquely human: emotional intelligence, ethical judgment, creative synthesis, and cross-domain innovation.

In this emerging paradigm, the competitive advantage shifts from organizations with the most experienced workforce to those with the most effective human–AI collaboration. The question becomes not "How many years of experience do you have?" but rather "How effectively can you cognitively upgrade?"

This represents not just a tactical shift but a philosophical one, challenging our deeply held assumptions about the relationship among time, learning, and mastery. As AI continues to compress the experience curve across domains, organizations will need to fundamentally rethink how they define expertise, structure roles, and develop talent. Those that cling to traditional experience-based models may find themselves outpaced by competitors who harness AI to create new forms of accelerated expertise development that were previously unimaginable.

AI-First Strategies

So much for human biases, compromises, and values that turn out to be less valuable in a business on its way to becoming autonomous. We've discussed stability, effort, and experience: three pillars of the human-first business. What about AI-first strategies? We've already described their potential impact via the Control Matrix. They can enable businesses to achieve high performance and high stability, two of the characteristics most desired by leaders, workers, and customers alike. We've already seen what they might look like when we apply them to product systems like cars. But let's look at what they might look like when we apply them to the future of core processes and strategic decision-making. Two examples of AI-first strategies are what we're calling autofacturing and enterprise-level digital twins. Let's look at these emerging capabilities, and we should stress that they are emerging, not yet mature in any systemic way, in more detail.

Autofacturing: Manufacturing Intelligence and Work in the Age of Autonomous Intelligence

Autofacturing envisions a future where manufacturing processes become fully self-operating, intelligent, and continuously adaptive. It aligns with the second phase of Autonomy in our Seven Levels of Autonomous Work framework, moving beyond AI and robotics simply assisting human workers to a point where they independently handle even the most repetitive tasks. In essence, the factory itself transforms into an Autonomous agent, capable of sensing, learning, deciding, acting, and improving without constant human intervention.

However, autofacturing goes beyond just automating physical work. It signifies a pivotal moment where we begin to "manufacture intelligence" itself. Rather than solely developing or applying intelligence, we'll produce it systematically and at scale as an integral part of the production process. In this paradigm, intelligence becomes both the driving force and the resulting output of manufacturing. Therefore, autofacturing can be defined as the intelligent production of work and the production of intelligence.

This shift fundamentally redefines what a factory is and its purpose, and this transformation may be closer than we think. The convergence of Agentic AI, advanced robotics, edge computing, and machine vision is already blurring the traditional lines between planning, making, inspecting, and delivering. We're witnessing the emergence of a new breed of Autonomous, intelligent factories—not just extensions of human effort, but self-contained production systems.

The groundwork for autofacturing is already being laid today. Consider 3D printing, which has evolved from a consumer fad to a vital tool for prototyping and even end-use production in industries like aerospace, medical, and automotive. Similarly, textile innovation is introducing 3D weaving systems capable of producing entire garments seamlessly. Initiatives like Nike's Flyknit and Adidas's Futurecraft hint at a future where shoes are manufactured on demand, customized for individual feet with minimal waste. These systems are data-driven, software-defined, and increasingly Autonomous.

Companies such as Tesla are also aggressively pursuing vertically integrated production lines where robots are central to the manufacturing process. Elon Musk's "Alien Dreadnought" concept, while initially facing challenges, represented an early vision of a high-speed, AI-coordinated factory building cars with minimal human involvement. While fully realizing this vision proved difficult initially, technology is rapidly catching up.

Other sectors are also making significant strides. In electronics, startups like Celus and JITX are pioneering automated circuit board design. In pharmaceuticals, companies like Insilico Medicine and Atomwise are using AI to design new molecules and optimize drug synthesis. In construction, 3D-printed homes from companies like ICON and WASP suggest a future where dwellings can be autonomously fabricated on-site.

Underlying these advancements is a broader shift in how intelligence functions within organizations. Traditionally, intelligence in manufacturing was human-driven, used for planning, problem-solving, and improvement. However, with advanced AI, intelligence is becoming the manufacturing process itself, aligning with the mSUDA model (machine-speed Sense, Understand, Decide, Act). A truly autonomous factory will execute this cycle in real time, sensing demand, understanding constraints, deciding on reconfiguration, and acting instantly and continuously.

Each stage of the mSUDA cycle is now being realized through machine capabilities. Internet of Things platforms enable real-time sensing, foundation models and digital twins facilitate deep understanding, reinforcement learning allows for optimal decision-making, and robotics execute the actions. This isn't a distant vision; it's happening in stages today and will likely converge into comprehensive system-level capabilities within this decade.

As autofacturing matures, its primary benefit will be adaptability. In a world characterized by fluctuating demand and supply chain disruptions, factories that can autonomously reconfigure themselves to adjust production volume, product type, and distribution will have a significant advantage.

There's also a geographical aspect to this. As AI and robotics become more compact and affordable, manufacturing can become more distributed. We're already seeing this with containerized microfactories and portable 3D printers. This trend could revitalize rural regions, enabling them to play a key role in production through remote diagnostics, cloud-based control, and autonomous transportation.

Autonomous trucking (e.g., Kodiak Robotics, Aurora) and aerial delivery (e.g., Zipline, Wing) further support this vision, enabling products to be made closer to where they're needed, on demand, and with a reduced carbon footprint. This distributed infrastructure also enhances resilience by creating a network of semi-Autonomous, redundant production nodes.

The social implications are profound, potentially leading to rural resurgence and enabling local communities to drive their economies through advanced, AI-augmented manufacturing.

An exciting related development is 4D design, where materials are programmed to change after fabrication in response to environmental stimuli. Research at MIT's Self-Assembly Lab is exploring materials that can fold or reconfigure themselves post-production, offering possibilities for self-assembling products and adaptive infrastructure. This aligns with the core principles of autofacturing: autonomous, adaptive, and context-aware creation.

This vision is further supported by the development of new materials at the molecular level, such as smart polymers and shape memory alloys, offering enhanced responsiveness, strength, and sustainability.

To fully realize autofacturing, our educational systems will need to evolve to include curricula focused on robotics, AI, systems thinking, ethical design, and distributed coordination. The future workforce will need a blend of digital and physical skills. Governments will also play a crucial role in supporting this transition through investments in infrastructure, connectivity, and interoperable standards.

While these technologies are still developing, the trajectory is clear, with consistent progress in areas like self-supervised learning and robotic capabilities. While challenges remain, the convergence of these advancements suggests a future where autofacturing becomes a reality.

In the long term, autofacturing will blur the lines between product and process, with intelligent products communicating directly with intelligent factories. Ultimately, factories themselves may evolve into distributed networks of AI-driven capabilities, assembled on demand.

The Digital Twin of the Business: A By-Product of AI-First Design

In traditional organizations, the idea of a digital twin is often applied to engineering, logistics, or manufacturing functions. A digital twin typically refers to a real-time, virtual replica of a physical system, such as a jet engine, a production line, or a delivery network, that enables engineers to monitor, test, and optimize operations before taking real-world actions. These systems are themselves relatively recent, and they hint at something still more powerful: a dynamic, continuously learning model of the business itself.

AI-first strategies do not merely digitize existing business functions, they re-architect the business as a system of interconnected, intelligent, and Autonomous agents. As sensing, understanding, decision-making, and acting are taken over by AI at scale, via the SUDA model, the company begins to operate more as a fully integrated, intelligent, coherent system. Its learning becomes continuous, and its operations become deeply instrumented. The result is the natural emergence of a new kind of twin: not of a process, or product, or factory, but of the entire company.

This is not a model you build; it is a model that emerges. It is the by-product of being truly AI-first. It arises when every core business capability is digitized, connected, and instrumented, and when each intelligent system feeds its status, predictions, and next actions into a shared operational nervous system. It is a living model of your business in motion, not a dashboard. It doesn't just simulate, it orchestrates.

This enterprise-level digital twin is the most compelling manifestation of the Autonomous business. It enables the business to simulate multiple strategies at once, to test and optimize decisions in a zero-risk environment, and to continuously refine its performance in the real world based on its virtual self-understanding. Instead of asking "what happened?" or even "what will happen?" the company can now ask "what could happen if we did this, and what else might we try?" It's a capability that the curious and the imaginative will love.

This is not science fiction. Leading-edge companies are already evolving toward this capability, even if they do not yet have the language to describe it. When logistics firms route goods dynamically based on live traffic, weather, and demand data, they are beginning to embody this twin logic. When manufacturers like Tesla and GE run self-optimizing factories and model system behavior end to end, they are taking early steps toward a business-wide twin. But to move from fragments to the full twin requires an AI-first strategy and a willingness to let go of human-centered control systems in favor of Autonomous orchestration.

Here, the Control Matrix comes into view again. Traditionally, businesses have had to choose: either build for stability and consistency (down-control) or build for agility and speed (up-control). But AI-first companies, guided by real-time digital twins, no longer have to choose. These systems enable both high performance and high stability by allowing for dynamic adaptation while preserving continuity. The digital twin becomes the interface that reconciles mission intent with machine execution. It is both a simulation engine and a coordination engine.

Autofacturing, 4D design, and distributed intelligence make this twin infrastructure not only possible but necessary. When AI systems manage production, supply chains, logistics, and customer interfaces with minimal human oversight, it becomes essential to have a coherent, integrated view of the whole enterprise. A business that acts Autonomously must also understand itself Autonomously. That is the role of the twin.

More than a tool, the digital twin of the business becomes the way a company knows itself. It is how the company observes, experiments, and evolves. In the same way that fly-by-wire systems freed aircraft from the constraints of human response time and AlphaGo Zero transcended the orthodoxies of human play, the digital twin frees the company from reacting slowly or flying blind. It becomes the company's second self, a mirror, a lab, and eventually a guide.

This future is not only coming, it will be an integral part of future business success. Any business that aspires to operate at the speed, scale, and intelligence of the AI economy will need a system-level twin. And any business that truly adopts an AI-first mindset will find that the twin emerges as a natural consequence of that mindset. In an Autonomous enterprise, intelligence does not sit on top of operations. It runs through them. The digital twin is how that intelligence sees itself.

> **Summary**
>
> AI integration requires a shift in design, moving beyond human-centered approaches to include intelligent agents. This necessitates reevaluating work structures, including enablement, supervision, measurement, rewards, and decision-making. The transition to Autonomous operations, like autonomous vehicles, demands redesigning human-centric aspects to integrate with AI. Leaders must adopt a "hands-off" approach, embracing strategic command and enabling organizational Autonomy. This chapter explores the trade-offs of human-first design and how AI-first strategies can offer alternatives, focusing on performance versus stability.
>
> The F-117 Nighthawk exemplifies prioritizing performance (stealth) over inherent stability, a trade-off historically balanced in aircraft design. Fly-by-wire technology and IFCS overcame this, managing stability to maximize performance. This concept applies broadly: beginners prefer stable down-control, while experts seek high-performance up-control. AI can handle stability, enabling pursuit of maximum performance without traditional trade-offs, leading to AI-first systems with high performance and high stability. The Control Matrix illustrates this, showing the limitations of up-control, down-control, and risky/failing systems compared to AI's potential.

Traditional hierarchical organizations (down-control) prioritize stability but can lack innovation. Flat, networked organizations (up-control) are innovative but may lack consistency. AI enables a new archetype blending both: adaptable, innovative like startups, but reliable like mature enterprises. These network-based structures use AI for coordination, establish outcome expectations, and push decision authority with AI support, achieving both speed and control.

Business models also reflect the stability-performance trade-off. Down-control models prioritize predictability (e.g., subscriptions), while up-control models emphasize customization (e.g., bespoke services). AI enables personalization at scale, combining individualization with standardization (e.g., Amazon recommendations). Future AI models will offer continuously adaptive, self-optimizing products with dynamic pricing, meeting demands for both perfect fit and reliability.

Leadership styles align with down-control (process-focused, stable) or up-control (visionary, autonomous). AI enables a hybrid model: setting intent and outcomes while AI manages boundaries. Leaders focus on capability building and system design, using algorithmic insights to balance judgment and data, providing clarity and empowerment.

Product design also reflects Control Matrix trade-offs. Consumer products use down-control (simplicity, reliability), while professional tools use up-control (complexity, capability). AI enables adaptive interfaces and intelligent assistance, creating custom-designed experiences without forcing users into categories. The result is accessible and high-performing products.

Embracing an AI-first strategy empowers businesses to automatically generate (autofacture) intelligence and streamline operations. These Autonomous entities will leverage digital labor to exponentially increase value creation, meeting demands with unprecedented speed. Welcome to an era of AI-driven abundance, enabling companies to achieve limitless potential and realize nonlinear results previously unattainable without Autonomous capabilities.

6

Autonomy and Boundless Principles

Becoming an <u>Autonomous business</u> requires the seven <u>Boundless principles</u> shaping the <u>mindset</u> and business operating <u>model</u>.

Autonomous businesses are not just healthy, they are also conditioned for high performance. This demands an operating model that enables routine, systemic speed to action. And in an age of Agentic artificial intelligence (AI), this means an operating system that supports both humans and machines but is tuned for the scale and speed that only AI and other advanced technologies can achieve.

Introduction

Our first book, *Boundless*, was an in-depth exploration of a new mindset for business success, and it laid out seven principles for the transformation of business. In the short time since it was published in September 2023, we have been struck by how this mindset and the principles are even more relevant and valuable than ever before. We encourage you to revisit *Boundless* alongside this new book of ours, but we have included a brief review of those principles in this chapter and how/why they are newly relevant in the age of Agentic AI.

In *Boundless* we made the case that traditional business structures are siloed, static, and built for control, and that they're already falling short in a connected world. We introduced a new model, one rooted in flow, adaptability, and shared success. The Boundless organization, we argued, was designed not for stability, but for movement. Not for command and control, but for connection and choreography. Not for predictability, but for possibility.

At the time, we believed this model was important for businesses navigating uncertainty, complexity, and digital transformation. But we didn't yet know how fast the world would change. We didn't know that within two years, Generative AI would explode into the mainstream, creating the most powerful accelerant to organizational change since the invention of the internet.

And now, with the arrival of Agentic AI, systems that can make decisions and take actions on our behalf, the Boundless principles are no longer just helpful. They are foundational, because autonomy, true autonomy for machines *and* for humans, is not just a technical upgrade. It's an organizational redesign as we will see in our other themes, especially those covering SUDA (Sense, Understand, Decide, Act), the seven-level AI maturity model, and relational intelligence. And without the right mindset to guide it, redesigns can become superficial embellishments on top of existing orthodoxies and conventions, not the transformations needed to achieve the nonlinear potential of AI.

The most effective way of positioning the Boundless mindset and its principles is to show the deliberate shift from economies of scale to ecosystems of success. A shift that gives birth to nonlinear outcomes, such as what we expect as the potential of AI.

Here's a thought experiment to showcase Boundless thinking and operating models: if you wanted to provide food relief to crises around the world, how would you start?

Most of us, wanting to do the most good possible, would look at the money we have available and go "Okay, how can I make as many meals as humanly possible with what I've got?" Reasonable right? You go in thinking that if you minimize the cost of each meal, you can feed the most people. This is standard, time-honored resource management at work. It's about being efficient and getting the most out of what you have. This is how all of our businesses and institutions are organized and run.

But, wait! If you start with the unit cost per meal as your key variable, you'll probably end up using centralized commissaries (food factories), the cheapest ingredients, and a volunteer meal production workforce. You'll probably airlift the meals to a safe place and arrange for them to be handed out to the locals from there.

And—this is in no way a criticism—when you start with your resources first and with a high-volume, low-unit-cost mindset, a mindset that's all about "doing more with less" and economies of scale, that's the operating model you'll end up with. You'll have unintentionally built a silo, an organization that is designed to accumulate resources and then protect and extract the most value from them possible.

The thing about silos is—they work. They're successful as we've said (at least for their owners and managers). And they're easy to implement. Silos are the simplest way to manage resources: centralize and protect. Organizations have done it this way for years—actually, for thousands of years.

Here's the problem: the success enjoyed by silos usually comes at the expense of the rest of the organization, business ecosystem, or community that needs those resources. Silos can slow down the systems of which they're a part and even cause their collapse. Silos kill. Especially in the age of AI where speed is going to become essential. More than ever, our companies, institutions, and ecosystems need another way.

We asked ourselves: what would it look like to manage resources without creating silos? Is it possible? Is anyone doing it? This was the driving question behind our book *Boundless*. Could we find any organizations in any industry who were thinking about their resources differently, in a way that prioritized things other than efficiency, things like value to customers and other stakeholders, things like speed to value, resilience, and sustainability?

We didn't find that many, to be honest. Those that we did find are very successful and differentiated in their respective industries. They're not small or obscure, they're leaders, and they've been around for a good while. We're talking here about industries as varied as high-tech, retail, product and process manufacturing, education, agriculture, and health care. And in the critical area of disaster and crisis relief, we found Chef Jose Andres and his organization, World Central Kitchen (WCK).

The World Central Kitchen Approach

Before 2010, José Andrés was best known as one of the world's greatest chefs. One night, watching the Hurricane Katrina disaster unfold on TV, he was struck by scenes at the New Orleans Superdome where hundreds of newly homeless people were sheltered but without any obvious signs of activity from relief organizations or volunteers. It was this inactivity that drove him to fly to Haiti—in the aftermath of the earthquake there—with no plan, no team, only a credit card, and a deep desire to act, to do something to help.

"Cooking alongside displaced families in a camp," according to Andrés "was guided on the proper way to cook black beans the way Haitians like to eat them: mashed and sieved into a creamy sauce. It wasn't just about feeding people in need—it was about listening, learning, and cooking side by side with the people impacted by the crisis."

That experience led Andrés to create WCK—to respond to humanitarian, climate, and community crises in the United States and around the world and provide food relief to the local people directly affected by these crises. That accomplishment by itself is worth recognizing and celebrating. But everyone in the crisis relief world is driven by the desire to help individuals and communities in need—that's a given. What's so interesting about WCK is the radically different approach it uses to get there—a new model for disaster relief.

WCK does not find the cheapest possible ingredients. It does not get unqualified volunteers to make vast batches in factory conditions. It does not optimize for scale in the way most of us would define it. It does not minimize unit cost and maximize volume output.

Here's what it does: it pays local restaurants, food trucks, and other related providers to source, cook, and deliver food in and for the communities in need. While significantly more expensive per meal, all the donor money goes straight to the local economy to help it recover faster rather than bypassing it with external services. In this way, WCK helps devastated communities recover and establish resilient food systems.

The importance of this cannot be overstated. By engaging with the affected community members themselves and making them a core part of the relief, Andrés and his team change the communities' perceptions of themselves. Rather than being powerless victims, they are enabled to be part of the solution, to act and to build their own resilience for the future. Their dignity, identity, and culture are never taken from them in the name of assistance. They become the heroes in their own story.

So what do we learn from all of this that is different from the conventional silo model of resource management? We see three major lessons.

Lesson 1: Shared Success

The first and most important difference is that everyone wins from this approach. The individuals in need get nourishing food that respects their traditions and culture. The local businesses, especially the restaurants, get paid for cooking the food, which means they can stay in business and pay their employees, who then, in turn, have money for their families and to spend in other local businesses.

The donors see that their funds go directly to the affected communities, not to building organizational infrastructure. Volunteers engage directly with people in need and support them emotionally, not work in kitchens doing work they're unqualified for.

WCK gets to deliver more than one million meals a day, every day, and to respond quickly to emerging crises and disasters around the world—with no infrastructure to slow them down. Some call this a win-win, others a zero-sum game. We call it shared success. And it's the guiding principle for all Boundless organizations, for-profit and nonprofit alike. Instead of the siloed focus on economies of scale, here we observed a focus on ecosystems of success.

When shared success is the guiding principle, it is most commonly the outcome as well.

Lesson 2: Scale Through Connection, Distribution, and Integration

The second thing we learned about is the principle of connection. WCK engages with its ecosystems and its communities far more intentionally and deeply than the traditional company. WCK listens, observes, respects, and learns—and in this way, it becomes connected to all its partners and other stakeholders. And through connection, it achieves scale.

Scale is as important to v as it is to any for-profit business, but WCK scales through the network and the ecosystem, not through its own organization and its own resources. By scaling through the community networks of restaurants, food trucks, individually owned cars, bicycles, and whatever other transportation options are available, they have access to far more resources than they could ever own and control—and they can distribute aid far more rapidly and to far more people.

So how big is WCK that it's able to deliver more than one million meals per day? Well, you can look at it in two ways: (1) you could use usual organizational metrics and say it's tiny. It employs just under 100 people and has no permanent physical infrastructure. Or (2), you can look at the ecosystem through Andres's eyes and declare WCK the "biggest organization in the history of mankind."

Lesson 3: Speed Through Flow and Designing for Movement

The third thing we learned is that WCK is built for speed. It aims to be among the first responders to crises and to have boots on the ground preparing and delivering food—even if it's only sandwiches—on the first day it's there. WCK can move fast because it needs minimal infrastructure, activating local resources wherever possible and working with whatever is available on site.

But if you want to be able to move at speed, first you have to be built to move—or flow, as we like to think of it. You have to be built like a car or an airplane, a runner, or a bird—and not like a house. When we talk about the *foundations* or *pillars* of an organization, these words describe an ancient Greek temple, not a 21st-century company. Speed is one of the currencies of the AI age, and you can't be fast—consistently and continuously fast—if you're not built to move in the first place.

In the tech industry, speed to value is of the essence. In other industries, speed suffers from its associations with the word *fast*, as in fast food and fast fashion, but we should be in no doubt about one thing: we're all missing our sustainability goals. According to a recent survey, only 17% of the sustainable development goals are currently being met. AI can help with both scale and speed. They say "Speed kills" but stoppages, blockages, and silos are the worst killers. We need continuous movement built into every core process. This is speed made routine. And that's what we need now if we're going to meet our sustainability goals before it's too late.

Chefs Versus Cooks

So let's try to sum this all up and join the dots. We live in a world dominated by the silo model of resource management. But there's another way, personified by Andrés and WCK, which achieves scale and speed by ignoring conventional wisdom, and which generates and shares success across all stakeholders. We call this becoming Boundless.

Silos measure success by their own health. Boundless entities measure success by the health of their ecosystems. Boundless organizations are sustainable organizations, even regenerative ones. Silos scale through centralization. Boundless entities scale through connection and distribution. Silos inhibit speed. Boundless entities enable it.

To be Boundless, we need to adopt a new mindset. We need to operate like chefs, not cooks. "I've been a cook all my life, but I am still learning to be a good chef. I'm always learning new techniques and improving beyond my own knowledge because there is always something new to learn and new horizons to discover," says Andrés. A cook uses recipes to create—learning by analogy. A chef does not need a recipe. A chef learns the taste of each ingredient and can combine the right ingredients to prepare a delicious plate—learning by first principles.

In a new world, defined by new killer ingredients like Generative and Agentic AI, we must all learn to be good chefs. This is the only way we can recognize new ingredients that are required to create new, beautiful, and impactful products and services. AI is electricity for the 21st century, and if we are not operating like chefs, we will be in the dark, unable to produce actions that scale.

WCK was able to scale its distribution and value-creation abilities by activating thousands of restaurants. Today, businesses are scaling their abilities by activating digital AI agents. AI agents are the most important strategic technology for 2025 and beyond. One-third of consumers would prefer working with AI agents for faster service, according to the latest Salesforce research.

Furthermore, research shows that chief information officers (CIOs) are learning to be more like chefs. CIOs must also serve as chief AI officers, according to a Salesforce survey. Even though the majority of chief information officers believe AI is a game changer, only 11% say they've fully implemented the technology—and the business wants more of them. Companies are looking for their CIOs to be AI experts. However, 61% of CIOs feel they're expected to know more about AI than they do, and their peers at other companies are their top sources of information.

We've been focused on ideas that scale—and ideas are important. But today, we need to go further than that. We need actions that scale. Become like Chef Jose Andrés. In a world of silos, become Boundless.

Let's revisit the Boundless mindset and its seven core principles—not as a retrospective, but as a forward-facing blueprint for the Autonomous, AI-first company.

The Boundless Mindset

Boundless companies, experiences, and mindsets have a compass that points outward toward customers, partners, and communities rather than inward toward their own processes. They aim to spread themselves out into those communities rather than distance and separate themselves from it. To be Boundless is to reorient ourselves, to use technology to reach out, to connect with each other, our customers, our business ecosystems, our communities, and our environment. Boundless is what you get when you bring together the power of networks and flow—an entirely new paradigm for next level success in this increasingly connected, increasingly smart, and increasingly at-risk world.

Boundless entities commonly disrupt industry norms and orthodoxies. Our research has found that these entities share, even if implicitly, a set of design principles that generate and guide this revolutionary business model: connection, distribution, integration, autonomy, mobility, continuity, and shared success.

These principles are not mutually exclusive, nor are they intended to be, although they are collectively exhaustive in the sense that together they explain the most salient features of any Boundless system. Not surprisingly, the principles are the exact opposites of the principles of silos. They can work for all companies, large and small, traditional and "modern," digital and analog. Better yet: we've observed that the more companies apply these principles, the greater the transformative or even disruptive impact they tend to have.

Guiding Principle: Shared Success

Silos are designed to accumulate, defend, and protect stocks of resources so as to extract their full value. They all share one overarching principle: they *measure success by the value extracted from their resources*. That their success is measured in terms of their own outcomes is reflected in how they operate.

Boundless entities foster sustainable or regenerative practices. They make non-zero-sum game decisions, seeking success for all members of their ecosystems, environments, and communities—including themselves. And so Boundless companies measure success very differently. Profit is still a priority for Boundless organizations (at least those in the commercial sector) but only so that they can continue to enable the success of all their stakeholders, including partners, customers, employees, communities, and the environment. We call this next level *shared success*. In other circles, the term *non-zero-sum game* is used. Colloquially the expression win-win, or win-win-win, reflects the idea behind shared success. It's not just organizations themselves that can be Boundless. Stakeholder experiences, products and services, organizational structures, and new business models can all be designed to achieve this goal. Regardless of industry or resource application, they nearly always produce the same win-win-win effect, reducing operational costs while simultaneously improving the customer experience and the environmental or community impact.

Connection

Whereas silos see themselves as stand-alone entities and work to maintain the distinction between themselves and the outside world, Boundless entities recognize that they are in fact connected to that outside world, market, or ecosystem of which they are a part.

They are able to sense what's happening in their environment and with all members and parts of it. They realize that their ability to be Autonomous depends, perhaps counterintuitively, on being more connected than ever before. This ability is almost entirely dependent on the effective use of sensing technologies, since there are too many moving parts, too much complexity, and too much real-time data for humans to sense and make sense of them without assistance.

They are able to connect and foster successful relationships. And they are able to move beyond a traditional and linear supply or value "chain" with their various vendors and suppliers and to instead build with them business ecosystems which they can co-create or co-innovate on behalf of their mutual customers.

Distribution

Silos create centers, taking resources out of their natural environments or local communities and accumulating them for scale. This creates an inward-facing, highly concentrated, intensive organization. By contrast, a Boundless entity is always looking outward. It's not just connected to the world—it distributes itself and its resources throughout it.

Boundless entities take advantage of, and become more like, decentralizing technologies that allow or will allow them to serve their customers where they are. Now, obviously older networks like TV, radio, or the power grid also deliver resources directly to their customers, but more modern networks allow new levels of interaction between provider and consumer—like tele-consults in health care—as well as enabling many-to-many communications and value flows. Technologies like solar power enable consumers to feed surplus energy back to the grid, and we can expect the Internet of Things to further accelerate and amplify the flow of information across our networks.

Boundless organizations question and even reverse the traditional relationship between headquarters (HQ) and "remote" workers. In a connected, networked world the HQ is remote and the remote worker is local. The HQ itself is no longer a center but a pump that ensures all its resources are continuously replenished to maintain efficacy. Since Boundless organizations meet and serve their customers where they are, they enable those customers to maintain their own flow.

Integration

Boundless entities integrate at both technological and human levels. They are purposeful and committed in integrating their systems to ensure seamless business process and customer journey flows and, most crucially in the age of AI, to ensure accurate, complete, and up-to-date data across and beyond their organization. They align their employees and other resources on a common mission, plan, or purpose to enable coherent and consistent actions and behaviors. Their aligned purpose and values drive their decision-making as well as their behaviors and communications.

Boundless organizations use their connections with the outside world to sense and understand what's happening, and they assimilate all the inputs from their sensing mechanisms—including all their customer-facing systems—and integrate them to create a synthesized view of customer journeys and market conditions. They are responsive to their customers' current needs and can even anticipate future needs based on the end-to-end vision and understanding of those customers' journeys.

In fact, Boundless organizations aspire to move beyond end-to-end integration and instead recognize the power of end-to-start integration, or circular integration, supported and enabled by the machine-scale Sense, Understand, Decide, Act (mSUDA) model (explained in Chapter 3). This can refer to understanding the customer journey as not just one iteration of a path from awareness to use but of multiple iterations, all adding up to a dynamic relationship. And this does not just refer to customers but also to other loops, like the journey of raw materials to end products to recycling and reuse.

Autonomy

In a silo, resources are stripped of all the support systems they would have enjoyed on the "outside" and are heavily controlled on the inside. The resources become dependent on the silo owner for direction and for support. They are treated as dumb. Obedience and rule following is rewarded and more highly prized than is creativity or innovation.

Boundless entities empower their resources—primarily employees in the business world—to make decisions and act in keeping with their unified mission, plan, or purpose and with their customer success as the primary goal. They support and empower their customers' autonomy, as well as that of their employees, through their experiences, offerings, and organizational models.

AI is a vital tool across multiple industries for supporting businesses both in decision-making and in delivering customer success. And AI is the primary means by which the autonomous vehicle currently, and the Autonomous business in the near future, gets its name. Autonomy is actually made possible by connection, its sister principle, and both principles are what will enable AI to become more teammates than tools, more part of the company and its decision-making capabilities itself.

A core aspect of AI that should be an inspiration to individuals and organizations is the focus on continuous learning. AI gets smarter as real-time data flows through it, and its algorithms improve their accuracy. Sensing and understanding becomes an increasingly important capability for the Autonomous enterprise as much as it does for an autonomous vehicle or individual human.

Mobility

Flow is essential to life. Within living systems, resources are pumped to where they are needed and are refreshed on a continuous basis. Without that movement, embolisms and other blockages would stop those flows, causing death to tissue, limbs, organs, or even the whole organism.

Boundless entities are modeled closely after living systems. They mobilize their resources to enable distribution to where they are needed and to enhance their responsiveness to emerging conditions and needs. They foster individual and collective well-being through movement, both literal and figurative. They extend this theme to their customers, designing experiences that enable them to stay in their flow without waiting or stopping and without friction. Movement also enables speed, which is the currency in the digital economy. As such, it is more or less impossible for a company to be fast if it is built on a worldview that promotes stability and control. However, note that speed is not equally applicable across all industries. For example, the Boundless model in agriculture emphasizes movement, partially because it improves the health of its animals and partially because it enables farmers to ensure that their animals enjoy and fertilize their pastures without exhausting or contaminating them. Speed is not a value to these farms.

Continuity

Boundless entities are organized for continuity of operations. This doesn't mean just that the lights stay on and the infrastructure needed to support the business maintains its availability, although of course all of that is important. It means that value creation, value transformation, and value exchange is always happening. Products are always being developed and delivered—driven by and driving customer demand. Decisions are always being made. Information is always being shared across the organization to enable those decisions. Expertise and all other important resources are always being made available to the parts of the organization that need them, and resources are always being refreshed to ensure their usefulness and well-being.

Continuity in computing has been an important principle in computing ever since the advent of multiuser systems in the 1960s. Since then we have seen shifts from a few centralized mainframes to billions of distributed devices, from nightly batch windows to 24/7 online availability, from hierarchical to relational to networked data, from proprietary to open systems, from waterfall methodologies to agile, from "monolithic" applications to microservices and application programming interfaces. In the age of AI, true $24 \times 7 \times 365$ business continuity will be possible, driven by the scalability and speed of the new digital workforce.

Summary

Boundless organizations are different. Unlike more conventional businesses that generate economic value from controlling access to accumulated resources, they are designed to encourage and optimize the flow of resources and to unlock the flow of value among customers, teams, partners, and platforms.

This makes it an ideal mindset for the AI economy, enabling it to work at its highest potential. AI depends on flow but it also amplifies flow. It senses faster. It acts faster. It learns faster. When the business is built to be Boundless and is driven by AI, the whole system becomes more intelligent—not just the tools within it.

The world of Autonomous is not a sequel to Boundless. It is an acceleration and amplification of its thesis. Together, they form a new model for business in the age of intelligent systems. A model not just for digital transformation but, powered by AI, for business revolution.

In Chapter 7 we introduce the seven levels of autonomous work. This framework shows the incremental increase in value that Agentic and physical AI will bring to an organization right up until the inflection point we have discussed previously where AI-first strategies and designs can lead to nonlinear outcomes, as long as the leaders of the business are willing to "let go of the steering wheel."

7
AI Is the New UI

Taking our hands off the steering wheel: the road to Autonomous maturity for AI, the company, and its humans requires bold leadership and a new playbook.

The journey to autonomy will feel gradual at first, the accumulation of capabilities that improve efficiency and productivity incrementally. But then all these improvements will suddenly add up to a brand-new business model with nonlinear impact. Leaders need to let go of the steering wheel.

Introduction

The autonomous car has been evolving before our very eyes since about 2004 or so with the launch of the DARPA Grand Challenge. Tesla is obviously the company we all tend to think of when it comes to Autonomy nowadays, and hundreds of thousands of Tesla owners have been participating in the development of its full-self-driving capabilities. But Waymo is also a very visible example, at least in the cities in which it operates its autonomous taxi service, and for its passengers it represents the most fully evolved level of autonomy so far. These levels have actually been described in the "6 Levels of Driving Automation" framework created by the Society of Automotive Engineers (SAE J3016, copyright 2021 SAE International).

It is worthwhile describing this framework and discussing the paradigm shift that it describes and that we are right on the cusp of experiencing.

Within this framework, the first level in this model is Level 0, No Automation, where the human driver is responsible for all aspects of operating the car while the car is capable of providing warnings about the environment.

At Level 1, Driver Assistance, the driver is responsible for all driving but with some basic support provided by the car such as automated emergency braking and lane assistance.

At Level 2, Partial Automation, the driver must stay fully alert with both hands on the steering wheel while the cart can perform basic tasks such as acceleration, steering, and braking in routine situations.

At Level 3, Conditional Automation, the car is capable of taking full control of steering, accelerating, and braking under normal conditions. The driver must still be at the wheel, able to take over control when the driving systems are unable to continue.

At the fifth level, Level 4, High Automation, can the human be "hands off," but still must be in a position to take over if the self-driving systems are unable to continue for whatever reason.

Only at the highest level, Level 5, Full Automation, is the human able to be a "passenger" and the steering wheel itself is optional. While this seems to be just one level up, the implications for the behavior and role of the human and for the design of the car are dramatic. The human has to be willing to let go of the steering wheel both in practice and as an emblem of control. For some people this will be easy and a non-issue. For others it will take a real leap of faith and some time before they feel safe with the vehicle itself being in control. But what they give up in operational control, they gain back in time and freedom. From driver to passenger may sound trivial at first but in actual fact it will be transformational, even revolutionary, in the possibilities it creates not only for the person with this sudden gift of time but also for the car and beyond, for whole industries in travel, shipping, and transportation, as well in automotive itself. In the design of cities and city living, and possibly it may even play a part in the resurgence of rural and small community living.

The car itself can be transformed. Not only can the steering wheel disappear but so can the pedals, the driver's seat itself, and even the dashboard. All the fixed interfaces that we have become long accustomed to, the gauges and dials, are unnecessary. The seat layout, the door design, the windshield and windscreen wipers, headlights, the mirrors, everything about the car design is available for reimagining. When we look at vehicles like the Zoox, which were designed to be autonomous from the get-go, we are reminded that they can also be bidirectional. They need not be designed with a specific front and back in mind.

As we continued to explore this model, we realized that it only applies to the ability of an autonomous car to complete a trip. It doesn't describe its ability to charge itself, prioritize and plan trips, schedule and complete maintenance, perform regular cleaning, or any other aspect of ownership and management of the car beyond its primary function of driving.

So while the SAE framework ends at Level 5 with full driving automation, we propose a conceptual "Level 6: Complete Vehicle Independence," where vehicles not only drive themselves but independently manage their entire operational life cycle without human intervention. At Level 6, the car is now capable of the following tasks (in addition to everything at Level 5):

- Self-initiated charging/refueling
- Autonomous scheduling of preventative maintenance
- Self-directed cleaning and sanitization
- Independent trip optimization and planning
- Automated fleet coordination with other vehicles
- Self-management of earning opportunities (ride-sharing, deliveries)
- Autonomous software updates and system optimization

Where Level 5 automation frees humans from the task of driving. Level 6 frees humans from vehicle management entirely. This represents not just a technical evolution but a complete reimagining of our relationship with vehicles—from owned possessions requiring constant attention to independent agents providing mobility services on demand.

It's important to recognize the full extent of the implication of decoupling the car from the human. Once a car is capable of finding its own way to a person requiring its services, it becomes possible to imagine different models of vehicle management and vehicle ownership. Once operation, management, and ownership of an individual car by an individual human are decoupled, both the car and the human become more free, with greater autonomy. The car can now take on new roles. It can take and pick up the kids from school, it can run errands for any member of the family, it can become a taxi or delivery vehicle, for last-mile or even long-distance runs, during those hours when the "owners" have no need of it. Carpooling takes on new possibilities as does fleet management. During peak hours and high traffic density, autonomous cars can choreograph their behavior to maximize the overall traffic flow and minimize journey times. The number of cars on the roads can be significantly reduced once cars spend all or most of their time moving rather than being stuck in parking lots, waiting for their humans to retrieve them. Parking and traffic jams are both transportation blockages, trapping a huge amount of value by rendering cars inert for most of the day, and Autonomy potentially removes those blockages as we discussed in Chapter 2.

There are few reliable stats for this but in Chicago alone there are about 36,000 metered parking spaces and tens of thousands of spaces in the public and private garages located throughout the city. And according to a new tool from the Parking Reform Network, "downtown Cleveland is 26% parking lot. The centers of nearby Columbus and Detroit are 27% and 30% parking lot, respectively. Although they each hover around one-third, these Midwestern cities lag behind San Bernardino, California, and Arlington, Texas, which currently lead the country when it comes to ceding city land to surface lots: 45% and 42% respectively." All of which is to say that a huge percentage of land in our cities is being used to store empty vehicles for hours, a massive waste of both resources, a massive trap of value, and therefore a massive opportunity for the future that will be unlocked by autonomous cars.

The point of this is that Levels 0–4 describe a linear progression in the capabilities of the car and the gradual, again linear, reduction in the requirements made of the human. But in the evolution of autonomy from Level 4 to Level 5, where the steering wheel becomes optional, and then from Level 5 to what we have described above as a potential Level 6, even though the change may appear linear again, the possibilities enabled are anything but linear. The decoupling of the car and the human from one another and the redesign of the car itself that this decoupling makes possible has huge implications for the redesign of everyday life, for transportation and travel, for accessibility, and even for our cities and rural areas alike. Removing the steering wheel (and pedals, and the driver's seat) enables a paradigm shift in what the car can become and what its relationships with humans can become.

The Evolution of the Autonomous Business

Similarly, the rapid evolution of artificial intelligence (AI) has the capacity to reshape how businesses operate, how they compete, and how they define work itself. Most conversations about AI in the workplace begin and end with automation. Faster data entry. Smoother customer service. A chatbot here, a predictive model there. These are useful steps forward but they only scratch the surface. They represent the early gains of a far more profound transformation, one that doesn't just change how work gets done but redefines what an organization is and how it functions. To see the full picture, we need a more comprehensive framework.

That's why we created the Seven levels of autonomous work: to offer a clear, strategic model of how AI capabilities evolve and, more importantly, what that evolution means for business design, performance, and leadership. Just as the automotive industry developed the six levels of autonomous driving to track progress from driver assistance to full autonomy, we need a comparable model for autonomous work that goes far beyond isolated tools or workflows to encompass the evolution of the organization as a whole.

The seven levels represent a progression from AI providing assistance to individuals with their more simple tasks to AI playing leading roles across businesses and even extending to their partners. They unfold in two distinct phases. The first is Augmentation, where AI enhances human capabilities and accelerates the speed of execution. The second is Autonomy, where AI begins to act, decide, lead, and ultimately orchestrate systems in ways no human team could match in speed or scale. But even though we describe this as a progression, the shift from Augmentation to Autonomy ushers in radical new possibilities for business with nonlinear impact and outcomes.

Let's walk through the successive levels of this model and the fundamental shift it represents (see Figure 7.1).

At Level 0, organizations operate without AI. All decisions, actions, and coordination are done by humans. Labor drives output, and everything depends on human time and attention.

Level 1 marks the beginning of automation. Here, AI handles simple, repetitive tasks including data entry, basic responses, and rule-based decisions. These are low-complexity activities, but their automation frees up

146 Autonomous

Level	LEVEL 0: No AI	LEVEL 1: TASK	LEVEL 2: SUB-PROCESS	LEVEL 3: PROCESS	LEVEL 4: ROLE	LEVEL 5: TEAM	LEVEL 6: BUSINESS	LEVEL 7+: ECOSYSTEM
Phase	N/A	AUGMENTATION / DIGITAL ASSISTANTS			AUTONOMY / DIGITAL AGENTS			
AI Role	None	AI retrieves data or content (read mode only) upon request and under direct supervision.	AI performs information retrieval activities under direct supervision using its knowledge of requester's needs and goals to deliver precise and highly relevant information.	AI completes certain activities without supervision. Makes recommendations for next action and in some cases makes the relevant decision.	AI performs most or all activities of an **individual worker** at human's request.	AI completes most or all activities of a **team of workers** at a human's request, including orchestration.	AI completes most or all activities of a **line-of-business (LoB)** at a human's request, including orchestration.	AI orchestrates and/or choreographs activities with ecosystem partner agents to optimize end-to-end flows of value to the customer.
Human Role	Human performs all work	Human performs all work, instructing AI to retrieve data.	Human works faster and more precisely using information contextualized and personalized by AI.	Human performs all discretionary work and entrusts rules-based work to AI.	Human delegates most activities to AI to enable them to focus on higher value work.	Human completes specific tasks requiring creativity as part of team partially or entirely powered by AI.	Human completes specific tasks requiring creativity as part of team partially or entirely powered by AI.	Human works with AI to imagine, model and test what else may be possible for their business and customers.
Example		Pre-programmed AI Chatbot can welcome and assist online customers.	Predictive AI can analyze case logs and sales histories to predict at-risk customers.	Gen AI assistant or co-pilot can summarize content, schedule appts., build web pages.	AI sales agent can open new territories, qualify leads, create detailed plans for a rep to beat quota.	AI marketing team agent can analyze campaign success and reset team priorities and budgets.	AI agent can predict increase in consumer demand and spin up new teams instantly to handle it.	AI procurement agent can notify their suppliers' agents of change in demand and re-optimize cross-ecosystem supply flows.
Adoption	N/A	2024	2024+	2024+	2025+	2030+	2035+	2035+

Figure 7.1 The seven levels of Autonomous work.

human bandwidth and reduces error. The impact is linear and familiar: a little more speed, a little more accuracy, a little less cost.

Level 2, Sub-Process Automation, builds on this foundation. AI begins to handle small clusters of related tasks, collections of activities that make up a functional part of a larger process. The efficiencies here compound, but the impact is still fundamentally about flow: faster, cleaner, more reliable execution of defined steps.

Level 3 takes this one step further with full Process Automation. AI now orchestrates entire business workflows across departments or systems, from intake to outcome. These processes may involve decisions, handoffs, and approvals, but they can now be executed end to end by an intelligent system. The benefits remain measurable and incremental: better throughput, lower cost, greater consistency. Together, Levels 1–3 make up the Augmentation phase. In this phase, AI doesn't change the structure of the organization. It simply helps it operate more efficiently.

But that begins to shift at Level 4, which introduces Role Automation. Here, AI takes on an entire job function performing work that would traditionally belong to a human in a defined role, like a claims processor, scheduling coordinator, or customer service rep. The automation now spans tasks, decisions, and accountability within a role. It's still relatively predictable in impact: lower labor costs, faster cycle times, improved service consistency. But it also lays the groundwork for a deeper shift. As AI begins to take on roles, the organization must reconsider how roles are defined and by whom.

At Level 5, we enter Team Automation. AI is no longer executing a single role; it is orchestrating a group. It assigns tasks, monitors performance, reallocates resources, and adjusts plans in real time. This is not Augmentation. This is leadership, at least in a narrow operational sense. At this level, AI becomes a coordinating force. Humans no longer oversee the work; they supervise the system. The returns are no longer linear. Productivity gains become exponential. Team-level AI can orchestrate performance across roles in a way no single human manager ever could.

Level 6, Business Automation. At this stage, AI can run entire business functions: marketing, logistics, procurement, even finance or HR. It makes decisions, executes strategies, adapts dynamically, and learns continuously. The human role becomes strategic rather than operational. And just as a driverless vehicle changes not just the act of driving but also the design of the car itself, a fully Autonomous business function invites, and in fact demands, a complete rethinking of the way the business is structured. This is no longer about tools or productivity. It's about new architectures of value creation.

At Level 7, we reach the Ecosystem level, which marks the second great break. Here, AI is not just orchestrating functions within a company but is also choreographing relationships across multiple businesses, systems, and partners. It communicates with supplier systems, customer interfaces, logistics platforms, and third-party tools in real time. It extends beyond the enterprise itself to optimize the entire value network. This is the level where competitive advantage becomes systemic. Businesses at Level 7 operate in a state of continuous flow and adaptation, shaped not by human limitations but by the dynamic intelligence of interconnected systems.

A Deeper Dive into the Seven Levels

Let's look at each of these levels more closely. Feel free to jump forward the next few pages if the introduction above was clear and informative enough for your current needs.

Level 0: No AI

Level 0 represents the baseline: an organization in which AI plays no meaningful role in operations, decision-making, or value creation. All Sensing, Understanding, Deciding, and Acting is performed by humans. No digital agents assist, augment, or automate the work. This is not to say that there's no information technology at all. You'd be hard pressed to find a company without enterprise software, databases, and digital tools, but at a level 0 business there's no technology that learns, adapts, or takes initiative.

This remains a common state across many industries. For some organizations, it reflects deliberate caution, concerns about compliance, brand trust, or the maturity of AI tools. For others, it's inertia. Teams are too busy to explore automation, leadership hasn't prioritized it, or existing processes seem to work well enough to avoid disruption.

Level 0 isn't inherently broken. Until recently, of course, this was the only way business was done or could be done. As we discussed in Chapter 5, business has always been designed by humans for humans. Decisions were made by people. Processes were designed, managed, and executed by teams.

Institutional knowledge lived in human minds, structured documents, and static systems. Many great companies were built this way, and many still operate largely within this paradigm.

But as AI capabilities become more accessible and more widely adopted, remaining at Level 0 starts to introduce risk.

That risk doesn't always appear as immediate failure. It often shows up in comparative performance. AI-enabled competitors begin to process routine work faster, personalize at scale, adjust to customer needs more quickly, and respond to shifting conditions with fewer delays. The challenge isn't that Level 0 companies stop delivering value, it's that others begin delivering the same value with greater speed, consistency, and margin.

Without embedded intelligence, organizations at this level rely heavily on human effort to maintain momentum. They carry significant coordination costs, with knowledge trapped in inboxes or individuals. Decision-making requires escalation. Exceptions are common. And as conditions change, teams must reorient manually, often without the support of real-time insights.

The good news is that the path forward doesn't require a complete overhaul. Most organizations begin by automating a small set of clearly defined, repetitive tasks, steps where the rules are known, the outcomes are predictable, and the time spent is disproportionate to the value created. That's the entry point into Level 1, where AI begins to act on behalf of the organization.

Level 1: Task Automation

Level 1 marks the beginning of automation. Here, AI handles simple, repetitive tasks including data entry, basic responses, and rule-based decisions. These are low-complexity activities, but their automation frees up human bandwidth and reduces errors. The impact is linear and familiar: a little more speed, a little more accuracy, a little less cost.

At Level 1, AI begins to play a visible role in the business, but only in narrow, well-defined ways. AI systems are used to perform specific tasks that follow predictable patterns, such as entering data, responding to routine inquiries, triaging service requests, or sorting incoming documents based on known criteria.

These are often the kinds of jobs that draw little attention when done by humans but accumulate significant cost and delay when scaled. They are repetitive, rule-based, and time-consuming. At this level, the goal isn't to redesign the organization. It's simply to remove friction from the edges.

The technologies that power Level 1 are widely available and relatively mature. Robotic process automation (RPA) tools replicate simple human interactions, filling in forms, moving files between systems, copying values from one screen to another. AI-powered chatbots answer frequently asked customer questions, handle basic transactions, or provide account information without needing a service agent. Digital assistants manage scheduling, reminders, and routine communications. Some tools use optical character recognition to extract structured data from scanned documents or PDFs, feeding it directly into workflow systems.

The use cases are specific, and the logic is predefined. AI at this stage does not learn from its actions or adapt its behavior. It operates based on rules, and it remains under supervision. But even these constrained deployments can yield real improvements in speed, accuracy, and reliability.

The advantage of Level 1 is that it provides a low-risk entry point. Automation can be introduced in small, modular ways, without requiring a full redesign of systems or processes. A single RPA bot might replace hours of low-value manual work each week. A chatbot might reduce call center volume by 15%. These results are rarely transformational, but they are measurable, and they build internal momentum.

What also begins to shift at this level is the allocation of attention. When software handles routine execution, human workers are freed to focus on what remains: exceptions, edge cases, creative work, relationship management. And as those boundaries become clearer, organizations start to see how much time was being spent on tasks that required no judgment at all.

Level 1 also introduces the first trace of machine-led action within the machine-scale Sense, Understand, Decide, Act (mSUDA) model. Although systems are not yet interpreting complex signals or making contextual decisions, they are beginning to take action on the organization's behalf. A trigger in one system leads to activity in another, without a person needing to intervene. That delegation, however narrow, marks a fundamental shift in how work is executed.

Still, progress at this level is not guaranteed. Many organizations install automation tools but fail to redesign the work connected to them. Processes remain fragmented. Exceptions are handled manually. Bottlenecks shift rather than disappear. In these cases, automation becomes a cosmetic layer on top of legacy problems, faster execution without any change in structure or logic.

Success at Level 1 comes from treating it not just as a cost-saving tool, but as an opportunity to experiment and as an opportunity to ask questions. We argued in Chapter 4 that a highly desirable human characteristic in the age of AI is not necessarily the ability to tell stories but the ability and willingness to ask questions. Every task that is automated raises a question about how that task fits into a larger flow. Is it still necessary? Can it be simplified? What comes before it, and what happens after? These questions begin to surface naturally as teams realize that the presence of automation changes not only how work gets done but also how it should be designed.

It's natural and perfectly acceptable to reach Level 1 gradually. A bot here, a scheduling assistant there, a small experiment tucked into the finance team or the HR function. But even these modest steps build internal fluency. They create trust in the technology. They shift expectations and prepare the organization to think more expansively about what could come next.

Level 2 begins when the focus moves from isolated tasks to sequences of work, when the business doesn't just automate the parts, but starts connecting them into something that moves.

Level 2: Sub-process Automation

By the time a business reaches Level 2, it has already seen that small automations can deliver tangible value. The next step is recognizing that value increases when those tasks are no longer isolated. At this level, AI begins to take responsibility not just for individual actions, but for short sequences of work, sets of tasks that follow a common logic and lead to a defined outcome.

A sub-process might be simple on the surface: verifying a document, scheduling a service, onboarding a customer, or updating a set of records across systems. But each of these actions typically involves more than one step, often across more than one platform. While Level 1 automates the steps, Level 2 starts to connect them. It shifts the focus from point solutions to flow.

The technologies involved at this stage include workflow automation tools capable of triggering actions across systems, often initiated by a single input. When a new request is submitted, for example, a customer record might be created, a confirmation sent, internal tasks assigned, and data distributed across the relevant platforms. AI-enhanced customer service management and enterprise resource planning systems can begin to manage these sequences with greater intelligence, responding to conditions, enforcing rules, and escalating exceptions automatically. And document processing tools, increasingly augmented with machine learning, extract structured data from incoming files and feed it directly into those flows.

These are not advanced systems in the abstract. They are becoming standard capabilities in modern platforms. But what makes them meaningful at Level 2 is the way they begin to reduce manual coordination. Instead of employees handing off work between systems, or between each other, the work begins to move on its own.

That movement has consequences. It reveals dependencies that were previously hidden. When AI is responsible for routing a case or assembling a record, the absence of a clean rule becomes visible. The exception is no longer handled quietly, it is flagged. The workflow no longer tolerates ambiguity. As automation takes over, edge cases become diagnostic. They show where the process was relying on informal knowledge, unspoken norms, or undocumented workarounds.

This is one of the quiet disciplines of Level 2. Before a process can be automated, it must be clarified. That often means revisiting steps that haven't been consciously examined in years. Teams must decide what "done" means, who owns which inputs, and how errors should be handled. In some organizations, this work is tedious. In others, it's illuminating. Sub-process automation begins to generate data about how work is actually performed, how long each step takes, where failures occur, and how the system behaves under different conditions. That information enables not only improvement but also anticipation. Work becomes more predictable and, after a while of dealing with them explicitly, exceptions become rarer.

In mSUDA terms, we begin to see AI contributing to multiple stages of the loop. It is not simply acting, it is sensing inputs, applying predefined logic to understand context, and triggering appropriate actions in response. The machine remains bounded by the rules it's been given, but those rules are increasingly applied across multistep workflows, not just single interactions.

Reaching Level 2 also forces a degree of technical maturity. Systems need to be integrated. Data must be clean, available, and consistent. Processes that were flexible in the hands of skilled employees need to be made consistent enough to be handed off to software. For some organizations, this means investing in better infrastructure. For others, it means redesigning how work is structured altogether.

Level 3: Process Automation

At Level 3, AI orchestrates entire business workflows across departments or systems, from intake to outcome. These processes may involve decisions, handoffs, and approvals, but they can now be executed end to end by an intelligent system. The benefits remain measurable and incremental: better throughput, lower cost, greater consistency. AI doesn't change the structure of the organization but it does help it operate more efficiently.

At Level 2, tasks were linked into short, self-contained sequences. At Level 3, those sequences expand to encompass the entire arc of a process. A customer request, for instance, can be received, validated, routed, resolved, and followed up on, automatically. A vendor onboarding process might collect credentials, verify compliance, trigger approvals, and initiate transactions without requiring anyone to chase down missing information or monitor progress. The work simply advances.

Technologically, this level depends on platforms that combine automation with orchestration. Business process management systems capable of modeling and running full workflows are central, often layered with event-driven architectures that allow for real-time responses to changing conditions. AI now supports not just rule execution but also dynamic coordination: adjusting timelines, triggering actions, reallocating tasks, and flagging exceptions as they occur. It may incorporate decision engines that apply logic based on data inputs or predictive models that anticipate downstream effects and optimize accordingly.

This isn't autonomy in a general sense. These systems don't choose the goals or redefine the strategy. But they do control the execution. In mSUDA terms, the AI isn't just acting or interpreting, it's managing a full cycle of activity, handling multiple decisions, and adjusting within boundaries. It Senses, Understands, and Acts in a closed loop. And when it does need human input, it knows exactly where to pause and wait.

One of the defining features of Level 3 is what it removes: the need for human oversight between steps. The process no longer advances through nudges and reminders. There is no inbox that needs clearing to move things forward. The workflow carries its own logic and timing. It doesn't stall unless something goes wrong, and even then, the system often knows where to look.

At Level 3 the role of the human workforce starts to change quite noticeably. People become process owners rather than process coordinators. They define the structure, tune the rules, and monitor performance. They no longer manage the details of execution, they manage its architecture. That shift opens space for different kinds of work, but it also creates new responsibilities. Teams must become more deliberate about how processes are designed and maintained. Automation at this level has the capacity to amplify both clarity and confusion, depending on how well the underlying system has been constructed.

Level 3 also introduces a new kind of fragility. When a process is fully automated, small errors in logic or data can propagate quickly. This means organizations must invest not only in building these systems but also in governing them. Testing, auditability, and exception handling become part of the design, not just the cleanup. It is possible that people will start to become frustrated when they experience cascading errors and their potential impact. We hope that this model will enable individuals, teams, and organizations to understand where they are in the journey to AI maturity and Autonomy and take these frustrations in their stride.

The payoff, when that fragility is overcome, is significant. Complete processes begin to operate with consistency, speed, and resilience. Work that once required dozens of emails, approvals, or escalations now runs smoothly in the background. Throughput increases without adding head count. And as processes generate more data in real time, optimization becomes continuous. Because AI is a learning system, it doesn't just execute, it gets better all the time.

Level 4: Role Automation

At Level 4 AI takes on an entire job function performing work that would traditionally belong to a human in a defined role, like a claims processor, scheduling coordinator, or customer service rep. The automation now spans tasks, decisions, and accountability within a role. It's still relatively predictable in impact: lower labor costs, faster cycle times, improved service consistency. But it also lays the groundwork for a deeper shift. As AI begins to take on roles, the organization must reconsider how roles are defined and by whom. This is the beginning of the Autonomous phase, where AI is not just doing the work but beginning to assume control of it. To the extent that the humans allow it to do so, AI starts to change the nature of the organization itself.

In most businesses we expect that this shift will begin in areas where work is highly structured, but still complex enough that full process automation was previously difficult to implement. Claims handling, tier-one customer support, appointment scheduling, and certain types of internal coordination often provide the first footholds. What these roles have in common is that they are composed of overlapping processes, governed by clear policies, and subject to frequent but manageable variation.

The technologies that support Level 4 are more adaptive than those used at earlier levels. AI systems at this stage combine structured automation with elements of contextual understanding.

- Domain-specific AI agents are trained to manage work within a defined scope, answering questions, applying rules, flagging exceptions, and resolving routine issues. These agents often operate on platforms that integrate decision trees, historical data, and real-time inputs to guide action.
- Generative AI tools may be used to draft responses, summarize information, or produce content as part of the role's output.
- And AI copilots, already common in software development and writing tools, begin to function more independently as they take on larger shares of the work.

In some organizations, AI at this level operates in parallel with human workers, taking on a share of the volume. In others, entire roles are reassigned. Teams that previously managed scheduling, routing, or triage functions may now supervise AI agents that do the same work faster and more consistently. And while people are still essential, their responsibilities shift. They handle the exceptions, oversee performance, refine the model, or take on more judgment-heavy roles adjacent to the ones the AI now performs.

This is where the structure of the organization begins to adjust. Job descriptions evolve. Capacity planning changes. The notion of "head count" becomes more fluid. It's no longer just a measure of employees, it becomes a hybrid metric, blending human and digital roles. A department may have fewer people, but more workers in total. Some of them just don't attend meetings.

From an mSUDA perspective, Level 4 represents a more complete loop. The AI now senses, understands, and acts, not only in response to isolated signals, but across the broader context of a job function. It weighs inputs, determines appropriate actions, and executes without needing direct supervision. It is still bounded by policy and logic. But within those bounds, it acts as an agent.

This is also the point where trust becomes a serious consideration. Handing over an entire role to a machine raises questions of accountability, transparency, and oversight. What happens when the AI makes a mistake? Who reviews its work? How do we know it's doing the right thing? These aren't just operational questions. They're cultural ones as well. The presence of a nonhuman colleague forces teams to rethink what roles mean, and what it means to perform them well. Metrics will need to evolve and escalation paths will potentially need to be redesigned. Someone must be accountable for the role, even if it's being executed by a machine. The question is, does the buck always stop with a human?

The benefits of getting to this level are substantial. Role automation brings consistency, availability, and speed. It enables businesses to scale without expanding payroll. It frees people to focus on work that requires insight, empathy, or creative thinking. But there's a deep cultural and/or structural impact as well. This generation of business leaders is likely the last to be managing only human talent. And that talent is likely the last to have only human peers, mentors, and managers.

Level 5 builds directly on this foundation. If AI can perform a role, what happens when it begins to manage multiple roles? What if it's not just a worker, but the one coordinating the work?

Level 5: Team Automation

Where Level 4 focused on the automation of individual roles, Level 5 is where AI takes on responsibility for managing how work is distributed among a group of people, agents, or both. It determines who does what, in what order, and under what conditions. The system becomes aware not only of what needs doing, but of how work is flowing across the team, and what needs to change to keep that flow efficient and aligned.

A clear signal of Level 5 maturity is the presence of an orchestration layer, a system or agent capable of dynamically assigning tasks based on inputs such as capacity, priority, time constraints, historical performance, or service-level agreements. These orchestrators rely on data streams from multiple sources: operational platforms, scheduling tools, communication systems, and case management systems. Using these inputs, they decide how to allocate resources, not as a one-time plan, but as a continuous adjustment.

Technologies at this level include AI-powered workflow orchestration platforms, often built on top of real-time analytics and rule-based optimization. In some environments, orchestration is handled by intelligent assistants that operate within team communication channels, monitoring workloads, assigning tasks, reminding contributors, and escalating delays when necessary. In others, the orchestration is invisible, embedded in back-end systems that simply reconfigure the work as conditions evolve.

From an mSUDA standpoint, the AI at this level is Sensing not only inputs, but interactions. It Understands not just what the work is, but how it's moving, where it's stuck, where it's accelerating, and where intervention is required. It acts not in isolation but as a system-level operator.

This has significant implications for the structure of teams. Human managers are no longer solely responsible for the allocation of effort. Instead, they shift toward setting goals, resolving edge cases, and managing exceptions, many of which are now surfaced by the system itself. They are still accountable for outcomes, but they are no longer manually coordinating inputs. That responsibility has been delegated to software.

In some cases, teams remain human-only, but are now guided by digital managers. In others, the teams themselves are hybrid, composed of human workers and AI agents performing defined roles. What matters is that the work is no longer being scheduled by committee or manually tracked in spreadsheets. It is being orchestrated, intelligently and adaptively.

The impact of this shift is operational, but also cultural. When an AI assigns work, employees may question its decisions, the way it makes them, or the way it communicates them. For the organization, this creates a new set of expectations. Transparency becomes important. Auditability matters. The system must be explainable, or at least trustworthy, if it is going to guide the efforts of a team.

Level 5 also introduces a different kind of scalability. At earlier levels, automation scaled linearly: more bots, more processes, more tasks completed. But orchestration scales systemically. As more processes are brought under coordinated management, the performance of the system as a whole improves. Bottlenecks are resolved before they form. Capacity is reallocated dynamically. And the organization begins to behave more like a responsive network than a series of discrete functions.

Level 6: Business Automation

At this level, AI moves from coordination to control. The orchestration introduced at Level 5 is extended across an entire function's operations. The system receives inputs, determines actions, executes them, monitors outcomes, and adapts in real time. Human involvement still exists, but it is intermittent and supervisory. In many cases, people remain accountable for goals and outcomes, but the execution of the function, the day-to-day decisions and actions that previously required management, is now the responsibility of software.

The technologies enabling this shift are not radically different from those seen in earlier levels. What changes is the level of integration, autonomy, and system-wide responsibility. A business function operating at Level 6 is built on a foundation of real-time data infrastructure, automated decision engines, embedded analytics, and systems that can sense context and respond without delay. The orchestration layer becomes more intelligent and expansive, incorporating dynamic rule sets, predictive models, and continuous learning loops.

For example, in a fully automated finance function, AI might manage accounts payable and receivable, monitor cash flow, optimize treasury operations, and produce real-time reporting, adjusting tactics in response to changes in demand, liquidity, or risk exposure. In operations, supply chain platforms powered by AI can forecast demand, negotiate pricing, trigger replenishment, and reroute logistics based on weather, traffic, or geopolitical shifts. These aren't isolated automations. They are tightly coupled systems running the function as a whole.

One of the defining features of this level is that AI begins to set priorities, not just follow them. Based on continuous sensing of internal and external signals, the system can adjust its strategy, shifting resources, rebalancing objectives, or pausing certain activities, without a meeting, a memo, or a request for approval. It is not autonomous in the philosophical sense, but it is operationally self-directed within its scope.

This changes the shape of the business. In earlier levels, teams remained essential intermediaries between decision and action. At Level 6, many of those teams no longer exist in the same form. The work still gets done, but the organizational layers that used to manage it are compressed or removed. Departments become smaller, more strategic, and more focused on exceptions, governance, and design. And in some cases, entire business units are replaced not by outsourcing, but by internally developed systems that outperform human teams on key metrics.

That shift introduces new challenges. Accountability becomes more abstract. When a system is running a function, and something goes wrong, it is not immediately obvious who is responsible. Questions about auditability, explainability, and compliance move from the edges to the center. Internal controls must be built not just for processes, but for entire systems. Governance becomes a design function, not just a regulatory requirement.

It also changes what it means to lead. Executives who previously managed by direct report now lead by intent, setting strategic direction and letting the system figure out how to get there. They are still essential, but their relationship to the function is different. They are no longer the hub through which all decisions pass. They define parameters, interpret signals, escalate critical issues, and reshape the structure when needed. But the motion of the function no longer depends on them.

The gains are substantial, even allowing for the questions of transparency and accountability we have raised previously. Level 6 enables businesses to run faster, leaner, and more precisely. It enables them to reallocate human talent to higher-leverage work (although the number of humans required to perform this higher-level work is unlikely to match those needed previously at the lower levels) and to compete at a scale and velocity that was previously out of reach for most firms. And perhaps most important, it enables organizations to respond to volatility, not just by reacting, but by recalibrating in real time.

Level 7: Ecosystem Automation

At Level 7, we reach the Ecosystem level, which marks the second great break. Here, AI is not just orchestrating functions within a company but is also choreographing relationships across multiple businesses, systems, and partners. It communicates with supplier systems, customer interfaces, logistics platforms, and third-party tools in real time. It extends beyond the enterprise itself to optimize the entire value network. This is the level where competitive advantage becomes systemic.

Businesses at Level 7 operate in a state of continuous flow and adaptation, shaped not by human limitations but by the dynamic intelligence of interconnected systems. AI agents communicate across organizational boundaries. They coordinate inventory and fulfillment between logistics networks. They negotiate prices, manage shared supply chains, update shared ledgers, or resolve conflicts between systems that operate under different rules but toward overlapping goals.

The technologies that enable this level are still emerging, but their foundations are already in place.

- Multi-agent orchestration frameworks allow AI agents from different organizations to collaborate across systems.
- Federated learning and privacy-preserving analytics enable firms to train models on distributed data without exposing sensitive information.
- Smart contracts and distributed ledgers provide real-time execution of agreements that are enforceable without direct human involvement.

These systems aren't hypothetical, they are being tested and deployed in sectors ranging from finance to manufacturing to logistics.

At Level 7, mSUDA becomes fully distributed, which means that each individual business has to be more sophisticated at each stage to communicate with the others effectively. Different agents handle different parts of the Sensing, Understanding, Deciding, and Acting cycle. In some cases, one AI senses a signal, like a change in customer demand, and another, in a partner firm, adjusts operations in response. The coordination is not top-down. It is emergent, based on shared goals, agreed-on interfaces, and real-time flows of information.

This shift introduces new opportunities for value creation. It enables businesses to deliver services that are more personalized, more efficient, and more synchronized across boundaries. Systems adjust together rather than in isolation and the benefits compound as more participants connect into the network.

But Level 7 also presents challenges that earlier stages do not. Interoperability becomes a strategic issue, not just a technical one. Firms must decide how much autonomy to grant their systems in negotiating with others, how much transparency to provide, and how to manage shared risk when things go wrong. When a decision made by one system affects outcomes for multiple companies, accountability must be traced and clarified. Legal frameworks, ethical boundaries, and regulatory standards all come under pressure as the line between "our business" and "theirs" begins to blur. Without shared governance, shared data standards, and aligned incentives, networks will break down faster than they scale.

Despite these challenges, the logic of the extended business at Level 7 is clear enough. In highly interconnected markets, isolated excellence is no longer enough. Businesses must be able to plug into networks, collaborate at speed, and deliver value as part of something larger. At this level, competitive advantage is not just a function of internal efficiency but also of ecosystem intelligence, the ability to participate in, adapt to, and shape the flows of value that span firms, industries, and systems.

Level 7 doesn't eliminate the need for human judgment, leadership, or strategic direction but it certainly does change the scope and boundaries of their influence and accountability. The business is no longer defined solely by what it controls. It is defined by how it connects, how it integrates, how it responds, and how it contributes to the performance of the system around it. In this context, the ability to collaborate intelligently becomes more important than the ability to operate independently.

For companies that reach this level, the organization becomes part of a wider fabric, an intelligent, responsive network of value creation. And while few businesses operate at this level today, those that understand it early will be best positioned to lead not just their teams or their functions, but the future shape of their industries.

From Linear Gains to Nonlinear Transformation

The shift from Augmentation to Autonomy is not just about doing more with AI. It's about rethinking what the business is for and how it runs. In the

Augmentation phase, gains are linear, manageable, measurable. But once Autonomy sets in, the underlying architecture of the firm begins to change. Removing the steering wheel doesn't just change the interface between human and vehicle. It changes the relationship between them. It changes the vehicle itself, and ultimately reshapes the world in which it operates. The same is true for the firm. Once AI leads the function, the team, or the ecosystem, the organization is no longer just better. It's different.

Having explored our model in detail, we want to offer up another aligned view of Autonomous maturity. We want to demonstrate that even if ways of thinking about Autonomy might differ in some of their details, we can have some confidence in the overall vision and our projections.

Silvio Savarese is the executive vice president and chief scientist at Salesforce, and a Stanford professor. Savarese is one of the most trusted voices in the world of AI research and the future of Autonomous businesses. Following are some of Savarese's most recent 2024–2025 projections, evolutionary and maturity definitions, and business considerations for adoption of Agentic AI in their journey toward building Autonomous businesses. The following excerpt is from Savarese's 2025 article on how enterprise general intelligence (EGI) will form a new business imperative—the model Savarese shows is aligned with how we define the fittest companies using athletic analogies to showcase the seven stages of the Autonomous enterprise.

What Is Enterprise General Intelligence?

Enterprise general intelligence is defined as AI, optimized for business applications, that excels in both capability and consistency, delivering reliable performance across complex business scenarios while maintaining seamless integration with existing systems. It can be defined through two critical dimensions: capability and consistency.

- **Capability.** The ability to navigate complex business environments, interface with multiple technology systems, reason through business rules, and deliver value aligned with business goals. This is the power to conduct complex research and operational tasks, but also create net new content to support objectives, refine knowledge based on

real-world feedback, and synthesize findings into coherent and highly relevant outputs. It must not only execute reliably but also adapt to changing conditions and pivot strategically when needed.
- **Consistency.** The delivery of reliable, predictable results with seamless integration into existing systems and rigorous adherence to governance frameworks. This consistency ensures that the system avoids "jaggedness," a term describing AI systems that excel at complex tasks but unexpectedly fail at simpler ones. A highly capable but inconsistent system would be useless for enterprise applications, regardless of its peak performance.

These dimensions create a framework with four quadrants encompassing low/high capability and low/high consistency; Let's use a metaphor of athletes to imagine how AI systems might fall across this framework:

- **The generalist (low capability, low consistency).** Systems that neither perform complex tasks nor deliver reliable results. These early-stage implementations typically have limited business value and represent stepping stones rather than solutions. Like a weekend tennis enthusiast, they may have basic skills, but they lack both the refinement and reliability needed for competitive play.
- **The prodigy (high capability, low consistency).** These systems have a "natural ability" to perform impressive, complex tasks but deliver inconsistent results, like a competitive soccer player with extraordinary gifts but unpredictable performance. When they do occasionally miss the mark, they can quickly erode trust, as users can't depend on them to deliver accurate results for mission-critical functions.
- **The workhorse (low capability, high consistency).** Some traditional software falls into this category: systems that perform a narrow range of simple tasks well, but cannot handle complex situations, like a reliable team player who executes their specific position perfectly every time, but can't perform every aspect of the sport. While reliable, these systems have limited adoption and potential, because they address only a fraction of today's business needs.

- **The champion (high capability, high consistency).** This is the goal for EGI: systems that can handle complex business scenarios flawlessly while delivering consistent, reliable results, like a true Olympic champion. These systems build and maintain trust through both their advanced capabilities and their dependable performance. And they are already beginning to emerge today.

You can see why enterprise leaders would want to have as many champions on their team as possible. Likewise, a prodigy might work well for consumer applications, but EGI follows a different development trajectory.

In business contexts, consistency can't be sacrificed for capability; both must advance in tandem for systems to deliver real value. And when they do, the trust gap that impedes AI adoption in enterprise settings will begin to close.

The Tennis Player Evolution: From Fundamentals to Championship Performance

The journey to EGI excellence parallels the development of an elite tennis player, a methodical progression through three distinct phases, each building on the last.

Phase 1: Fundamental Skills Training (Pretraining) Most people learn to play various sports at school or with friends. They develop general athletic capabilities, running, jumping, catching, but not at a level where they could compete professionally. Similarly, EGI begins with broad pretraining, creating a foundation of general capabilities like language understanding, pattern recognition, and basic reasoning. This is the frontier model stage, where systems learn general principles that will later be refined for specific business applications.

Phase 2: Sport-Specific Training (Fine-tuning) Athletes who pursue higher-level training become more specialized. In tennis, for example, players who take lessons and enter competitions receive rankings from organizations like the Association of Tennis Professionals or the Women's Tennis Association. Similarly, EGI undergoes fine-tuning for specific industry contexts and business functions. A model pretrained on general data now specializes in understanding financial regulations, supply chain terminology, or health care protocols, becoming proficient in the specific "sport" it will play within your enterprise.

Phase 3: Elite Performance Development (Ultrafine Tuning) The difference between a decent tennis player and one who can compete with the best in the world, a Grand Slam champion, requires thousands of hours of specialized practice that optimize every aspect of performance for specific competitive environments. For EGI, this translates to ultrafine tuning within your specific organizational context.

What might this look like?

Consider how elite tennis players, like my fellow Italian and Grand Slam champion Jannik Sinner, might review match footage and work with his coach to identify specific weaknesses in his game, then focus training specifically on those aspects. The level of performance he seeks requires excellence in both consistency and capability. It's not enough to display power and accuracy on the court. He must maintain optimal strategic thinking during matches, quickly develop intuition about opponents' weaknesses, and consistently adapt his gameplay on the fly. Similarly, EGI must not only perform tasks reliably but also demonstrate quick reactions, strategic pivoting, and adaptability when encountering new information or challenges. EGI, like a champion, succeeds by combining reliable execution with intelligent, adaptive strategy.

Importantly, this evolution isn't about creating a single "general" system that does everything. Just as sports have specialized variants (singles tennis, doubles tennis, squash, and the ever-popular pickleball!), enterprises will likely deploy multiple specialized agents rather than a single general-purpose system, with each agent reaching "championship level" performance in its specific domain. Different types of businesses and use cases may require different specialized agents, much like how various sports require different skill sets from their athletes.

Will Autonomous Businesses Need Us? Asking for a Horse

One of the questions that the emergence of the Autonomous business raises, in fact maybe the most important question, is what it all means for us humans. Throughout the discussion of the seven levels, we've tried to be clear that the role of the human, both employee and manager, changes. We've identified an increasing role in strategy and design, in relationship management, and a freedom for us to focus more on the mission or purpose of our companies. But we also recognize that companies need far fewer strategists and thinkers and transformation specialists than people who get stuff done. So what does it mean?

It is clear that AI will have an impact on human jobs. Some people like to talk about the effect of technologies on creating new, unimagined jobs and about the Jevons paradox. Remember the Industrial Revolution. Consider the prompt engineer. We understand these arguments and readily admit that we have no crystal ball but we think there's another story to consider, and that's a story about the horse.

The Manure Crisis of 1894

According to public legend, in 1894 the *London Times* published an article claiming that, if nothing was done about it, London would be buried in nine feet of horse dung within the next 30 years. Just four years later, with the same concern in mind, the Mayor of New York George E. Waring organized the first ever international congress on urban planning. The congress was attended by delegates from as far away as London and Paris. The main theme of the meeting was horse manure and its goal was to develop ways to combat the ever-worsening situation. The story goes that the congress was planned to last 10 days but the problem was so intractable that everyone left after 3 days, frustrated at being unable to reach any solutions.

Now, the problem with the legend is that it seems to be precisely that: a legend and largely apocryphal. No one at the *London Times* has ever found the alleged "dung crisis" article, George E. Waring was never the mayor of New York City, and there is no direct evidence that any such planning meeting ever took place in 1898. But whether we believe the story or not, its inspiration was real enough. The streets of New York and other major cities around the world really were in crisis, due in part at least to the working horses that had become part and parcel of urban life.

By the late 19th century there were tens of thousands of horses working in New York, London, and other major cities around the world, providing the backbone of their transportation systems. They had been providing these services in cities for centuries already, pulling private coaches as early as 1580 and then coaches for hire from the early 1600s, first the four-wheeled hackney carriage (from which we get the word *car*) and then the two-wheeled hansom cabriolet, or *cab*. But with the Industrial Revolution the need for horsepower increased significantly and the population of working horses rose rapidly and by 1900 had reached an estimated 24 million in the United States alone.

"The draft animal population—the vast majority of which were horses and mules, grew six-fold between 1840 and 1900, from 4 to 24 million. This outpaced the growth in human population, which merely tripled during those same decades. By 1900, there was one horse or mule for every three humans in the United States. The majority of work animals lived and worked in cities and their surrounding hinterlands. The greatest uses of animal power were in agriculture and transportation."[1]

With this increase in demand for power came everything else that comes with horses. Urine, dung or manure, and a lot of both. And, unfortunately, a lot of corpses in the streets as thousands of horses died every year from being overworked and were left quite literally to rot where they fell.

The same George E. Waring who was not the mayor of New York was in real life a sanitary engineer and he was in fact responsible for leading the efforts to clean up New York in the mid-1890s, prior to the real-or-not international symposium. He set up teams of sanitary engineers who cleaned the streets and who were recognized for their important efforts with a public parade in 1896. But the horse crisis was kept at bay rather than solved, and the continued growth of New York City as well as other cities around the world seemed to demand ever more horses and ever more filth. Even without the symposium, it's perfectly reasonable to think that the residents of the great cities of the world were justifiably worried. The final solution had, in fact, already been invented, but was still a novelty and few people, if anyone, could have imagined that it would come to replace, and redefine, horsepower.

The Phantom Phaeton and the Rise of the Automobile

While the *London Times* article of 1893 decrying the horse dung crisis may have been a fabrication, an article in the *New York World* newspaper in late November of the same year hinted at the technological innovation that would finally solve that crisis. The article was titled "A Phantom Phaeton" and subtitled "Without horses, it glides through the park, noiseless and rapid."

In the late 19th-century city, everyone would have known what a phaeton was: a horse-drawn carriage with short sides and oversize wheels. Wealthier New Yorkers tended to be the ones riding and driving this light, sporty vehicle. But the phantom phaeton *The World* wrote about had no horses pulling it, and its driver went unidentified. "For the past week a mysterious, self-propelling carriage has astonished the afternoon throng in Central Park," the article stated. "It threads its way easily among the crush of equipages on the East Drive, turning, winding in and out, and checking or increasing speed as readily as any of the vehicles drawn by horses."[2]

This mysterious, horseless carriage was, of course, an early automobile. Not the first in New York City but still early enough to have caused quite a stir and to have been considered newsworthy.

With the advent of the internal combustion engine the number of literal workhorses in the United States had fallen to six million in 1960. That figure has since fallen further to only about 1.5 million, of a total US horse population of about 10 million, most of whom are owned as pets and/or used in competition. The story is similar in Europe. In England for instance there were some 3.25 million horses working at the beginning of the 20th century but that number had fallen below 2 million within a quarter of a century—despite the loss of human laborers to the first world war and to the flu pandemic of 1918–1920 that took some 25–50 million lives globally. And a century later, in 2020, it is estimated that there are less than a 10th of that figure, about 160,000 horses, some 70% of which are pets and the rest are mostly engaged in racing and in some niche areas like mounted police and brewery dray horses. There are, in short, nearly no horses today in regular employment from a heyday of tens of millions fully employed.

Another likely apocryphal part of this story is the Henry Ford quote, which has passed into innovation and design lore that "if I had asked people what they wanted, they would have said faster horses." Quite apart from the fact that there is no evidence he actually uttered those words, it seems historically unlikely, given what we know about the horse dung crisis, that they would have said any such thing. In fact, the lesson of this story about the horse and car is clear. If a new way of fulfilling a need is better (cheaper, safer, cleaner, less effort, etc.) than the old way, people will hardly hesitate to choose it over the old way.

The car quickly became a more cost-effective alternative to the horse. It did not require stabling or feeding or a staff to care for it and drive it and its carriage. And it was much cleaner and more sanitary than the horse, and significantly more compact than the horse and carriage combined. It solved many of the pressing problems that beset the fast-growing cities and their inhabitants. And so the old solution for travel and transportation was quickly discarded. Within 20 years of the singular appearance of the phantom phaeton there were as many cars on the streets of New York as there were horses and within a few years more the horse had disappeared from them more or less entirely. We have to ask ourselves whether AI will be able to fulfil a whole range of business needs better than humans, without the additional costs associated with maintaining those humans. Because if the answer is that it will, it's clear that the humans will be freed up from having to perform those tasks within the not-too-distant future.

A Place for Humans?

Taking this unconventional approach of thinking beyond humans and recognizing horses as other suppliers of effort into our economy, in other words, as other members of the workforce, we are inclined to take the view that successful technology does indeed create opportunities but that it is entirely agnostic about who or what does the work associated with them. In fact we can go further and state that successful technology creates opportunities for itself. And only to the extent that it requires designers, builders, maintainers, supporters, and operators itself—human or otherwise—does it create opportunities for them, too.

In the past, all these designers, builders, maintainers, supporters, and operators were human (or equine!) and so it felt that in aggregate technology was creating opportunities for us. Think about the age of computers. Thomas Watson, the legendary president of IBM, said in 1943, "I think there is a world market for maybe five computers." Computing devices now far outnumber humans, meaning that computers are a very successful technology. And they've needed us to help them be successful. There are tens of millions of jobs for humans worldwide designing, building, supporting, maintaining, and operating them.

And this is why the argument from history seems compelling at first glance. After all, the Industrial Revolution really did create a vast number of new jobs. The same is true of the printing press hundreds of years earlier.

But the invention of the car absolutely did not create more work opportunities for the horse, and likewise the invention of the combine harvester in agriculture about 1800 absolutely did not create new jobs for humans. Over the last 200 years this technology has continued to evolve and improve, creating new opportunities for itself and yet destroying the industry from a human perspective. In 1800 the US population was about 5.3 million and over half of that population was engaged in agriculture. Two hundred years later the population was 282.2 million, with only 2% of it farming. In other words, in 2000 it took only twice as many farmers as in 1800 to feed a population 50 times larger. A case could be made that technology has eliminated more than 100 million human jobs. The only significant counterexample of technology increasing the demand for human labor in agriculture is, sadly but instructively, the invention of the cotton gin in 1800 by Eli Whitney. This invention increased the demand for American cotton in the United Kingdom and beyond, and this demand was met by a significant increase in the enslaved population in the Southern states to pick the cotton.

And now we've taken the next step. We are creating a whole suite of technologies that enable the automobile to live up to its name even more fully. *Auto* means self, and it originally implied a carriage (hence the word *car*) freed from the power of the horse. Now it means freed from the control of the human. It is technology by itself, Autonomous, "under its own steam" so to speak, and in that sense it is starting to become something new. And the implications are going to be felt far beyond the world of travel and transportation.

So does the Autonomous company have a place for humans if they're designed for machines? We think the answer is yes, at least for now. As with the plane or the car, in an autonomous company the AI controls the operations and the human controls the mission. While being a passenger in a car could be regarded as being more passive than being the driver, from another perspective the passenger has freedom that the driver does not. And more relevantly, the pilot of a plane with intelligent flight control systems has the freedom to focus on completing their mission, not on operating the plane itself. We may lose control but we gain a higher level of autonomy.

Until very recently, technology was first and foremost a tool. It was something that humans built and then used to do a job. To do it better, faster, easier than we could without it. But still, we used it. What's new is that with AI we are not creating new tools to help us do a job. We are creating a new workforce to do the job for us. This is not an absolute, of course, and we can always point to older technologies that may have done part of our job for us (factory automation began at least 200 years ago) but we are now creating a cheaper, faster, better, scalable workforce, not a cheaper, faster, better, scalable tool set.

This new workforce is not going to replace us all any time soon. There are two main reasons for this. The first is that the hype of AI far exceeds its current capabilities except in some narrow, rules-based scenarios (e.g., games, in which it can now far outperform even the greatest human players). It is clear that Generative AI in particular appears almost magical in its ability to render text, images, and even video, and yet its inability to actually understand any of it, along with the volume of data and the power needed to train it, surely limits it from achieving much more of practical use to humans in its current architecture.

The second is quite simply the time it takes our institutions to fully understand and embrace the capabilities of technology that actually are proven. We saw this most clearly in 2020 when schools districts and businesses alike had to cease operations altogether during the COVID pandemic because they had not yet implemented full online operations despite the capabilities being in existence for a good 15 years at least (being kind). We can expect late adopters to wait again until they're presented with an existential threat before embracing AI and this lag will affect the whole population.

Given those two major caveats, we can track the gradual integration of AI into the workforce and the eventual, inevitable reduction in the number of human employees as AI becomes cheaper, more efficient, and more accurate than us at performing a wide range of functions. It may be true that AI will create new opportunities that we can't yet imagine but they won't necessarily be opportunities for more of us humans. In the short term, of course, we may well see an increase in jobs for us as not all technologies will develop at the same speed and will need our help to work with them. We expect this to be true for at least the next five years and possible for the entire period covered by our book. One day though—and we expect that the real watershed moment will once again be fully autonomous mobility, from the vehicle to the android robot—the measure of manpower (mp) will become as figurative as horsepower (hp) is now and we will likely be startled by the number of mps the average robot will operate at. There'll likely be fewer of us, but hopefully healthier and happier. We'll be able to live more fully as long as we take seriously our one "job" of finding a new sense of purpose and joy once employment no longer sets our course and we go the way of the horse.

Summary

Businesses receive a variety of signals from customers every day. These signals, which are the fundamental unit of business intelligence, can range from a customer contacting support or visiting your website to downloading content, scheduling meetings, attending events, or making purchases. These interactions across various touchpoints all provide valuable information, but all too often the information is either missed, overlooked or handled too narrowly by one part of the organization working in its own silo, independently of all other parts. And when these signals are coming in thick and fast, they can overwhelm our human abilities to deal with them all effectively, accurately, and in real time.

But with the near-future potential of multi-Agentic AI, a single customer signal can be instantly Sensed, Understood, Acted on, and shared across all relevant parts of your organization. What if your company could deliver precisely what a customer needs, the moment they need it, based on just one signal, across every relevant department like sales, service, marketing, commerce, HR, supply chain, and engineering? An unprecedented and deeply contextualized understanding of both historical and real-time data and the ability to predict future outcomes through seamless knowledge sharing, would enable a "one-to-many" scenario previously unimaginable. A single customer signal could trigger a coordinated set of actions across multiple lines of business in real time.

This is just part of what we call the nonlinear impact of an Autonomous business, once it hits Level 5 of our maturity framework, powered by orchestrated AI agents individually and collectively capable of mSUDA. And it's not fanciful or wishful thinking or clickbait. It's a real capability emerging now. To truly reach their Boundless potential, businesses must adopt an Agentic AI layer throughout their entire organization. The companies that do will leverage digital labor powered by Agentic AI with abilities far beyond the reach of human intelligence and labor alone. And it will almost immediately separate businesses into those who are positioned to win and those who aren't.

In Chapter 8, we will recap everything that we have covered throughout the book in the hope of firmly embedding its insights into the broader AI conversation.

8

Summary of Key Insights

This is what defines the world's most successful companies: Autonomy.

Our aim in writing this book has been to demonstrate to business leaders, strategists, and designers the reality and urgency of the evolving role of artificial intelligence (AI), transitioning from a mere digital tool to a form of digital labor. This fundamental shift necessitates a corresponding change in human roles, moving away from day-to-day operational control toward a higher-level function of mission control. Throughout this book, we have outlined the significant implications of this evolution. Our goal has been to provide a clear road map for the transformation of your companies toward an AI-first approach, which requires a significant departure from the traditional human-first model that has long been the standard.

To effectively facilitate this significant and often complex change, we have identified seven key insights that we believe are crucial for navigating this new landscape. The entirety of this book has been dedicated to thoroughly explaining and exploring each of these insights. Our intention has been to equip you, as leaders, with the knowledge and understanding necessary to confidently prepare for the inevitable journey toward greater business Autonomy.

As we reach the conclusion of this work, we want to reiterate these seven key insights one final time. We do this to ensure that the most critical messages and takeaways from our exploration remain firmly with you as you embark on this transformative path.

Insight 1

> In an <u>AI-powered</u> economy, the companies that are the <u>fittest</u> (most likely to win) are <u>Autonomous</u> using <u>digital labor</u>.

To thrive in the AI economy, companies need to be fit in two key ways. First, they must be adaptable and responsive to the evolving demands of customers, the market, and the broader economy. Second, they need to be in peak operational condition: healthy, agile, and driven by talent.

The fittest companies operate without internal inefficiencies that hinder progress and erode value. They are conditioned for consistently high performance and can execute at speed as a standard practice, not as an exceptional effort. They cultivate a talented workforce that integrates digital AI capabilities—predictive, Generative, Agentic, and physical AI—with human expertise, creating a powerful hybrid resource that leverages the strengths of both. Furthermore, these leading companies prioritize AI in their strategies and designs, aiming for significant, transformative results.

Crucially, the leaders of these fit companies are forward-thinking and willing to empower their teams, enabling the organization to achieve exponential growth using a hybrid talent—people and AI agents co-creating highly scalable stakeholder value at the speed of need. We call these highly adapted and future-ready organizations *Autonomous*.

Insight 2

> <u>Blockages</u> are the number one cause of <u>death</u> in living organisms and businesses alike. <u>Autonomous</u> companies are <u>living organisms</u> that are <u>immune</u> to blockages.

Our research explored the significant and increasingly critical effects of various blockages on a company's ability to succeed. We believe that by shifting our perspective, businesses can leverage the power of AI to proactively identify, mitigate, and ultimately overcome these hurdles.

Consider the parallels between a thriving organism and a successful company. From the complexity of the human body down to its individual cells, health is maintained through optimized flow. Whether it's the movement of matter, energy, or information within the organism and between it and its environment, these flows are essential for vitality.

We've previously delved into one specific type of blockage in our book *Boundless*: organizational silos. These are often deeply entrenched because they can appear to function effectively, at least for those managing them. Furthermore, managing resources through silos tends to be our default approach, often an unconscious choice. Overcoming these requires a fundamental shift in mindset, one we've termed *Boundless*.

However, addressing other business blockages doesn't necessarily require such a profound initial change. A sense of urgency, stemming from the understanding of how critical unimpeded flow is to any living system, can be the catalyst. Just as blockages in the human body can lead to severe health issues and the ultimate cessation of life through the stopping of breath and blood flow, companies too are living entities dependent on various flows for their well-being.

Blockages in business—whether of information, capital, expertise, decision-making processes, or human resources—inevitably lead to slowdowns and reduced effectiveness. We contend that these obstructions have a similarly detrimental impact on a company's success as they do on individual health, even if their precise impact is yet to be rigorously measured.

The principle of optimal flow extends beyond living organisms to the machines and systems we build. The uninterrupted flow of electricity, hydraulics, data, fuel, and air is fundamental to their proper operation.

This same principle is crucial for healthy businesses. Optimal flows of incoming resources like money, raw materials, energy, expertise, and data, coupled with outgoing flows of value to customers (products, services, information), and the subsequent flow of money back to providers and investors, are vital. When these flows are impeded, businesses suffer in numerous ways, potentially leading to deterioration and even failure, regardless of their size or structure.

Fortunately, AI offers not only a catalyst for change in removing these blockages but also a powerful tool for identifying and eliminating them across various aspects of business operations. AI can effectively remove bottlenecks, streamline workflows, and enhance a company's agility, enabling rapid responses to both internal and external pressures.

In conclusion, there are significant opportunities, both easily achievable and more substantial, for any company looking to accelerate its performance, gain a competitive edge, and thrive in this era of rapid change. The speed demanded by today's business environment aligns perfectly with the solutions AI can provide to ensure optimal flow and overcome the detrimental effects of blockages.

A healthy living organism, from complex ones like humans to the individual cells that we're composed of, is one that optimizes flow. Optimal flows of matter, energy, and information between the organism and its environment, and flows within the organism itself, keep us all alive and healthy.

Optimal flow is also essential to the health or optimal functioning of a whole variety of machines and systems. From the flow of electricity that animates nearly all systems nowadays, to hydraulic flows, data flows, fuel flows, airflow, and so on, our constructed and built world relies on uninterrupted flow to work properly.

This same principle of optimal flow also applies to business. Healthy companies have optimal flows of money, raw materials, electricity, expertise, data, and other resources coming in and flows of value to the customer coming out (product, service, information, and so on), as well as flows of money back out to providers, investors, and so on. When these flows are obstructed business suffers in all sorts of ways. Blockages cause the deterioration and even death of companies of all shapes and sizes

Insight 3

> **Autonomous companies have <u>operating models</u> for <u>decision dominance</u> and action at <u>machine speed and scale</u> (mSUDA).**

The concept of "decision dominance," highlighted by US Army Futures Command chief General John Murray, is defined as a commander's ability to sense, understand, decide, act, and assess more rapidly and effectively than any adversary. The US military emphasizes its importance and the critical elements required, including speed, range, and convergence.

Speed encompasses both the physical velocity of weapons and the cognitive speed of AI in offering commanders options. This enables faster and better-informed decisions, potentially leaving adversaries at a significant disadvantage. Range refers to the capacity to outmaneuver the enemy physically and strategically position forces, equipment, and resources effectively. Convergence involves connecting diverse Army and even non-Army systems through a shared data network, exemplified by exercises like Project Convergence. It also extends to fostering collaboration across different institutions, both within the Army and between the Army and private sector.

Achieving a SUDA (Sense, Understand, Decide, Act) model that operates at machine speed involves more than just advanced technology and AI. According to General Murray, it encompasses not only the tools of warfare but also the strategies and organizational structures employed in combat, emphasizing the importance of scalability.

Just as overall health is fundamental to fitness, conditioning distinguishes high-performing autonomous entities. Their ability to act swiftly and routinely stems from being built around the mSUDA (machine-scale Sense, Understand, Decide, Act) model. This serves as the operational framework for decision dominance and competitive advantage in the age of AI, designed to minimize the time gap between sensing an event and taking action. Embracing mSUDA necessitates predictive, Generative, Agentic, and physical AI-powered solutions, driving the evolution of enterprise applications toward systems of engagement, action, and impact.

With the increasing adoption of Agentic AI in business, capable of 24/7 autonomous actions, a new measure of productivity, perhaps termed *machine power*, will likely emerge. This metric will reflect machines' capacity not only to perform human tasks faster and more efficiently but also to undertake tasks of greater complexity, managing more variables and demanding quicker resolutions.

The management of robo-taxi fleets represents an early manifestation of this new machine power, showcasing a transportation service devoid of human drivers. Similarly, managing fully Autonomous companies will exemplify this capability further.

Decision dominance, achieved through mSUDA models and powered by Agentic AI, will enable businesses to drastically reduce the time between Sensing, Understanding, Deciding, and Acting, approaching near-zero latency. To thrive in an AI-driven economy, the most critical currencies will be speed, scale, intelligence, personalization, and, crucially, trust.

Businesses must proactively plan and design for an environment of continuous change. AI will be instrumental in assisting leaders and their teams in making both strategic and immediate data-driven decisions, leading to more effective action.

Insight 4

Autonomous companies are <u>hyper-talented</u>, integrating <u>human and digital resources</u> and building deep <u>relational intelligence</u>.

At the heart of every thriving business lies a network of strong relationships, built on trust and commitment, that consistently create positive experiences and deliver lasting mutual value. As AI evolves into a form of digital labor and becomes an integral part of our workforce, it will introduce both new avenues and unique challenges for cultivating these crucial connections. We must consider how these technological advancements will affect the personal interactions that are fundamental to our success.

This is where relational intelligence (RI) becomes essential. We define RI as the capacity to intentionally develop, foster, and strengthen successful relationships in an era defined by AI and intelligent automation. RI uniquely combines human qualities like individuality, creativity, and empathy with the speed, scale, contextual understanding, and data-driven insights offered by AI agents. By doing so, we can deepen our most important connections: with our customers, our employees, and all our valued stakeholders, ensuring that technology serves to enhance, not replace, the human element of our business.

The integration of AI represents a significant expansion of our company's capabilities, offering unprecedented levels of performance in terms of speed and scale. To truly leverage this new talent pool, we must adopt a thoughtful and strategic approach to integration. Rather than simply applying AI to isolated problems, we should focus on how these resources can be effectively harnessed to enhance the performance and overall effectiveness of our entire organization. This holistic approach will enable us to maximize the benefits of AI while preserving the relational aspects that drive long-term value.

Summary of Key Insights 181

Insight 5

> Adopting an **AI-first** strategy is the **only** path from assistive to **Autonomous** capabilities, producing **nonlinear**, exponential outcomes.

The conventional design of airplanes has historically involved a significant trade-off. Due to the inherent limitations of human pilots in managing unstable flight, engineers had to prioritize stability. While highly skilled pilots could certainly manage aircraft with a degree of instability, this focus on stability inherently restricted the potential performance of the aircraft. As a result, the physiological and cognitive capabilities of human pilots placed fundamental constraints on the types of airplanes that could be developed and the overall limits of their speed and maneuverability.

The introduction and widespread adoption of fly-by-wire technology has largely circumvented this long-standing compromise. By replacing mechanical flight controls with electronic interfaces, fly-by-wire systems have enabled the development of aircraft with significantly reduced inherent stability. This shift has unlocked remarkable advancements across a range of critical attributes, including increased speed, enhanced stealth capabilities, superior maneuverability, and improved recoverability from extreme flight conditions. Furthermore, the ongoing and rapid development of Intelligent Flight Control Systems, increasingly powered by sophisticated AI, holds the exciting promise of pushing the boundaries of aircraft capabilities even further, potentially into realms previously considered impossible.

Considering the world of business through this analogous lens reveals a potentially transformative insight: certain human qualities and organizational structures, which have traditionally been viewed as either neutral or even distinctly advantageous, may now be reevaluated as potential limitations in an era increasingly defined by the capabilities of AI. For instance, the value traditionally placed on extensive human experience in certain roles might become less critical when advanced AI systems can rapidly learn and master intricate tasks, processing vast datasets and continuously enhancing their performance at a pace unmatched by human learning curves. Similarly, the fundamental significance of human effort, particularly in routine and repetitive tasks, could diminish as AI systems can operate tirelessly, 24/7, without the inherent needs for compensation, rest, or traditional motivational structures. Even long-established corporate hierarchies and traditional management structures, built on human oversight and motivation, might become less relevant as AI demonstrates the potential to efficiently coordinate, manage complex operations, and provide data-driven guidance without the typical human incentives or hierarchical dependencies.

In essence, the increasing sophistication and pervasiveness of AI are compelling us to subject many established and deeply ingrained business practices to fundamental reevaluation. The concept of an Autonomous company, an organization designed from the ground up to leverage the strengths of AI and machine-driven strategies—and perhaps even designed and optimized by AI in the future—is rapidly moving from a theoretical possibility to an increasingly pertinent and potentially inevitable reality.

Insight 6

> **Becoming an <u>Autonomous business</u> requires the seven <u>Boundless principles</u> shaping the <u>mindset</u> and business <u>operating model</u>.**

We currently operate in a business environment largely defined by resource management silos. However, the approach exemplified by Chef Jose Andrés and World Central Kitchen (WCK) offers an alternative. Their model achieves significant scale and speed by challenging traditional norms and fostering shared success across all involved parties. We call this "becoming Boundless."

Traditional silos measure their success internally. By contrast, Boundless entities gauge their success by the overall health of their surrounding ecosystems. Boundless organizations are inherently sustainable, even regenerative. Silos grow through centralization, whereas Boundless entities expand through connection and distribution. Silos tend to impede speed, while Boundless entities actively enable it.

Transitioning to a Boundless approach necessitates a fundamental shift in mindset. We must learn to think and operate like chefs, not merely cooks. As Andrés eloquently stated, even with extensive experience, continuous learning and exploration beyond current knowledge are essential for growth and discovery. A cook follows established recipes, learning through imitation. A chef, however, understands the core elements of each ingredient and can creatively combine them to produce exceptional results, learning from first principles.

Summary of Key Insights 183

In today's evolving landscape, marked by transformative technologies like Generative and Agentic AI, adopting the chef mindset is crucial for everyone. This perspective enables us to recognize and effectively use new ingredients to develop innovative and impactful products and services. Just as electricity powered the 20th century, AI is the driving force of the 21st. Without a chef's understanding, we risk being unable to harness AI's potential for scalable action.

WCK's remarkable ability to scale its operations and value creation was achieved by empowering thousands of restaurants. Similarly, businesses today are expanding their capabilities by leveraging digital AI agents. Our latest Salesforce research indicates that one-third of consumers already prefer interacting with AI agents for quicker service, underscoring their strategic importance in 2025 and beyond.

While focusing on scalable ideas has been valuable, we must now prioritize scalable actions. We need to emulate Andrés's Boundless approach in a world often defined by silos.

The foundation of autonomous companies will rest on the principles of connection, integration, distribution, Autonomy, mobility, continuity, and shared success. Agentic AI inherently brings new and enhanced connections. Data, the vital element for AI success, necessitates integration for seamless access. Distribution becomes automated and more extensive. Mobility and continuity accelerate Autonomy, and shared success now encompasses both human and digital contributions, shifting the focus from mere economies of scale to thriving ecosystems of success.

We initially introduced these principles in our book *Boundless* to articulate a business philosophy that stands in direct contrast to conventional, siloed structures. We now recognize that these very principles provide the ideal framework for building the AI-first company. Boundless principles show us how to successfully build Autonomous businesses.

Insight 7

Taking our hands off the steering wheel: the road to Autonomous maturity for AI, the company, and its humans requires a bold vision and a new playbook.

The shift from human-led to AI-led Autonomous companies won't happen overnight. It's going to be a step-by-step evolution, and to make it successfully, organizations need a clear understanding of the path ahead and a new way of thinking. To help with this, we've created a seven-level maturity model. This framework is designed to help businesses like yours see what's coming, plan accordingly, and measure your progress as you integrate digital labor and move toward greater Autonomy.

Our model highlights two critical stages in this journey. These stages represent turning points where AI's impact moves from being helpful to truly transformative. Think about autonomous vehicles. In the early stages, even with self-driving features, a human driver is still in charge, and the autonomous capabilities offer improvements but not a fundamental change. The real game changer happens when the vehicle can operate entirely on its own.

The same principle applies to AI in your company. Its influence will grow steadily, providing increasing benefits, until you reach a specific level of Autonomous maturity. It's at this point that we can really start to imagine the future possibilities—a future where we can confidently rely on our AI systems as not just tools but also as true digital colleagues, collaborators, mentors, and even orchestrators of our operations.

Summary

What will define the world's most successful and healthiest companies: Autonomy. Driven by leadership dedicated to future-proofing their organizations, these companies are developing a digital workforce leveraging Agentic AI. This allows for the nonlinear scaling of their teams', business', and ecosystem's health, conditioning, and talent.

The result is continuous operation and responsiveness around the clock, the elimination of obstacles and inefficiencies that hinder value creation, and a strong position for unlimited business success in an AI-driven economy. In these organizations, operations are machine-led and human-assisted, marking a shift from the traditional model.

This is the Autonomous business.

9 | Ten Tenets of Autonomous Businesses

These are the 10 key takeaways from this book.

Business survival in an AI-powered economy is not guaranteed. We believe a bold and different approach is required for businesses to thrive, unlike anything we've seen in the past. The fittest businesses are Autonomous. They need to adopt AI-first strategies and embrace digital labor to succeed. Those that don't leverage artificial intelligence—whether predictive, generative, Agentic, or physical—will likely not survive.

Our goal with this book is to educate, inspire, and encourage proactive steps toward building the fittest businesses of the future, and we believe strongly that these 10 tenets of Autonomous businesses should be a guide for you on your own journey to Autonomy:

1. **Superior performance.** The fittest companies are Autonomous businesses—scaling health, conditioning, and talent to achieve Boundless potential for value creation and winning.

2. **Boundless mindset.** The path to becoming an Autonomous business requires the seven Boundless principles shaping the mindset and business operating model.
3. **Blockage prevention and waste elimination.** Autonomous businesses are best able to identify waste and to identify, root case, remediate, and prevent blockages.
4. **AI-driven foundation.** The path to full Autonomy (versus assistive artificial intelligence [AI]) requires AI-first design principles; AI is the user interface.
5. **Exponential growth.** Autonomous capabilities are the *only* path to nonlinear optionality (autonomous vehicle: driver → rider).
6. **Machine-scale operations.** Autonomous businesses can Sense, Understand, Decide, and Act at machine scale (mSUDA).
7. **Digital workforce.** Autonomous businesses achieve mSUDA by using AI agents and digital labor.
8. **Resilience and performance.** Autonomous businesses are optimally designed to respond to instability, without making trade-offs between their own stability and performance.
9. **Human-digital synergy.** A successful autonomous strategy is about cognitive transfer of low-value work to digital labor and cognitive upgrade of high-value work for human labor.
10. **Dynamic orchestration.** Autonomous businesses can orchestrate and choreograph actions and value creation, using one or many input signals, at optimal scale and speed.

Notes

Chapter 1

1. For a good summary of the history of AI, see Salesforce, Inc. n.d. *What is the History of Artificial Intelligence (AI)?* Salesforce, Inc.
2. Goldman Sachs. 2023. *Generative AI Could Raise Global GDP by 7%.*
3. Michael Franzino, Alan Guarino, and Jean-Marc Laouchez. 2018. *The $8.5 Trillion Talent Shortage.* Korn Ferry.
4. Karen Semone and Denise Pérez. 2025. *2024 in AI Research: Building Blocks for the Agentic Era Ahead.* Salesforce, Inc.
5. Alex Singla, Alexander Sukharevsky, Lareina Yee, Michael Chui, and Bryce Hall. 2025. *The State of AI: How Organizations are Rewiring to Capture Value.* McKinsey & Company.
6. Salesforce, Inc. n.d. The Sixth Edition Connected Shoppers Report.
7. World Economic Forum. 2018. Machines Will Do More Tasks Than Humans by 2025 but Robot Revolution Will Still Create 58 Million Net New Jobs in Next Five Years.
8. Hyo-Eun Kim, Hak Hee Kim, Boo-Kyung Han, Ki Hwan Kim, Kyunghwa Han, Hyeonseob Nam, Eun Hye Lee, and Eun-Kyung Kim. 2020. Changes in cancer detection and false-positive recall in mammography using artificial intelligence: a retrospective, multireader study. *The Lancet* 2 (3): E13–E148.

9. Jacques Bughin, Jeongmin Seong, James Manyika, Michael Chui, and Raoul Joshi. 2018. *Notes From the AI Frontier Modeling the Impact of AI on the World Economy*. McKinsey & Company.
10. Capital One Tech. 2024. AI Readiness Survey: Are Companies Ready for AI Adoption?
11. Gartner, Inc. 2025. Gartner Predicts Half of Supply Chain Management Solutions Will Include Agentic AI Capabilities by 2030.
12. MuleSoft from Salesforce, Inc. n.d. 2025 Connectivity Benchmark Report.
13. Salesforce, Inc. 2024. Just 11% of CIOs Have Fully Implemented AI as Data and Security Concerns Hinder Adoption.
14. Scott Mayer McKinney, Marcin Sieniek, Varun Godbole, Jonathan Godwin, Natasha Antropova, Hutan Ashrafian, et al. 2020. International evaluation of an AI system for breast cancer screening. *Nature* 577(7788): 89–94.
15. PwC's 27th Annual Global CEO Survey. 2024. Thriving in an Age of Continuous Reinvention.
16. Accenture. 2025. Technology Vision 2025. AI: A Declaration of Autonomy-Is Trust the Limit of AI's Limitless Possibilities?

Chapter 2

1. Wikipedia. n.d. Clinical Death.
2. CDC National Center for Healthcare Statistics. 2025. Leading Causes of Death.
3. See, for instance, this 2024 research by BCG on costs and growth: Boston Consulting Group. 2024. What Leaders Are Saying About Costs and Growth in 2024.
4. See also: Suzanne Heywood, Dennis Layton, and Risto Penttinen. 2009. *A Better Way to Cut Costs*. McKinsey Quarterly.
5. Salesforce, Inc. 2023. *New IDC Study Details 'AI Boost' to Salesforce Economy Revenue and Job Growth*. Salesforce, Inc.
6. Hector M. Garcia-Garcia. 2024. *Research: Hands-free AI Can Identify Coronary Blockages After Angiogram*. MedStar Health.
7. BBC News. 2024. "Game Changer" AI Detects Hidden Heart Attack Risk.

Chapter 3

1. Sydney J. Freedberg. 2021. *Army's New Aim Is "Decision Dominance."* Breaking Media, Inc.

Chapter 4

1. Gartner, Inc. 2024. Gartner Forecasts Worldwide IT Spending to Grow 9.3% in 2025.
2. MuleSoft from Salesforce, Inc. n.d. 2025 Connectivity Benchmark Report.
3. IDC. 2025. The CIO Imperative: Six Priorities for the AI-Fueled Organization.
4. Gartner, Inc. 2025. Gartner Predicts Agentic AI Will Autonomously Resolve 80% of Common Customer Service Issues Without Human Intervention by 2029.
5. Amie M. Gordon. 2022. The Top 5 Predictors of Relationship Quality. Psychology Today.
6. K. K. Ganguly. 2019. Life of M.K. Gandhi: a message to youth of modern India. *The Indian Journal of Medical Research* 149: S145-S151.

Chapter 7

1. Greene, Ann Norton. 2023. *Overview: Animal Power. Energy History Online.* Yale University.
2. Ephemeral New York. 2024. The Great Upper Manhattan Sleigh Races That Thrilled the Wintertime City.

Glossary of AI Terms

This book is obviously about artificial intelligence (AI), but its clear focus is on the impact of AI—in particular predictive, Generative, Agentic, and physical AI, as their capabilities continue to develop—on the organization and operation of today's businesses. It is not a technical book or a manual or a primer on AI. There are plenty of those as well as videos and blogs. And we can also go directly to the source and ask AI about itself. Curiosity is, as we will see, one of the most important traits a human can have in the AI age and is well rewarded by AI itself, which "lives" to be able to answer our questions.

But we will be using terms that may still not be well understood by the general reader. For that reason, here is a brief glossary of those terms.

Core AI Concepts

Artificial intelligence (AI)   A broad term referring to machines or software systems that mimic aspects of human intelligence such as learning, reasoning, problem-solving, or language understanding. AI can be rule-based, statistical, or adaptive (learning from data over time).

Deep learning   A specialized branch of machine learning using neural networks with multiple layers (hence *deep*). Particularly effective for processing unstructured data like images, audio, and text. Powers many recent AI breakthroughs including computer vision and speech recognition.

Foundation model A large, general-purpose AI model trained on vast amounts of data and capable of being adapted to a wide range of downstream tasks. Examples include GPT (OpenAI), Claude (Anthropic), and Gemini (Google). These models are the basis for many LLM-based applications.

Machine learning (ML) A subset of AI where algorithms learn patterns from data rather than being explicitly programmed. ML models improve performance over time with more data and feedback, and are used in prediction, classification, and personalization.

AI Types and Approaches

Agentic AI An AI system that not only analyzes or predicts, but can initiate actions, pursue goals, and interact autonomously within digital environments. Unlike passive models, Agentic AI is capable of operating independently, planning tasks, making decisions, and executing workflows.

Artificial general intelligence (AGI) A theoretical form of AI with human-like ability to understand, learn, and apply knowledge across diverse domains. Would demonstrate flexible problem-solving and transfer learning across different contexts.

Generative AI (GenAI) AI systems that can create new content including text, images, code, audio, or video based on learned patterns. Unlike traditional analytics or classification models, Generative AI produces original outputs in response to prompts or instructions.

Narrow/weak AI AI systems designed for specific tasks without general intelligence capabilities. All current commercial AI falls into this category, even sophisticated systems like ChatGPT or autonomous vehicles.

Physical AI AI systems that interact with the physical world through robotics, sensors, and actuators. Includes autonomous vehicles, warehouse robots, manufacturing automation, and other embodied AI applications.

Predictive AI Systems that analyze historical data to forecast future outcomes. Used in demand planning, risk assessment, maintenance scheduling, and customer behavior prediction.

Language and Communication AI

Chatbot A conversational AI interface that can simulate text- or voice-based dialogue with users. Used in customer service, sales, and HR to answer questions, provide guidance, or triage requests. Can be rule-based or powered by large language models.

Hallucination (in AI)   When a Generative AI system produces outputs that are factually incorrect, nonsensical, or fabricated, despite sounding plausible. A common issue with large language models, particularly in complex or specialized domains.

Large language model (LLM)   A type of AI model trained on massive amounts of text data to understand and generate human-like language. Examples include GPT-4.5, Claude 4 Sonnet, and LLaMA 4 Scout. LLMs are the backbone of many conversational and Generative AI applications.

Natural language processing (NLP)   The field of AI focused on enabling machines to understand, interpret, and generate human language. Used in search, translation, summarization, sentiment analysis, and conversational interfaces.

Prompt engineering   The practice of crafting inputs (prompts) to guide a Generative AI model's output. In business, prompt engineering helps generate better results from LLMs for use cases like summarization, drafting, or analysis.

Retrieval-augmented generation (RAG)   A technique that combines LLMs with external knowledge sources. Before generating a response, the model retrieves relevant documents or data, increasing accuracy and grounding outputs in verifiable information.

Semantic search   An AI-enhanced search method that understands the meaning of queries rather than matching exact keywords. Enables better discovery across documents, chats, or knowledge bases.

Zero-shot/few-shot learning   The ability of an AI model to perform tasks it was not explicitly trained on (zero-shot), or with very few examples (few-shot). A hallmark of advanced foundation models and LLMs.

AI Development and Implementation

Fine-tuning   The process of taking a pretrained AI model and adjusting it for a specific use case by training it on a smaller, domain-specific dataset. Fine-tuning improves accuracy and relevance in specialized tasks.

Federated learning   A type of machine learning where AI models are trained across multiple devices or organizations without sharing raw data. Useful for privacy-sensitive environments like health care or financial services.

Inference The process of using a trained AI model to make predictions or generate outputs. In contrast to training (learning from data), inference happens during the model's use, when it answers a query or takes an action.

Model drift The gradual degradation in AI model performance as real-world conditions change from those in the training data. Requires monitoring and periodic retraining to maintain accuracy.

Synthetic data Data generated by AI models to simulate real-world information. Used to train models when real data is limited, sensitive, or unavailable.

Training data The dataset used to "teach" an AI model during development. The quality, quantity, and diversity of training data heavily influence model performance.

Responsible AI Frameworks and practices ensuring AI systems are ethical, transparent, fair, and accountable. Includes bias mitigation, explainability, privacy protection, and human oversight.

Vector database A type of database optimized to store and retrieve high-dimensional data, like the numeric embeddings generated by AI models. Commonly used in LLM applications for fast semantic search and contextual memory.

Business Applications and Integration

AI alignment The process of ensuring AI systems act in accordance with human values and intentions. Critical for preventing unintended consequences as AI becomes more powerful.

Augmentation The use of AI to enhance, rather than replace, human capabilities. In business, this often refers to AI assisting employees by speeding up tasks, surfacing insights, or reducing manual effort, while keeping humans in control of decisions.

Autonomy (in AI) The degree to which an AI system can operate independently. At higher levels, autonomy means the system can make decisions, adapt to changes, and execute actions without supervision, often seen in robotics, autonomous vehicles, and Agentic enterprise tools.

Autonomous agent A software entity capable of perceiving its environment, making decisions, and taking actions to achieve defined objectives, without ongoing human input. Autonomous agents can operate on behalf of users, businesses, or other agents in dynamic environments.

Copilot A category of AI tool designed to work alongside a human user in real time. Copilots generate suggestions, automate routine tasks, and help complete work across writing, coding, design, or communication platforms. Examples: GitHub Copilot, Microsoft 365 Copilot.

Cognitive load The mental effort required to perform a task or process information. AI systems can reduce cognitive load by automating routine steps, summarizing data, or filtering information, freeing humans to focus on creative or strategic thinking.

Decision automation The use of AI systems to make or support decisions without human involvement. Decision automation often combines business rules with predictive models or real-time data, and is used in areas like underwriting, fraud detection, and supply chain optimization.

Digital worker/labor An AI agent or software bot that performs tasks traditionally done by a human employee, such as reviewing documents, responding to emails, or resolving service requests. Often integrated into enterprise systems as part of automation strategies.

Edge AI AI processing that occurs on local devices rather than in the cloud. Enables faster responses, works without internet connectivity, and enhances privacy by keeping data local.

Explainable AI (XAI) AI systems designed to make their decision-making process transparent and interpretable to humans. Critical for trust and adoption in regulated industries.

Human-in-the-loop AI systems that incorporate human judgment at key decision points. Balances automation efficiency with human oversight for complex or sensitive decisions.

Orchestration (AI) The coordination of multiple tasks, systems, or agents, typically across teams or functions, by an AI system. Orchestration platforms assign work, monitor performance, and optimize execution in real time.

Multi-agent system An architecture in which multiple AI agents interact, collaborate, or compete to achieve individual or collective goals. In business, this enables complex workflows where different AI systems coordinate across departments or ecosystems.

Reinforcement learning from human feedback (RLHF) A technique where AI models are refined based on human evaluations of their outputs. Helps align AI behavior with human preferences and values.

Robotic process automation (RPA) Software that mimics human actions to automate structured, repetitive tasks like form entry, system updates, or data migration. Often used as a first step in enterprise automation.

Acknowledgments

We would like to thank our team at Wiley, especially Jeanenne Ray, Michelle Hacker, and Kim Wimpsett, and we are grateful to Dan Farber and John Taschek at Salesforce for their continued support.

About the Authors

Vala Afshar and **Henry King** are the authors of the bestselling book *Boundless*. With a combined 60+ years of experience, both are award-winning executives and technology practitioners specializing in business strategy, digital transformation, cloud computing, CRM, data, and AI technologies.

Vala Afshar is currently Chief Digital Evangelist at Salesforce, where he advises customers on the rise of Agentic AI and the future of advanced technologies. Previously, he has served as Vice President of Engineering, Chief Customer Officer, and Chief Marketing Officer. Recognized as a leading industry thought leader, Vala boasts over a million followers on X and LinkedIn, holds multiple US patents, writes a weekly column for ZDNET, and has hosted the popular enterprise podcast *DisrupTV* for over a decade.

Henry King is an Innovation Strategist and Chief Information Officer with a distinguished career at Salesforce, Accenture, Deloitte Consulting, and other top technology firms. He is also a regular blog columnist and trusted advisor to organizations navigating digital transformation and AI adoption.

Together, as proven authors, technology practitioners, and advisors, Afshar and King are uniquely positioned to offer leaders, strategists, and designers actionable insights for positioning their companies for success in the age of AI.

Index

4D design, development/usage, 121, 123
"6 Levels of Driving Automation"
    framework (SAE), 141–144

A

A1000, cutting-edge tools (usage), 77
Action
  examples, 70–72
  optimization, AI-enabled digital twins
    (technological pillar), 70
  scope, 67–69
Adaptive AI workflow orchestration
    (technological pillar), 70
Adaptive learning systems (analytical
    area), 59
Advanced sensing, computer vision usage
    (company need)
Aerial delivery, impact, 121
Agentic artificial intelligence (agentic AI),
    1–2
  business adoption, 179
    increase, 50
    predictions, 77
  capabilities, 9, 128
  impact, forecasts, 76–77
  mindset, adoption, 183
  opportunities, 75
  usage, 39, 133
Agents, team approach, 99–100

Age of Intelligence, entry, 116
AI-orchestrated IT operations (AIOps)
    (technological capability), 68
Airflow systems, blockages, 22
Alien Dreadnought concept (Musk), 120
AlphaGo Zero, success/learning process,
    4, 115–117
Andre, José, 130–134, 182–183
Anomaly detection (analytical area), 58
Application Programming Interfaces (APIs),
    impact, 10
Artificial intelligence (AI)
  absence (Level 0), 145
  AI-augmented decision intelligence
    (analytical area), 59
  AI-driven edge computing
    (technological pillar), 69
  AI-driven foundation, 186
  AI-driven personalized marketing
    execution (technological
    capability), 68
  AI-driven predictive analytics (company
    need), 54
  AI-enabled training programs,
    deployment, 118
  AI-first design, 103, 122–124
  AI-first strategies, 119–124, 181–182
  AI-guided field operations
    (technological capability), 68

Artificial intelligence (*continued*)
  AI-integrated IoT execution networks (technological pillar), 70
  AI-powered action, 67–72
    scope, 67–69
    technological components, 69–70
  AI-powered autonomous robotics (technological pillar), 70
  AI-powered decision-making, 62–66
    technological components, 65–66
  AI-powered economy, changes, 176
  AI-powered market intelligence (analytical area), 59
  AI-powered robotics (technological capability), 68
  AI-powered sensing, 51–53
    technological components, 53–55
  AI-powered understanding, 56–62
    technological components, 60–61
  AI-powered workflow orchestration, 157
  assistance, 40–42
  boom (2022), 4–5
  code assistants, usage, 77
  copilots, usage, 155
  evolution, importance (understanding), 8–12
  global economy contribution, 9
  implementation, 94
  implications, 13–14
  integration, 2–3, 7
  partnership, imagination (usage), 91
  risks, policies/oversight (formalization), 76
  usage, expansion (preparation), 11
  user interface (UI), 141
Artificial intelligence (AI) adoption, 5–8
  benefits, 12
  projections, 9–10
Artificial intelligence (AI) agents
  adoption, integration (challenge), 10
  advantages, 75
  importance, 6
  team approach, 99–100

Assistive AI, cognitive upgrade, 95
Assistive technology, objective, 93
Augmentation, shift, 161–162
Autofacturing, 119–122
Automated decision engines (AI-powered decision strategy), 63
Automation
  AI usage, absence (Level 0), 145, 148–149
  beginning stage (Level 1), 145, 147.
    See also Task automation.
AutoML (analytical area), 59
Automobiles
  evolution/autonomy, 113–114, 141–143
  rise, 167–169
Autonomous AI agents (technological capability), 68
Autonomous AI, cognitive upgrade, 95
Autonomous business
  dynamic orchestration, 186
  entry, 14–17
  evolution, 145–161, 182–183
  mSUDA
    operating model, 51f
    usage, 50
  performance, superiority, 185
  resilience/performance, improvement, 186
Autonomous companies
  blockages, impact (impossibility), 19
  foundation, 183
  operating models, 43, 178–180
  talent/resources/RI, 180
Autonomous decision execution systems (technological pillar), 69
Autonomous intelligence, work (defining), 119–122
Autonomous intelligent agents, AI revolution, 79
Autonomous maturity, approach, 183–184
Autonomous operating model, 43–50
Autonomous process automation (technological capability), 67
Autonomous trucking, impact, 121

Index

Autonomous vehicles, self-choreography, 144
Autonomous Work framework, levels, 119
Autonomous work, levels, 47, 145–148, 146f
 examination, depth, 148–161
Autonomy
 approach, 14
 boundless principles, 127
 evolution, 144–145
 impact, 175–176
 importance, 3
 usage, 137–138, 161–162

B

Bayesian decision networks (AI-based decision-making technology), 65
Behavioral analysis (analytical area), 58
Benioff, Marc, 5, 17, 76, 79
Binary Big Bang, 15–16
Blockages
 experience, 22–23
 identification/action, 31–38
 impact, 19–22, 176–178
 prevention, 186
 removal, 40
  AI assistance, 40–42, 177–178
Blockchain (company need), 54
Boundless (Afshar), 46, 84, 127–129
Boundless mindset, 134–139, 182–183, 186
 adoption, 133
 goals/outcomes, 32–33
Boundless thinking, 128
Boyd, John, 44
Business
 agentic AI adoption, 5–8, 50
 AI role, 7–8
 automation (AI control, increase) (Level 6), 147–148, 158–159
 digital twin, 122–124
 models (transformation), Control Matrix (usage), 110–111
 operating principle, 182–183
 shape, change, 159

C

Capability (EGI dimension), 162–163
 low/high capability, 163–164
Carpooling, possibilities, 144
Causal AI models (core technology), 60
Causal inference (analytical area), 58
Change management blockages, 29
ChatGPT (OpenAI), launch, 4–5
Chief human resources officers (CHROs), digital labor adoption forecast, 97–101
Chief information officers (CIOs)
 chef-like roles, 133–134
 impact, 77
Clinical death, definition, 20–21
Cloud AI (company need), 55
Cognitive capabilities, 181
Cognitive downloads, cognitive upgrades (contrast), 92–97
Commitment
 defining, 85
 impact, 84–88
 phases, 86–87
Companies
 death, blockages (impact), 19, 23–31
 performance, origin, 83
Competitive intelligence, 52
Competitive strategy, redefining, 112–113
Complete Vehicle Independence (SAE Level 6), 143
Complex data analysis (acceleration), agentic AI (impact), 75
Computer vision (company need), 55
Connection, usage, 131–132, 135–136
Consistency (EGI dimension), 163
 low/high consistency, 163–164
Context-aware decision making (AI-powered decision strategy), 64
Contextual data analysis (analytical area), 57
Continuous learning AI execution systems, 70
Continuity, importance, 138–139

Control Matrix, 109f
  creation, 108
  usage, 110–113, 123
Control, meaning, 106–107
Crisis/resilience blockages, 31
Cross-domain intelligence fusion (analytical area), 59
Cultural blockages, 26
Curiosity, importance, 88–90
Customer experiences, customization, 75
Customer sensing, 52
Customer service, autonomous AI agents (technological capability), 68

D

Darwin, Charles, 2
Data
  flow, blockages, 23
  fusion, multimodal AI (company need), 54
  integrity (company need), 54
  trapping, 10
Death, blockages (relationship), 21–22
Decision
  automation (core technology), 61
  dominance, definition/components, 47–48
  modeling (analytical area), 58
  optimization (AI-based decision-making technology), 65
  systems, explainable AI (XAI) (AI-powered decision strategy), 64
Decision-making
  automation, 75
  enhancement, agentic AI (impact), 75
  examples, 66
  process, blockages, 27–28
  scope, 63–64
Declaration (commitment phase), 86
Deep Blue (IBM), 4
Deep reinforcement learning (DRL)
  AI-based decision-making technology, 65
  core technology, 60

Demonstration (commitment phase), 86–87
Design (commitment phase), 86
Digital labor
  benefits, 78
  defining, 78
  examples, 78–79
  integration, 100
  relational intelligence, usage, 73
Digital twins, 122–124
  AI-enabled digital twins (technological pillar), 70
  company need, 54
Digital workforce, impact, 186
Distributed decision intelligence, federated learning (AI-based decision-making technology), 65
Distributed intelligence, 123
Distributed ledgers, usage, 160
Distribution, usage, 131–132, 136
Domain-specific AI agents, training, 155
Down-control business models, 110
Down-control leaders, emphasis, 111
Down-control positioning, 113

E

Economic/financial sensing, usage, 523
Ecosystem level (AI choreography) (Level 7), 148, 160–163
Edge computing (company need), 54
Edison, Thomas, 114
Effort
  culture, 114–116
  pursuit, problems, 115
Elite performance development (ultrafine tuning), 165
Emerging technology monitoring, 53
Employee sensing, 53
Enterprise general intelligence (EGI), 162–172
  defining, dimensions, 162–163
  phases, 164–165
Enterprise-level digital twin, usage, 123

Enterprise software applications, agentic AI (inclusion), 77
Environmental awareness, 53
Ethical AI (core technology), 61
Expertise, time (decoupling), 117
Explainable AI (XAI)
  AI-powered decision strategy, 64
  core technology, 61
Exponential growth, 186
Externalities
  impact, 34–35
  negative externalities, identification/mitigation, 35–36
  positive externalities, design, 36–37
  practice, examples, 37–38
External relationship blockages, 28

F

Federated decision-making (AI-powered decision strategy), 64
Federated learning
  AI-based decision-making technology, 65
  core technology, 61
  usage, 160
Finance, AI (impact), 12
Fit company, definition, 1
Fittest, definition, 2–3
Flow, usage, 132, 138
Fluid systems, blockages, 22
Fly-by-wire, usage, 106, 113–114, 181
Fractals, autonomous systems (comparison), 46
Fragility, AI (impact), 154
Fuel systems, blockages, 23
Fundamental skills training (pretraining), 164

G

Game-theoretic decision models (AI-powered decision strategy), 63
Gandhi, Mahatma, 96
Generative AI
  capabilities, 73
  impact, 4–5
  mindset adoption, 183
  tools, usage, 155
  usage, 133
Geopolitical/risk sensing, 53
Geospatial AI (company need), 55
Global GDP growth, Benioff/Goldman Sachs prediction, 5
Guardian agents, availability (CIO demand), 77

H

Health care, AI (impact), 11
High-value service center (HVSC), usage, 39
Huang, Jensen, 114
Human-AI hybrid decision systems (AI-powered decision strategy), 64
Human-centric key performance indicators, evolution, 76
Human-digital synergy, 186
Human resources, digital resources (integration), 73, 180
Humans
  edge, impact, 88–92
  future, 169–172
  judgment, continuation, 161
  workforce, role (change), 154
Hybrid AI
  AI-based decision-making technology, 65
  core technology, 61

I

Imagination, importance, 88, 90–92
Industrial Revolution, 170
Information Technology (IT)
  expenditures, increase, 74
  workload, increase, 10
Innovation blockages, 30
Integrated user experience (integrated UX), elusiveness, 10
Integration, usage, 131–132, 136–137
Intelligence
  demonstration, diminishment, 115–116
  manufacturing, 119–122

Intelligent Flight Control Systems (IFCSs), usage, 106, 181
Intelligent RPA 2.0 (technological pillar), 69
Intelligent supply chain execution (technological capability), 68
Intention-based architectures, usage, 16
Internet of Things (IoT), 52–53
 IoT-enabled sensor, edge computing (company need), 54

K
Kasparov, Gary, 4
Knowledge graphs (analytical area), 58
Knowledge management blockages, 27

L
Large language model (LLM), 4
 core technology, 60
 discussion, 79
Leadership
 approaches, evolution, 111–112
Leadership blockages, 23–25
Linear gains, shift, 161–162
Logistics
 AI, impact, 12
 optimization, 75
 tracking, 53
Low/high capability, 163–164
Low/high consistency, 163–164

M
Machine health, flow dependence, 22–23
Machine Intelligence test (Turing), 4
Machine-scale operations, 186
Machine-scale Sense, Understand, Decide, Act (mSUDA), 43, 50, 120–121, 178–180
 action stage, 67–72
 chain, 39
 decision-making stage, 62–66
 levels, perspective, 156, 157
 operating model, 51f, 179
 sensing stage, 51–56
 understanding stage, 56–62
 usage, initiation, 150
Manufacturing equipment, clogs/blockages, 23
Manure crisis (1894), 166–167
Market/industry trends, examination, 52
McCarthy, John, 4
Minimum viable cost center (MVCC), usage, 38–40
Mobility, importance, 138
Movement, designing, 132
Multi-agent AI decision systems (AI-powered decision strategy), 63
Multi-agent AI simulations (AI-based decision-making technology), 65
Multi-agent orchestration frameworks, usage, 160
Multimodal AI (company need), 54
Murray, John, 47–48, 178
Musk, Elon, 114
 Alien Dreadnought concept, 120

N
Nadella, Satya, 9
Natural language processing (NLP), 52
 company need, 54
Natural selection, 2
Negative externalities, identification/mitigation, 35–36
Neural networks (AI-based decision-making technology), 65
Neurosymbolic AI (core technology), 60
Nonlinearity, 103
Nonlinear transformation, arrival, 161–162

O
Observe-Orient-Decide-Act (OODA)
 loop, 44–46, 49
 Sense-Perceive-Decide-Actuate model, comparison, 45
Open inquiry, 88–90
Operational blockages, 25–26

Operational control, ceding, 3–4
Optimal flow, impact, 20, 177
Organizational design, reimagining, 109–110
Organizational imagination, development, 91–92
Origin of Species, The (Darwin), 2

P

Parking Reform Network, 144
People/employees
  autonomous business need, (question), 165–172
  importance, 81–84
Performance, 104–114
  characteristics, stability (contrast), 105
  objective, 105–106
Personalized AI recommendations (analytical area), 58–59
Phantom Phaeton, arrival, 167–169
Planes, evolution/autonomy, 113–114
Policy/regulatory interpretation (analytical area), 59
Positive externalities, design, 36–37
Possible, envisioning, 90–92
Predictive analytics (analytical area), 57
Prescriptive analytics (analytical area), 57–58
Prescriptive analytics/optimization (AI-powered decision strategy), 64
Privacy-preserving analytics, usage, 160
Probabilistic decision-making (AI-powered decision strategy), 63
Process Automation, AI involvement (Level 3), 147, 153–154
Process optimization, prioritization, 116
Product design, reimagining, 112
Product monitoring, usage, 52–53
Psychological blockages, 30–31

Q

Quantum AI (AI-based decision-making technology), 65

R

Real-time AI decision loops (AI-powered decision strategy), 64
Real-time AI inference/decision execution (AI-based decision-making technology), 66
Real-time AI inference/response mechanisms (technological pillar), 70
Real-time data pipelines (core technology), 61
Real-time data streaming/processing (company need), 54
Real-time sentiment (analytical area), 58
Regulatory/policy changes, knowledge, 52
Reinforcement learning (RL) (AI-powered decision strategy), 63
Relational design, 83
Relational intelligence (RI), 180
  ability, 83
  usage, 73
Relationships
  commitment, impact, 84–88
  importance, 79–81
  strengths, 83–84
  success, requirements, 84
Research and development (R&D), acceleration, 75
Resource allocation blockages, 29–30
Retail, AI (impact), 11–12
Risk detection (analytical area), 58
Robotic process automation (RPA), 73, 150
Role Automation, AI control (Level 4), 147, 154–156
Rule-based logic (AI-based decision-making technology), 65

S

Salesforce, AI exploration/implementation, 94
Satellite data processing (company need), 55
Savarese, Silvio, 162
Scalable machine learning infrastructure (company need), 55

Index

Scaling, connection/distribution/integration (usage), 131–132
Scenario-based decision modeling (AI-powered decision strategy), 64
Sedol, Lee, 4, 115, 117
Self-driving, 3
Semantic AI (analytical area), 58
Sense-Perceive-Decide-Actuate model, 45, 49
Sense, Understand, Decide, Act (SUDA), 39, 46–50
  achievement, 179
  model, 48, 122
Sensing
  data integrity, blockchain usage (company need), 54
  examples, 55–56
  mSUDA stage, 51–56
  scope, 51–53
  technological components, 53–55
Sensing, Understanding, Deciding, and Acting cycle, 160, 179
Service design, reimagining, 112
Service performance monitoring, 52–53
Shared success, importance, 131, 135
Silos
  success measurement, 133
  usage, 129
Sinner, Jannik, 165
Smart contracts, usage, 160
Smart factories (technological capability), 68
Social/cultural trends, importance, 53
Society of Automotive Engineers (SAE), "6 Levels of Driving Automation" framework, 141–144
Software, expenditures (increase), 74
Sport-specific training (fine-tuning), 164–165
Stability, 104–114
  performance compromise (disappearance), AI (impact), 108

Strategic planning, reinforcement learning (AI-powered decision strategy), 63
Strategic road map, creation (CIO leadership), 77
Sub-process automation, AI (usage increase) (Level 2), 147, 151–153
Supplier tracking, usage, 53
Supply chains, optimization, 75
Sustainability awareness, 53

T

Talent, reskilling/redeploying, 98–99
Task automation, AI introduction (Level 1), 149–151
Team Automation, AI orchestration (Level 5), 147, 156–158
Teams (upskilling), agentic AI (impact), 75
Team structure, change, 157
Technical debt
  blockages, 28–29
  drag, 76
Technological pillars, 69–70
Tennis player evolution, 164–165
Tesla
  autonomy, 141
  vertical integration production lines, 120
Time, requirement (diminishment), 116–119
Transformer AI (core technology), 60
Turing, Alan, 4

U

Understanding
  examples, 61–62
  mSUDA stage, 56–62
  scope, 57–59
Unstructured data, NLP usage (company need), 54
Up-control business models, 110
Up-control leaders, emphasis, 111
Up-control positioning, 113
User interface (UI), 141

W

Waring, George E., 166–167
Waste
  cost, contrast, 32–34
  elimination, 186
Watson, Thomas, 169
Waymo, usage, 141–143
Whitney, Eli, 170
Workforce
  impact, 171
  sensing, 53

Work, hybrid future, 98
World Central Kitchen, 182–183
  approach, 130–134
  community members, engagement, 130–131
  creation, 130
  flow, usage, 132
  movement, designing, 132
  scaling, connection/distribution/integration (usage), 131–132
  shared success, 131

ALSO FROM
VALA AFSHAR
HENRY KING

Boundless • ISBN: 978-1-394-17179-8

WILEY